LIESELOTTE AND THEO ENGL   Twilight of ancient Peru

1 *Gold and copper alloy mummy mask with mother of pearl eyes.*

Lieselotte and Theo Engl

TWILIGHT OF ANCIENT PERU

the glory and decline of the Inca Empire

translated by Alisa Jaffe

McGraw-Hill Book Company

New York · Toronto · London · Sydney

to our daughter Eva Maria

Published by McGraw-Hill Book Company, 1969 · © Verlag Georg D. W. Callwey, Munich · All rights reserved · No part of this work may be reproduced without the permission of the publishers · Library of Congress Catalog Card No. 75-76143 · Printed in West Germany · 19478.

CONTENTS

The world of Ancient Peru — The great shrines — Mythical and semi-mythical landings and migrations — Inca Pachacútec Yupanqui (1438—1471) is shown the provinces of the future Great Empire in a crystal — The original hierarchy is rejected — Inca Túpac (1471—1493) conquers Chile and Ecuador — Sister-marriage and succession to the throne — Divine worship of the rulers and their mummies.

"There was once a time when the earth lay in darkness. Men suffered terribly from the absence of light and called upon their gods with lengthy lamentations and prayers . . . Then the sun in all its splendor rose above the island of Titicaca and all the people burst into great jubilation . . . then there came a man from the south, white and tall of stature, who was worshiped everywhere; he displayed great powers over nature; he reduced mountains to plains and made plains into mountains; he caused water to gush out of the bare rock . . . and so men called him the Creator and the Beginning of all Things and Father of the Sun . . . he gave life to men and creatures and established the order whereby they should live."[1]

The Peruvian Indians have various myths that give highly graphic descriptions of how the creator god, worshiped by the name of Conticiviracocha or Viracocha, first created light and thereafter created the peoples of Peru, modeling them in stone at Tiahuanaco on Lake Titicaca. Then, aided by two acolytes, whom he sent out to the north and the west, to the Andes and to the coast, he summoned the peoples out of lakes, streams, valleys, caves, trees, rocks, and mountains, which later became tribal shrines, or *pacarinas*.[2]

Viracocha himself finally set out on the long journey from the Bolivian highlands through the different lands and varying climatic zones of what was to become the Inca empire. This journey followed the "royal highway," by way of Cuzco and Cajamarca, as far as Ecuador. The people of Cacha in the Collao (Titicaca highlands) rebelled against him, whereupon he called fire down from heaven. To the penitent he was a gentle teacher and benefactor[2]. On the Pacific coast, "near the equator, in the vicinity of present-day Puerto Viejo and Manta, he joined company once more with his two acolytes and left the Peruvian earth. He spoke to his creatures of the future: people would come claiming to be Viracocha, their creator, but they must place no trust in these; in time he himself would send them emissaries, to protect and teach them. Then he and his two companions turned to the sea and strode forth over the water, as if it were dry land, without sinking . . . this is the origin of the name 'Huira-cocha', which means 'foam on the sea.'"[3]

This is the most beautiful of the ancient Peruvian myths, and its meaning is also the most disputed. It was known throughout Peru and occurred in many versions, interwoven with legends about the creation of the cosmos and mankind, the deeds of rival deities, and stories about the origins of the individual tribes. The passage at the beginning of our text, taken from the earlier chronicle of Cieza de León, is a synthesis of various texts. It begins with a world without light, or with very little light, in which man is already present, and goes on to describe the birth and glorification of the sun. The subsequent appearance of the figure of Viracocha is only gradually recognized by men as that of the creator. Other versions make a firm distinction between a first and second creation. In some cases several further creations of mankind, before and after a flood and other world catastrophes, are distinguished. Moreover, the divine creator and the great wanderer and teacher are not always one and the same person. Occult traditions of the ancient Peruvian priesthood and popular Indian folk mythology are interwoven with European Christian allusions to form a wonderfully colored fabric. Against this background of rich imagery, the figure of the divine stranger, familiar to so many religions of the world, emerges with rare clarity.

By a tragic chain of circumstances, the name Viracocha, with which the Peruvian history of creation begins, was to become the token of the fall of the Inca empire. In 1532, while Cuzco, the capital of the Tahuantinsuyu, the "Land of the Four Quarters," was enduring bitter degradation, and Huáscar, the Inca of the time, was being ill-treated and dragged off as a prisoner by the generals of his half-brother Atahualpa, Pizarro and his small expeditionary force of white-faced, bearded men were landing in the extreme northwest of the Inca empire, on the same coastline that was revered as the place of Viracocha's departure and the promised return of his emissaries. In northern Peru, and in Atahualpa's entourage, the Spaniards were known simply as the "bearded ones." For the vanquished party of Huáscar in Cuzco, imploring the aid of the supreme god with costly sacrifices and great supplication, they were the "Viracochas." The name spread rapidly, and in some areas it is still used for Europeans to this day.[4]

This is the practical explanation offered by the Jesuit father Bernabé Cobo, in his famous 17th-century chronicle, for the baffling way in which the white men were held in undeserved esteem by some of the Peruvian Indians.

For a long time the physical appearance of Viracocha, and the pale skin and bearded face attributed to him, so alien to America, was considered a falsification or religious deception fabricated by the conquistadors and missionaries. The idea that this legend might have any Indian origin was firmly rejected.

Yet Cieza, the Spanish soldier who traveled through Peru in about 1550 and is generally regarded as the most impartial of all the chroniclers, described the Chachapoya tribe living in the Andes of northeastern Peru with the words: "These Chachapoya Indians are paler-skinned and more charming than any of the others I have seen in the parts of America through which I have traveled."

In 1966, the mountaineer and scholar Gene Savoy took part in the Peruvian expedition to the ruins of Pajatén, where he met "hundreds of blond, blue-eyed, tall men with long faces and aristocractic noses" in the remote jungle villages south of the city of Chachapoya. These features could of course date back to forgotten European settlements of the early colonial period. However, in Pajatén the expedition found pottery figurines with moustaches and ostensibly Semitic or Phoenician facial features similar to those familiar from Mayan sculpture. Here we see how remnants of theories and myths about the racial kinship between Europe, America, and Asia long thought extinct, still persist. The early Spanish, Dutch, and English conquerors and settlers "sought the lost tribes of Israel on the soil of the New World and quite literally looked for the footprints of the Apostles" (Trimborn).

Unfortunately it is impossible for us to examine more closely here the intricate problems of the prehistoric and early wanderings in America that have occupied the archaeologists, ethnologists, and mythologists for decades. Current research is of the opinion that there were a great number of landings at different times and in numerous places.

Between 500 B.C. and A.D. 333 strong influences came to Peru and Mexico, as the Heine-Geldern investigations seek to show, from southern China, still very much a maritime nation at that time, and later from what today is Vietnam. This movement from west to east is supposed to have been partly balanced out by the so-called Pontic wandering of European peoples from the Danube area and the Caucasus, who brought elements of the Hallstatt culture as far as China. Seafarers from eastern Asia are thought to have introduced many moral and material cultural elements into Central and South America, such as the construction of the state according to model plans, the sacred division into Four Quarters, weaving techniques, the discovery of bronze, and the working of gold. Garcilaso, the Spanish-Inca chronicler, describes the very same artificial trees or branches of silver with golden leaves that appear in the fables of the *Thousand and One Nights*, which were still being paid as tribute by Laos to the king of Siam in the 1860s, and were described by that famous English governess at the court in Bangkok. One strong incentive for the Chinese and Asiatic seafarers may have been the presence of tin and gold in the Peruvian Andes.

Well into the twentieth century historians still regarded the Inca state as the only great empire in old Peru. Before Max Uhle, the grand master of Peruvian archaeology (who began his scientific career with discoveries in southern Asia), carried out the first excavations at the Pyramid of Pachacámac, all ancient Peruvian art was considered to be Inca. Since that time, however, other great Peruvian cultures have been discovered indicating that common myths, certain life styles, craft techniques, and artistic forms were spread over large areas of the Andes.

One of these civilizations is called Chavín after the site in northern Peru where great stone buildings and sculpture, dating from the first millenium B. C. (ca. 900

to 500 B. C.) have been found. The other revolved around the religious and artistic center of Tiahuanaco on Lake Titicaca, but extended from the southern coast near Arequipa to middle and north Peru, and lasted from 950 to 1200 A. D., the century preceding the mighty military expansion of the Inca state.

Because we lack a secure historical basis, and because the Incas, like the Spaniards, only reluctantly acknowledged the traditions of earlier dynasties, it is only through archaeology that we have adequate information about the cultural side of those great expansions of Chavín and Tiahuanaco-Huari. The late Peru scholars R. Larce Heyle and W. C. Bennett, and more recently Dorothy Menzel, hypothesize an organized empire of Tiahuanican culture with the center (Huari) at Ayacucho in middle Peru that was, to a certain extent, a predecessor of the competing empires of the Chimú and the Inca. The regard that the later Inca rulers Túpac and Huayna Cápac gave the centers on Lake Titicaca and Vilcas near Huari supports this theory. As a consequence of the valuable textile and ceramic finds from corresponding sites on the northern and southern coasts of Peru, the local cultures of the intermediate epochs of Mochica, Paracas, Nazca, and Chimú are much better understood than the history of the great expansions.

Only one hundred years before the Spanish discovery of America, there was still a series of politically independent minor and major centers of power in greater Peru. They shared many common features which were then brought together under the subsequent Tahuantinsuyu. The great oracle shrines of Tiahuanaco on Lake Titicaca, Pachacámac near Lima, and the island of La Plata on the coast of Ecuador, were meeting places for pilgrims and emissaries from tribes and states, often from remote areas. These cultural centers, like the pilgrim stations of the Old World, presumably lived on the rich sacrificial offerings, and their monuments are thought to have been built with the aid of the many pilgrims who assembled there.[5]

Ruins of a house in Inca style, Ollantaytambo.

Trading and pilgrimages were responsible for the spread of cult symbols, styles, and ways of life from the coast to the highlands, and in the reverse direction, and possibly even as far as the Polynesian Islands, as Thor Heyerdahl attempted to prove by his Kon Tiki voyage. Apart from the commonly shared shrines, dedicated to the chief divinities, such as Viracocha, Pachacámac, the sun, the moon, thunder, and lightning, there was an endless variety of sacred rocks, lakes, glaciers, and other natural phenomena hallowed by different local cults. Interwoven with these was the strange realm of ancestor worship.

Some important dynasties of western South America, such as the Chimú along the coast, the Caranqui in northern Ecuador, and the Inca in the southern Peruvian highlands, traced their ancestry back to strangers, who either by physical or cultural superiority, by the manipulation of symbols, or by breaking existing taboos or establishing new ones, asserted themselves as priest-kings. Legend has it that these strangers or new tribes came from unknown lands across the sea in rafts or boats and landed on the coast, settling there or penetrating further inland into the highlands. References to major overland wanderings are comparatively rare in these fragments of history.[5a]

The legends surrounding the emergence of Manco Cápac, the founder of the dynasty of the princes of Cuzco and the subsequent Inca kings, are particularly impressive and appear highly authentic from an ethnological and historical point of view. They tell of the wandering of a clan in search of a permanent place to settle. The final halt before the appearance of Manco Cápac in the region of Cuzco is at the island sanctuary on Lake Titicaca; voyages in *balsas* across lakes and oceans, and even along subterranean watercourses, play an important role here. Anello Oliva, the Jesuit father, has a vivid description of the origin of Manco, which he claimed to have heard personally from the lips of a tribal elder in Bolivia who knew the *quipu* (knot-records):[6]

Having come ashore, after much wandering, Manco took leave of his 200 companions by Lake Titicaca, with the assurance that they would find him again if they asked for the "Son of the Sun and Moon." In solitude, "he fed upon Chucan and Pilli plants" — the latter a poisonous variety of lobelia, with a reputedly stimulant effect — and wandered slowly in a northwesterly direction as far as the shrine of Pacaritampu, two days march from Cuzco. There, at dawn, hung with golden disks, he stepped from the "royal window," the central one of three sacred niches in the rock, to the amazement of the onlooking peasants of the region.[7]

Inca Roca with his son Yahuar Huacac. On the coat of arms the *mascapaycha*.

According to the version of another chronicler, Ramos Gavilán, Manco Cápac was prepared for his future vocation by a magician, and then, in the splendor of the sunrise against the golden background of the cave, he was presented to the people, who had held a ceremonial orgy to celebrate the awaited arrival of the son of the sun. The robes in which the young Cápac appeared are described in great detail: hanging ornaments of gold and silver disks that call to mind the Shamanite attire still worn to this day in Siberia and blue and yellow feathers from exotic birds symbolizing heaven and the light of the sun.[8]

Yet the intruders' seizure of power over the community did not go entirely without resistance. We learn of bloodthirsty rites and horrors of war during this early period. Mama Guaco, sister of the mother of the dynasty, and probably a priestess, is portrayed tearing out the heart and lungs of an enemy, inflating the lung, and driving the terrified peasants to flight with her sling and stones.[9]

In pre-Columbian times the word "Inca" was never the name of a people, but from the start was used to denote only the ruler, his blood relations, and a few privileged families whose ancestry derived from companions or kinsfolk of Manco Capác, the founder of the dynasty, or other original inhabitants of Cuzco. With every generation this caste grew in numbers, while new *ayllus* grew up (the *ayllu* being an extended family or sub-tribe). As soon as he became Inca, the successor to the throne left his father's *ayllu*, and with his progeny founded his own *ayllu* and established a new royal area. The *ayllu* of a deceased Inca continued to exist. Its symbolic head was the mummy of the dead king with his *huaoqui* — an idol worshiped as the "brother" or protective spirit — of the ruler,

Inca Yahuar Huacac.

Wall of exactly fitting stone blocks with trapezoid niches in Ollantaytambo.

Inca Viracocha, son of Yahuar Huacac.

whose harem and offspring continued to occupy the old palace and lived from the lands and incomes that went with it. Accordingly, when the Spaniards came to Cuzco, they found a great number of palaces of varying ages filled with fabulous riches of gold and silver, which they called "casas de muertos" ("houses of the dead"). The chronicler Pedro Pizarro described in amazement how "the greater part of the people and the wealth were in the possession of the dead, in whose honor fabulous luxury and waste were displayed."

The subjugation of further tribes increased the possessions and the privileges of the ruling families, who soon came to form a class similar to the Spartans in ancient Hellas. Members of the Inca nobility wore heavy ornaments in their pierced earlobes, and this is why in all the Spanish sources they are referred to as "orejones" ("great ears"). The highest priestly offices were reserved for them, as well as the higher military and administrative posts.

If we are to go by the most credible of the chroniclers, there were altogether thirteen ruling Incas, including Atahualpa. At the time of the seventh Inca, Yahuar Huácac, the influence of the city-state of Cuzco in the southeast extended as far as Lake Titicaca; the remaining geographical frontiers are hard to establish, since at that time there was no unified state, but rather a system, admittedly far-reaching but dependent on changing constellations, consisting of alliances and the obligations of major and minor political units. There were numerous temple cities and small towns in the immediate vicinity of Cuzco, such as Chincheros, Písac, Yucay, Calca, and Ollantaytambo in the Urubamba valley, controlled by secular and spiritual lords of impressive independence[10] whose contribution of local manpower for feudal service in the Inca army was heavily rewarded in the form of special privileges.

The strong Chanca people, who lived in the neighboring region of Andahuaylas, to the west, were the Inca's most dangerous vassals and competitors for power in the highlands. For two generations they were a mortal danger to the Inca state. In their first assault they penetrated as far as the very alleys of Cuzco; the Inca Yahuar Huácac, "he who shed tears of blood," had given the city up for lost and retreated to Sacsayhuaman.[11] Contrary to all expectations, the Inca, led by young princes, succeeded in his counterattack and won back his allies.

This is the version of Spanish chroniclers following the heroic sagas of the Incas. Possibly a powerful state stands behind the name Chanca; perhaps they were vassals, or even successors to a Huari empire in middle Peru and the earlier Incas paid them tribute.

The difference between them did not merely consist of the weapons employed on the battlefield — the Inca used mainly stone clubs and slings, while the Chanca used long lances[12] — but was also one of cult and religion. The Chanca brought the *huaoqui* of their two dynastic founders with them into the field;[13] the Inca who bore the proud name of Viracocha, gloried in the special favor of the creator divinity, who created warriors out of the stones of the mountainside and changed them back again.[14]

Yahuar Huácac's son, Cusi Yupanqui, who later became the most famous of the Incas under the name of Pachacútec ("transformer of the globe"), received more than encouragement in time of need from the spirit world. He received the call to become ruler of the future great empire of the Tahuantinsuyu in a dream in which the sun god appeared to him. As the young prince, after much fasting, was praying at the well of Susurpuquio in Sacsayhuaman,[15] ". . . he saw a crystal fall into the water, and in it he perceived the face of an Indian . . . he was wearing a headband across his forehead, like the *llautu* of the Incas, and his earlobes were pierced and adorned with heavy earplugs; he was attired exactly like an Inca. There were three rays radiating outwards from him like the rays of the sun; snakes coiled themselves round his arms; there was a puma's head growing between his legs, a second puma on his back grasped his shoulders with its paws, and a kind of snake hung down the length of his back.

"The sight of this apparition so terrified Pachacútec that he took flight. But the figure spoke to him from out of the well, calling him by his name: 'Come hither, my son, and do not be afraid! I am your father, the sun.' And in the crystal the god showed him the provinces that he was to conquer[15] and called out to him further, saying: 'Take care, that you honor me and remember me with sacrifices!' Then the apparition vanished, but the crystal remained. Pachacútec lifted it out of the water and is supposed to have kept it by him always, in war and in peace, and discovered from it all that he wanted to know."[16] It is said that during his reign relief maps of pottery were made of the provinces he had seen.

Some scholars regard the famous oracle stone of Concacha to be something of a similar nature, namely a kind of representative model of the Tahuantinsuyu. Between 9 and 12 feet in diameter, its surface is chiseled with representations of towns, fortresses, temples, terraces, people, and animals. In the chronicle of Pe-

Inca ceramic. Berlin Museum.

13

Chimú warrior's helmet of woven basket-work, leather armor, and sandals (below). Berlin Museum.

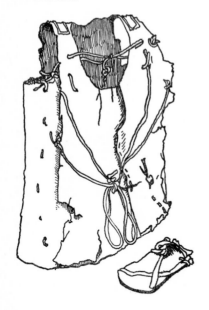

dro Sarmiento de Gamboa, Pachacútec appears as a second Pericles, who immediately after the Chanca wars were ended, began on the building of Cuzco. He replanned the districts and established the basic features of the town, giving it the appearance it had when the Spaniards discovered it, which can moreover still be detected in the present-day plan of the town. In place of the former small and modest Sun Temple, he erected the famous "Golden Court" (Coricancha) and founded similar, splendid temples in honor of the sun throughout all the provinces, endowing them with generous revenues and making it the duty of all his subjects to worship there.[17]

To start with, Pachacútec was still *primus inter pares* for the elders of his tribe and its allies. Before each campaign, he would distribute golden weapons among them that he himself had used.[18] In the *Suma y narración de los Incas* Betanzos, the early Quechua specialist and chronicler, gives an impression of the exultation and presumption of the Cuzco nobility at that time: "Pachacútec had assembled all the *curacas* and lords of the city and of the neighboring region, in Cuzco. He impressed upon them the number of towns and rich areas that lay within reach of their city. He intended to conquer them and annex them, for he could not see why he, who was strong and mighty, should content himself with little. Furthermore, it was wrong that every little prince should call himself Cápac; he alone was entitled to this name. His plan was to depart in two months' time and begin his conquests. However, in the event that he should encounter a prince who proved himself superior in battle, then he would gladly enter the service of the other. He did not, however, anticipate in the slightest that this would occur, for during the war against the Chanca they had all seen that the sun was with him. For the forthcoming enterprises he now required a large number of people and provisions of all kinds."

The elders asked for a period of three months in which to prepare themselves, but otherwise they were in agreement. An enterprise of such proportions could not be tackled without previously consulting the *huacas* — the name these peoples used to denote everything that was sacred to them — and offering them sacrifices.

At this point, Betánzos describes how the Incas revered the river Huatanay, which flowed through Cuzco, by having two cups of *chicha* brought, drinking one themselves and casting the other into the river, as if drinking to the river, which then reciprocated.[19]

However, the Incas Viracocha and Pachacútec frequently broke the peace with the allied feudal lords. Cuzco eventually became the sole domain of the Inca and was for the most part inhabited by outsiders.[20] Chincheros, Písac, Calca, and Yucay became places of ceremonial assembly and pleasure seats of the ruler. Pachacútec's armies were soon to fight in regions more than 600 miles away, and not long after, the territories conquered by them formed a united empire, as provinces under the supremacy of Cuzco. Thanks to the organizational talent of the ruling class, vast areas came under the Inca's scepter almost without resistance.

These gains were not made by this Inca alone, but were achieved in two generations. It is virtually impossible to distinguish his own acquisitions from those made by his brothers or his sons — by Túpac, in particular. The most striking feature of that period, however, is the remarkable total of individual achievements and the number of outstandingly gifted personalities.

In Pachacútec's lifetime his brothers Cápac and Huayna conquered the north Peruvian province of Cajamarca, thereby bringing the entire hinterland of the coastal empire of the Chimú under Inca rule.

Despite its military strength, this complex state system, composed of numerous formerly independent city-states, was extremely vulnerable from the direction of the Cordillera, whose snows provided the reservoirs for the system of canals used in agricultural irrigation and for the water supply to the cities.

Although Pachacútec in Cuzco had foregone all expansion in that direction (there may well have been a non-aggression pact between him and the Chimú), his brothers were not content to halt at this border of the empire and moved on to conquer and plunder Chanchán, the Peruvian Nineveh. Immeasurable gold treasure fell into their hands and was assembled in the main square of Cajamarca on the very spot where, three generations later, the Spaniards melted down the sacred treasures of the Inca empire. The politicians in Cuzco did their utmost to restore the order that had been shattered by this attack; the princes of Cajamarca and Chimú were allowed to continue to rule their lands under Inca supremacy, while their sons were detained and educated in Cuzco and were married to supposed daughters of the Inca. The two generals, Cápac and Huayna Yupanqui, were executed for insubordination at the order their brother, the Inca Pachacútec.[21]

The coastal peoples had already exercised a strong cultural influence and this now affected the political and social structure of the conquering state. Many technical achievements, such as the great highways, are thought to have been taken over from them. Although such claims for precedence are always open to dispute — for example, agricultural irrigation with meticulously planned sloping terraces had long existed in the highlands — it is quite certain that the Chimú culture possessed a particularly rich tradition and an advanced level of civilization.

There appear to have been especially strong external influences on the Chimú. Here too, the dynasty dated back to a landing in *balsas* in the not too distant past. The similarities with Central America in the style of architecture and minor arts are striking.[22]

Chanchán, the capital, already had streets and a central square; the city was divided up on a rectangular plan and, in addition to the terraced temples, the king's palaces, and the cemeteries of the nobility, there were parks, gardens, and irrigated and cultivated areas. A city center of this size is unthinkable without a highly organized social order and a strong political authority.[23]

Brutal Chimú punishment — flaying and exposure.

Palace in Chanchán.

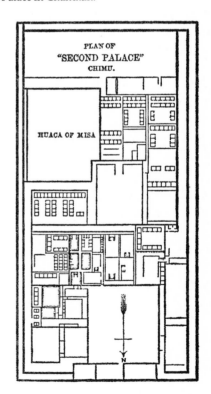

15

The Apucuna of Chinchaysuyu.

Quipucamayo with knot record and "counting board."

The major architectural works were richly adorned with reliefs in clay. The abundance of ceramic and goldwork found there suggests nothing short of mass production.

The task of retaining the territories gained by conquest and preventing their subsequent loss must have been more formidable for Pachacútec and the Incas than the initial conquests. The hierarchical structure and the maintenance of the numerous garrisons required immense resources. The Incas could never have held their empire by military means alone. They adopted measures involving all areas of life and were backed by existing institutions.

The structure of the Inca state can be described as an adaptation of the existing regional agrarian and social structure to mythical cosmic concepts of the state, which probably originated from Asia. There is the significance of the number four and the division of the empire, not on ethnic grounds, but into the four *suyus* — that is, the winds, directions of heaven, the four governors, and the ancient throne, umbrella, and litter symbols of majesty, (Heine-Geldern, Trimborn). For the most part, agricultural land was collectively owned and the Inca and sun temples now claimed their share of it. Similarly, the village communities had their own communal labor system, which the Spaniards continued to use.

Throughout the major provinces the population was subject to a hierarchical system and was divided into groups ranging from the family unit to units of 100, 500, and 1000. The only communication that existed between the different social levels was by the delivery of orders and reports. The implementation of authority was for the most part left to the leaders of families and chieftains, even in the case of former deadly enemies, such as the Chanca.[24]

Naturally, the conditions were constantly changing with the acquisition or loss of different territories, so that a great deal of improvisation was essential. So, although scholars and writers are forever seeking to construct a picture of an all-embracing, total Inca bureaucracy, this picture must, of necessity, remain incomplete.

The higher administrative and military posts, such as the *apucuracas* of units of 10,000 men, were filled by *orejones*, the Inca nobility. The governors of the great provinces, the traveling inspector generals (*tucuyricuc*, the all-seeing ones), and the ministers in Cuzco (the *apucunas*) responsible for the four parts of the empire — Chinchaysuyu, Contisuyu, Collasuyu Antisuyu — were almost always closely related to the reigning Inca.

The sons of *curacas* were educated at the Yachahuasi, the Inca college in Cuzco. This boys' school had had an outstanding reputation in Peru since the time of the fourth Inca, Mayta Cápac. Here, in the company of the imperial princes and sons of the Inca nobility, they received instruction in all the sciences, which the sons of common folk were not allowed to learn. For four years they were taught the religion and its ceremonial and learned elegant style in the use of the imperial language Quechua, as well as oratory, history, and knot-records. In the event of an uprising, they were valuable hostages.

II   Portrayal of a demon or god.

1 and 2   Manco Cápac and his sister Mama Ocllo, the legendary ancestors of the Inca dynasty. Colonial painting, showing the traditional Inca symbols (disk of the sun, headband and tuft, feather sunshade, puma heads, metal ornaments, and geometric decoration.

3　Part of the mountain city of Machu Picchu, restored from the jungle, with terraced walls and gabled houses of white granite, and the sun sanctuary behind on the left (Intihuatana sun seat).

4　Farming terraces near Ichupampa.

5   *Bastions of the fortress of Sacsayhuaman above Cuzco.*

6   *Tampu Machay ("cave of refuge"), a sanctuary by a spring and a healing bath near Cuzco, traditionally a favorite resort of Inca Túpac.*

7 Wooden goblet in the form of a jaguar's head.

8 Wooden ritual container. The bowl with the bird's head symbolizes a spring.

9 *Monolithic oracle stone from Concacha or Sayhuite, on the height of the pass between the Apurímac and Abancay (west of Cuzco). Length: 14′ 5,″ width: 9′ 9,″ height: 7′ 10.″ The figures on the upper surface are severely damaged.*

10   *One of the rare portraits from the Inca period.*

From the study of similar institutions in the Byzantine and Turkish empires, we know that these young people usually gained extensive privileges for their families and native communities.

The liberty of the subject peoples was greatly curtailed by the compulsory resettlement of entire population groups and by the prohibition against changing their domicile. The trading sections of the population were presumably permitted greater mobility. Trade and commerce were in some cases even stimulated by these resettlements. De Soto, Pizarro's famous captain, observed the lively coming and going of Indians carrying wares across the suspension bridge over the river Huancabamba, and Xerez states that the Indians had to pay a certain share of the merchandise that they carried as a bridge toll. Some groups of *mitmac*, the name for those who had been transferred from their homes to other regions, succeeded in gaining influence in their new surroundings; thus we see the Cañari and Chachapoya, who had been transferred to Cuzco, as Huáscar's bodyguard.

The resettlements, the labor tax, and other compulsory measures may have temporarily strengthened the security of the state and even raised the general prosperity, but in the long run they must have severely impaired the efficiency of the people. They could not hope to control the chaos that resulted when the rigid organization from above could no longer be maintained. This may account, to a certain extent at least, for the passivity of the Indians when confronted by the few hundred Europeans who invaded their land.

As in the ancient Persian empire of Darius and in the case of the Romans, the maintenance of order and economic stability was possible only by solving the problem of communications by opening up the country. The geographical nature of the Andean region was most unfavorable for the formation of a unified state. In this land, divided by countless mountain ranges, valleys, and ravines, political disunity would have seemed the natural outcome.

It is well known how the Chimú and the Incas surmounted these obstacles. There were the highways with their ever more lavishly equipped wayside resthouses, storehouses, and arsenals (*tampus*), and the punctual and incredibly rapid delivery of messages by relay runners (*chasqui*). There were steps to scale the steep ascents (the roads led over passes of up to 13,500 feet), since there was only foot and llama traffic, and rivers and ravines were crossed by paved roads and rope bridges. Long stretches of these roads have been maintained to this day, and 19th-century travelers still used a suspension bridge that spanned the deep ravine of the Apurímac river at Limatambo. These technical achievements seem all the more astounding to us when we consider that in all their activities these peoples were dependent on human labor alone.

The main preoccupation during this period of conquest and great creative achievements must surely have been the spiritual and religious encounter with the cultures of the Chimú empire and the coastal regions, with their sacred shrine of Pachacámac on the shores of the Pacific Ocean.

Legendary procession by litter across the night sky. Lizard and fox carry a star divinity (moon?), radiating rays with snakes' heads. The moon's orbit is depicted in the form of the famous two-headed snake.

25

Inca Sinchi Roca.

Inca Túpac with a Quipucamayo.

Whereas the Incas of the cooler highlands worshiped the sun, the inhabitants of the hot, rainless Pacific coast, featured the moon in their legends as the healing, benevolent element personifying the moistness and cool of the night, while the sun was the destroyer.

Their highest god, Pachacámac, the creator, shares many common features with Viracocha, the god the Incas revered as their creator. The Spanish sources frequently make no clear distinction between the names, Viracocha and Pachacámac, indicating a fusion of the cults of the highland and coastal peoples. Although the sun cult was generally imposed as the official religion, the Incas were largely tolerant of the religions of their subject peoples, since it was in their own interest to have the major and minor local divinities acting on their behalf. They took the *huacas* of the conquered peoples from the temples in the provinces and brought them to Cuzco, which became the holy city for the whole of the Tahuantinsuyu.

This transfer of gods was also strategically intended to insure the state against insurrections; at the first sign of unrest in a province, the *huacas* revered by the inhabitants of that particular province would be publicly scourged in Cuzco. Such measures had a very strong impact on the believers. It is hard to suppress a shudder at this intermingling of religion and political expediency. A characteristic of the ruling people appears to have been a certain sobriety, which is evident in their art. "Vase painting and the decoration of textiles lack that breath of mysticism that the potters and weavers of the ancient Peruvian cultures were able to inject into their works. The mastery of the Inca potters lies in their unerring feeling for color and proportion and in restricting themselves to vessels of few and strictly determined forms. The weavers worked the same recurring designs and decorations into the brilliant robes of their nobility. The patterns are always attractive and decorative, but they are simple and show none of the wealth of imagination and uncanny mystery of some of the ceremonial garments of the Tiahuanaco period or the burial cloths of Paracas."[25]

The status of the shrine of Pachacámac in Peruvian history, before and during the Conquest, shows us that cultural exchange took place between the conquerors and the conquered. Initially of secondary importance, its significance increased immensely as fate turned its back on the Incas and their belief that the sun would always be on their side was shattered. In their most desperate need, Huayna Cápac, Huáscar, and Atahualpa turned to this oracle and accepted its pronouncements.

We can well imagine that the incorporation of such heterogenous elements made it increasingly difficult for the conquerors in Cuzco to overlook this interplay of forces and adjust to the changing situation, without compromising their own values.

But there was no halting this development, whether or not it boded well for the future.

In the next to last generation there was a reversal of fortune against the ruling Incas.

During the lifetime of Pachacútec Inca Yupanqui there was a second wave of conquests, led this time by the crown prince Túpac and his brother Tilca Yupanqui.[26] The garrison of Quito, some 1200 miles from Cuzco, was established in the course of this undertaking, although it was lost once more after Túpac's departure. He also marched through the coastal lowlands of Ecuador that were to present Huayna Cápac with such problems. Túpac's travels did not serve military purposes alone. In Sarmiento's chronicle he is portrayed as a great discoverer. From Ecuador he put out to sea in *balsas* and is supposed to have been away for so long that there was fear for his safe return. The islands of Avachumbi and Ninachumbi, mentioned by Sarmiento, have not been localized to this day.[27]

It is not known whether the objective was a visit to one of the famous ocean shrines or whether the voyage took him much further afield. (The potsherds in Chimú and Inca style found by Thor Heyerdahl in the Galapagos Islands, some 600 miles from the mainland, increase the likelihood of its having been the major venture.)

During their six-year absence in the northern lands,[27] the successor to the throne and his brother Amaru devoted themselves to an intensive cultural and construction program. At Tumibamba, his headquarters in southern Ecuador, Coya Mama Ocllo granted him the inheritance of Huayna Cápac. At the insistence of the aging Inca Pachacútec, Túpac finally returned to Cuzco "and there he led the most triumphal entry into the city that any Inca had ever held . . . he brought with him captives of all different tribes, decked out in their ceremonial attire, and strange animals, and incalculable treasures."[27]

Again, as after the victory over the Chimú empire, reasons of state and the mistrust of the aged Inca and his advisers towards the successful general demanded a sacrifice from the Inca family itself — this time it was Túpac's brother and closest associate, Tilca Yupanqui.

The victory celebrations, which lasted for more than a year, and Túpac's accession to power during his father's lifetime, helped divert attention from this sacrifice.

Battle scenes, probably a festival, with sling-throwers, archers, conch blowers, heraldic birds and plants. In the center, under the feather sun shade, is the leader (Inca?) with ritual battle-ax.

The triumphal procession has been described in such graphic and illuminating detail by Santa Cruz Pachacuti, the Indian *curaca*, that, despite its primitive style, we are including a literal translation here:[28] "Túpac is on the homeward march to Cuzco; he brings with him the Cayambi, Cañari, and Chachapoya as halberdiers; these are followed by many maidens from Quito, from Quilaco, and from the tribes of the Quillasinga, Chachapoya, Yunga, Hualla, and Huanca, to wait on the *coya* (queen) and to serve as temple virgins for Viracocha-Pachayacháchic (the creator deity). The good, aged Pachacútec Inca Yupanqui was waiting in Cuzco with 30,000 warriors, and as he (the victorious son) approached the city, the father went out in person as far as Vilcaconga to meet him, leading his men in battle formation, the high *apucuracas* in their litters shaded by feather umbrellas. And the two armies, shimmering with gold and silver and in the glowing colors of their feather decorations, swarm about each other in spiral or serpentine maneuvers, and the good, old man appoints himself general and his son commander in the field. The half of the troops leading the captured *curacas* and all the *apucuracas* are ordered to the fortress of Sacsayhuaman and instructed to remain there in a state of readiness for the defense of Cuzco, and the young prince Huayna Cápac, his grandson, is to fight them with his 50,000 men. At last the war game begins — those who had gone to Sacsayhuaman are conquered, the young Huayna Cápac climbs the fortress and takes captive all the Cayambi and Pasto and whatever other tribes there were, and also the heads of the decapitated foes, sprinkling them with llama blood and impaling them on lances. To end with, they cry out their 'haylli' at the conquered and lead them in triumph along the great processional road to the Coricancha (sun temple) in Cuzco; there, all the war leaders do homage to the simple image of the creator and go out by another door into the two great squares, Haucaypata and Cusipata, singing the 'Quichu' hymn; the *curacas* take their seats beneath feather umbrellas, while Pachacútec Inca Yupanqui with his two sons, Túpac Inca Yupanqui and Amaru Túpac Inca, sit on golden *tianas* (lower seats), all three adorned with the *llautu* (the multicolored fillet wound around the head) and the *mascapaycha* (headfringe), Pachacútec bearing the *sunturpaucar* (the scepter adorned with the feathers of the Coriquenque bird, worn by the highest Inca), and whereas Túpac Inca also has a scepter, Amaru has none, and simply holds two small golden *champis* (clubs) in his hands."

Like the external developments in the empire and its provinces, occurrences within the ruling dynasty itself determined subsequent events and crises.

The acquisition of absolute power brought in its train a fundamental change in the way of life of the ruling family. The royal household was extended and palace life became increasingly dominated by ceremonial. From the time of Pachacútec onwards the number of royal wives and children became considerable. Subject peoples would present the Inca with maidens by way of tribute, and he could choose concubines for himself or as gifts to favored followers from the sun "convents," which commanded the most beautiful girls from all parts of the empire and from all social levels.

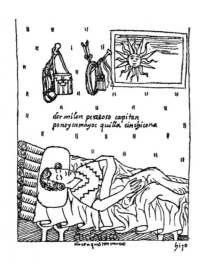

Not all the Incas were conquerors. Prince Yupanqui was a "sleeper and lazy captain and died without conquering anything."

The main wife, the *coya*, was the only person equal in rank to the Inca, and her sons alone had the right of inheritance.

Pachacútec, whose main wife was the daughter of a chieftain, married his son Túpac, the successor to the throne, to his daughter Mama Ocllo. In subsequent generations sister-marriage was obligatory, but was restricted to the Inca alone. In this way, children of the sun were completely separate from all others, even from the powerful Inca nobility. Pachacútec had already felt himself to be the favored son of the sun and in various guises had conversed with the deities. When Túpac Inca marched through Chinchaysuyu, he was worshiped as a god. He was brought burnt offerings, just like the sun and the royal mummies, and no onlooker was permitted to approach him.[29]

Little is known of the earlier *coyas*, who still came from *curaca* families. At that time, the Inca's eldest sister appears to have occupied a more important position than the women of the seraglio, including the first wife. She may possibly have performed the role of a priestess.[30] Túpac's sister and queen, Mama Ocllo, became the most famous Inca *coya* and was among the outstanding personalities of her generation.[31] When Túpac wished to put all the men of the Yanayaco tribe to death on account of a revolt, the sentence was mitigated as a result of her intervention.[32]

Mama Ocllo, the dominant queen mother.

Above all, however, she would mediate in the conflicts between the priesthood and the ruler, and just after the birth of Huayna Cápac, the Inca's heir, she succeeded in averting a bloody punishment that Túpac had imposed on a large number of *humus* and *laycas*, representatives of the lower ranks of the priesthood.[33]

The interrelation between the Inca, the *coya*, and the servants of the cults and oracles is strikingly reminiscent of alignments in similar disputes in the ancient Persian empire. Among the Achaemenids the "magi" were a strong force; Darius was unable to prevail by waging war on them and so adopted a more political brand of piety that did not run counter to the principles of the great kingdom. His chief wife and sister Atossa, however, protected the magi, who subsequently regained ground.

After Túpac's death, Mama Ocllo, the *coya*, exerted great influence over the destinies of the land, since her son Huayna Cápac was not yet of age.[34] Many years after her death, when the nobility lost faith in her son as their Inca and he stood in danger of losing control of power, the divinely worshiped *huaca* of this woman was the source of the reviving force that brought everyone to their senses and restored the authority of the Inca.[35]

After Túpac and Mama Ocllo, the strength of the dynasty rapidly declined and signs of degeneration began to appear.

Among the great Incas, the principle of succession, touched upon above, was in fact only followed in the case of Huayna Cápac, the son of Túpac and Mama Ocllo, and was taken up once again after the death of Manco II. Pachacútec and Túpac were both younger sons; the former came to power by a coup d'état and the latter when his older brother Túpac Amaru stood aside. After the death of Huayna Cápac, followed almost immediately by that of his legitimate heir Ninan

Cuyuchi, two sons of differing legitimacy — Huáscar and Atahualpa, who subsequently became famous — hotly fought for the succession. Even at Huáscar's accession, there were palace revolutions caused by other pretenders.[36] The Spaniards, accustomed to the European preoccupation with questions of succession, could hardly have been very convinced by the "legitimacy" of the individual accessions to the throne of the Inca.

The contradictions in the different Spanish accounts of the system of succession in the Tahuantinsuyu arise mainly out of the multiplicity of factors which governed the choice of the successor to the throne — namely legitimacy, the father's decision, the preference of the *ayllus*, and the judgment of the deities, which was established by the *calpa* (augury made by scrutinizing the heart and lungs of llama).[37] On this occasion, the *villac-humu* (the high priest) himself performed the sacrifice and was thus one of the most important participants.[38]

Huayna Cápac (1493–1527) — Accession to power and marriage — Display of magnificent opulence — The Inca assumes office of high priest — Importance of the individual shrines is determined by the loyalty of their priests to the ruling house — Privileges of the Orejones are curtailed — Removal of the royal household to Ecuador increases the influences of new groups — Uprisings and an epidemic of the plague strike at the core of the complicated state structure — First landing of the Spaniards at Túmbez in 1527 — Hallucinations of armies of the dead and visions of imminent ruin afflict the sovereign, who dies of the plague at the age of forty.

Shortly before 1500, at the time when Columbus was sailing the Caribbean, Huayna Cápac (in the Inca language the name means the "sublime youth") came to the throne of the vast empire of Túpac and Pachacútec.

The young ruler's accession to the throne took place at the same time as his marriage to his sister Mama Cusi Rimay. Preparations for the festivities are supposed to have lasted three years.[1] The Inca prepared himself by fasting for four weeks — the so-called *zaziz*. During this period he had to withdraw to one room and remain there in total darkness.

The women of the royal *ayllus* prepared the *chicha* beer, and between the beginning and end of the *zaziz* all four of the Inca's new ritual robes had to be completed. While he was observing the rules of the fast, the queen mother and the sisters of the Inca performed this task, including all the preparations involved, such as dressing the skins and the vicuña wool, and also the spinning and dyeing.

The first garment consisted of a black, collarless tunic with a red design and a long cloak, which may have been a puma skin or dyed to resemble one. The second had an undergarment with the puma design, while the cloak was snow-white. For the third robe both the undergarment and the cloak were snow-white. The fourth was a blue color edged with fringes and had cord fastenings.

At the end of the *zazis*, the future Inca, attired in the first of his garments, left the room and made his way out of the city to the oldest shrine of Huanacauri and the hill Anahuarqui. Thousands of warriors were assembled there awaiting his arrival.

On the sacred hill of Yahuira, the young Inca put on his second robe and the *llautu*, the emperor's headband of red vicuña wool to which the feather decora-

Curved terminating wall (apse) of the main temple (Coricancha) in Cuzco.

tion, consisting of three erect feathers from the sacred Coriquenque bird, were attached. The heavy golden earrings hung down from under the *llautu*. A gold band, reaching down to the ground, hung from the great lance that he carried, and his breast was covered by a gold disk in the shape of the sun (Cieza describes it as moonshaped). Outside the city, the Inca killed a llama with his own hands and thereby inaugurated the great sacrifices.

It is hard for Europeans of today to form any idea of the color and magnificence of those festivities. Santa Cruz Pachacuti describes[2] how all the public buildings and houses were decked out with feather decorations and how the streets of the procession shone with gold and silver.

On the day of the wedding there were two processions moving through the city. Carried on his litter, Huayna Cápac emerged from the palace of his grandfather, Pachacútec Inca Yupanqui, accompanied by his advisers and by the nobility, the *apucuracas* of Collasuyu. From the palace of her father Túpac Inca, came Mama Cusi Rimay in her litter, accompanied by many *orejones* and the *apucuracas* of Chinchaysuyu, Contisuyu, and Antisuyu. The two processions used two separate gateways to enter the temple, where they merged. The high priest united the Inca and *coya* by placing golden shoes on their feet.

What we would call the coronation took place three days later. The Inca received the *mascapaycha* (the head fringe) and the *sunturpaucar* (scepter) from the hands of the high priest, who then placed the royal diadem upon the *coya*. Kissing the earth and shaking his mantle, the young Inca swore that he, like his forefathers, would do his utmost for the improvement of the temple and for the welfare of the empire and that he would protect and defend it, that he would uphold the privileges granted by previous Incas and recognize their laws. And he promised rights and favors to those who served him faithfully.

There followed the great prayer of the high priest for the well-being of the Inca, in which all those present joined.

In conclusion, Huayna Cápac received homage from the *orejones*, the *curacas*, and the officers in the Haucaypata square, in front of the Sun Temple in Cuzco.

The *coya*, Mama Cusi Rimay, is said to have died very young. She gave the king one son, Ninan Cuyuchi, who should have been heir to the throne. Huayna Cápac already had older sons by women of his seraglio, of whom Atahualpa and Huáscar are the most famous.[3]

In the early years of Huayna Cápac's reign, the strong personality of his mother Mama Ocllo made itself felt. During her lifetime, the Inca was never absent from the capital for long. It was not until after her death that the Inca embarked on his extensive travels, first in the south, in present-day Bolivia and Chile.

The inspection of the northern part of the Chinchaysuyu was at this time undertaken by one of his brothers. The sovereign visited the royal households of the individual *tucuyricuc* (governors of the provinces), deposing some who had not been successful and appointing new ones in their place. It is worth noting that in this he relied on the *curaca* tribes for support and entrusted these high posts to men who had recently been fighting against his father.[4] He made fresh conquests in Chile and he had to advance with armed forces into the southeast, where the border peoples, and in particular the Chiriguano, were repeatedly threatening the empire. To secure the border, he settled *mitmacs* there. Cochabamba, in southern Bolivia, was another important colony of this kind. He extended and improved[5] the border garrisons established by his father and promoted an ambitious building program everywhere, ranging from shrines to important military objectives, such as fortresses, roads, *tampus*, arsenals, and storehouses. Not content with these, however, he also, as we read, built summer residences, hunting lodges, and baths.

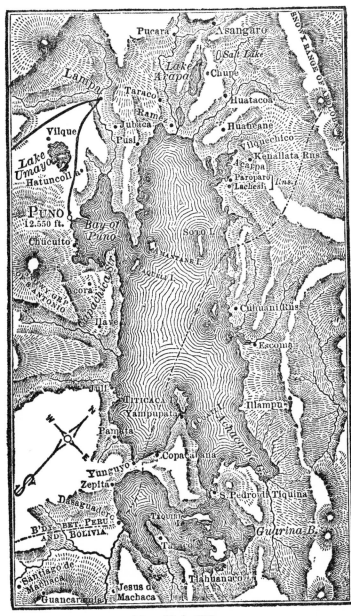

Map of Lake Titicaca.

Huayna Cápac, the "Young Ruler."

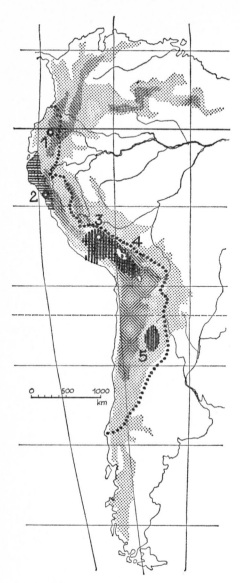

Tahuantinsuyu(Inca Empire)

Altitudes over 1,000 meters

Altitudes over 3,000 meters

Chimú states alliance
(ca. 1400)

Area of influence of Inca
(ca. 1400) (according to information of the chronicler,
A. Vásquez de Espinoza).

Empire of the Inca Huayna
Cápac (ca. 1500)

1 Quito
2 Chanchán
3 Cuzco
4 Lake Titicaca
5 Tucma (Tucumán)

The larger *tampus* were equipped with everything that a visit from the large and demanding royal household could possibly require. At each of the numerous shrines along the road to Collasuyu, almost all of which were connected with the origins and history of the Inca dynasty, he performed memorial rites for his parents and ancestors. He fasted and prayed for many days at the island shrine on Lake Titicaca[6] and offered captives taken in war to the father sun.[7]

During his long expedition to Collao and Chile he received frequent reports of a large-scale uprising in the northern highlands of Ecuador, which his father had conquered.

The many contemporary accounts are mostly unreliable as far as the early history of Ecuador is concerned, and they are not explicit as to whether this uprising consisted of a temporary alliance of independent tribes or cities, or whether it was an organized confederacy or the insurrection of one of the kingdoms conquered by the Inca. The official Inca tradition recognized no supra-regional allegiance except to itself. The Indian clans in sympathy with Atahualpa, the Spanish chroniclers, and subsequent historians of Ecuador all believe in a traditional monarchy centered at Quito; Atahualpa's mother is supposed to have been its princess and to have brought the province to the Inca Huayna Cápac as a form of dowry. The uprising was probably the result of an alliance, whose central authority was weak in peace time, but rallied to strong leadership in times of crisis.

The ethnographic composition and the origin of the population of the territory presents many problems. From earliest times down to the very recent past, Ecuador has been beset by unrest and ferment, and in those generations just before and during the Conquest many tribes were exterminated.

Before the Inca conquest, most of the inhabitants must have belonged to the Chibcha language group.

At various times, also during the reign of Huayna Cápac, the coast and hinterland were harrassed by seafaring foreign tribes and splinter groups. This is confirmed by legends and accounts, the best known of which is the legend of the origin of the Cara or Scyri, which was not actually written down until much later, in the 19th century.

The invaders are supposed to have arrived on rafts in about 700 or 800 A.D., landing at the Bay of Caraques. They led a nomadic life on the coast for about 200 years, and then, following the Esmeralda River, they penetrated the highlands. There they established a kingdom and united it through marriage to the older principality of Puruhá, on its southern border.[8]

The political significance of the Cara may be uncertain; their name does not appear in the records of battles with the Inca, though there is reference to the similar sounding Caranqui. Nevertheless, recent research is lending increasing weight to the traditional accounts of immigration from overseas. Ceramic finds suggest a Mexican influence and maritime trading with Central America.[9] Some Bonn ethnologists are at present conducting a special investigation into the peoples of Ecuador which should provide some interesting conclusions on this point, when their findings are published.

The great snow-capped mountains and volcanoes along the equator had the same mythical importance for the highland peoples as places of communal worship, as Lake Titicaca had for the Peruvians. Well into the 18th century, children were still sacrificed to the gods in certain mountain caves.[10] For the Indians, Chimborazo and the volcano of Tungurahua facing it embodied the chief male and female deities.[11] Alexander von Humboldt, who traveled through the "equinoctial regions of the New Continent" in about 1800, was deeply impressed by the violence of the myths surrounding the high mountains of Ecuador, which an Indian friend had disclosed to him.[11a]

Huayna Cápac spent one and half years preparing for the great war in Ecuador. He assembled the *curacas* in Tiahuanaco and called them into service. He proceeded in much the same way as his grandfather Pachacútec had once done, informing the feudal lords of the neighborhood of Cuzco of his plans for the conquest of the northwest Peruvian plateaus, while distributing weapons and apparel amongst them and promising them increased privileges.[12]

Huayna Cápac must have been intent on more than simply putting down the uprising and from the outset must have thought in terms of conquering fresh territories in the north. He may well have been swayed by economic considerations too, for the traveling Chibcha merchants must surely have informed the Inca of the great wealth of Colombia.

Now the organization of the Inca empire set to work. The *tampus* were prepared, the camps filled, and provisions and arms procured.

The *curacas* set out for the native regions to assemble their contingents, meanwhile imposing a certain quota of able-bodied fighting men to be raised by the chieftains immediately responsible to them, right down to those in charge of 100 families.

At the appointed time, the troops from all four *suyus* met at the heart of the empire, assembled according to their tribes, and camped outside the capital.[13]

The departure coincided with one of the holy festivals of the year.

In Cuzco life no longer pursued its customary course. The extent to which religion intruded into everyday life, and the way in which the major festivals were not restricted to individual places and areas, but involved and embraced the entire Tahuantinsuyu, can be seen from the two descriptions by the chroniclers Cieza and Cobo,[14] which have been collated here:

All the *huacas* that were housed in Cuzco were brought out into the Haucaypata square; beside the oldest and most revered Inca idols stood the mummies of the dead Incas, surrounded by the *huacas* of the tribes they had conquered in their lifetime. The royal mummies, seated beneath feather umbrellas, had been washed, clothed, and adorned in honor of the day, for they too participated in the banquet and the sacrifices.

Churches: 1. St. Christopher. 2. Santa Ana. 3. The Nazarene Church. 4. S. Antonio. 5. St. Blaise. 6. Devotee's House, Aropata. 7. Jesus Mary. 8. Cathedral. 9. Chapel of St. Jacob. 10. St. Francis. 11. Memorial Church. 12. La Companía. 13. St. Augustine. 14. Hospital de Hombres. 15. Santa Clara. 16. Santa Catalina. 17. Devotee's House of Santa Rosa. 19. St. Dominic. 20. Devotee's House of Ahuacpinta. 21. St. James. 22. Bethlehem Church. 23. Pantheon Church. 24. University. 25. Prefecture. 26. Town Hall. 27. Prison.

Inca Ruins: A. Sun Temple. B. Palace of the Virgins of the Sun. C. Palace of Inca Túpac Yupanqui. D. Palace of Inca Yupanqui. E. Palace of Inca Rocca. F. Palace of Inca Viracocha. G. Palace of Yachahuasi, or the schools. H. Palace of Inca Pachacútec. I. Palace of Huayna Cápac. J. Palace of Manco Cápac. K. House of Garcilaso de la Vega. L. The Intihuatana, or Sun Circle. M. Ruins of an Inca building. N. Chungana, or the rock with chambers. O. Hewn rock with chambers. P. Steep road leading to the stone quarries. O. Pila or the bath of the Incas. The black lines show the old Inca walls (after Squier).

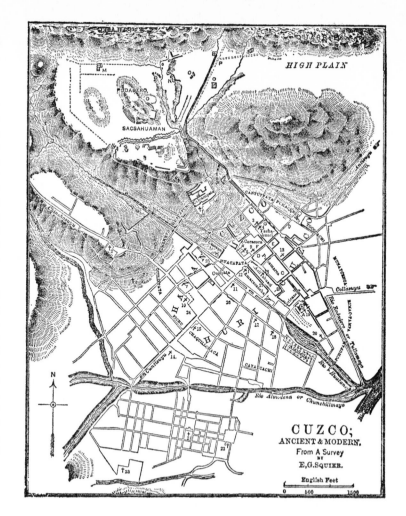

Sacrificial offerings arrived from all regions of the Tahuantinsuyu, even from the poorest and most remote areas — live llamas, guinea pigs, field produce, provisions, simple and splendid textiles, feather and shell ornaments, pottery vessels, and gold and silver figurines of people, llamas, and everyday articles. A cosmos of the entire life and diverse cultures of the western part of South America was to be seen in the Inca metropolis at these festivals.

At important occasions, such as the imminent war against Ecuador, the usual sacrifices of animals, objects, and drink were not considered adequate, and the event called for *capacocha*, or human sacrifice.[15]

In each of the main towns of the provinces, a girl and a youth aged between ten and twelve years and of noble birth and especial beauty would be chosen and then sent to Cuzco, magnificently adorned at the center of a festival procession bringing the other sacrificial gifts.

On arrival at the capital, the sacrificial trains would circle twice around the Haucaypata square, passing in front of the images of the deities, the mummies of the kings, and the reigning Inca.

At the behest of the ruler, the priests decided which sacrifices were to be made in Cuzco and at shrines in the vicinity and which were to be returned for sacrifice in their place of origin.

In Cuzco the ceremonies were performed according to the following procedure:

"The high priest selected four llamas and sacrificed one for the creator, one for the god of thunder, one for the sun, and one for Huanacauri ... in front of him stood great gold and silver vessels of *sancu* (a maize dish); he sprinkled them with the blood of the animal offerings ... and, facing all those assembled about him pronounced the following prayer:

'Take care, when you partake of this *sancu,* that you do so not in a melancholy or half-hearted fashion; for the sun, our father, will see this and make you suffer dearly for it. However, he who eats and believes with his whole heart, he will be richly rewarded by the creator, the sun, and the thunder god, who will grant him sons and happy years, and he will never want for food or anything else ...'

All swore, henceforth, to desist from evil, not to grumble against the creator and the thunder god, and always to be loyal to the Inca, and the priest gave each one who had sworn the *yahuar-sancu,* picking up a small portion with three fingers and pushing it into his mouth."[16]

The sacrifices were connected with *calpa,* the inspection and interpretation of the condition of the entrails of the animal offering; moreover, the *huaoqui* and the Inca mummies would immediately be questioned by the priests about imminent events, the prospects of victory, weather, harvest, and the life and death of the Inca.[17]

The individual deputations now left Cuzco with the selected children and dedicated gift offerings, moving at first in four great processions along the imperial roads to Chinchaysuyu, Contisuyu, Collasuyu, and Antisuyu; these then split up and each group took its shortest homeward route.

At the head of the line went the llama herds, followed by the children selected for sacrifice and the people bearing the dedicated offerings. From time to time, choir leaders would strike up prayers and litanies in praise of the Inca and the rest would join in the responses.

If any person met the procession in the open country, they would avert their gaze and fall to the ground; villagers filled with awe would remain in their houses until the procession had passed by. The offerings dedicated in Cuzco were so deeply venerated that people no more dared to lay eyes on them than on the divine person of the Inca himself. In this way the procession crossed mountains, forests, and ravines.[18]

We are told that the children selected for human sacrifice were made numb with coca and were then suffocated. Molina says that their hearts were extracted and the blood sprinkled over the *huacas.* Elsewhere we read that the victims were buried alive in rock graves.[19] The animal and food offerings were burned, while the remaining dedicated offerings were presented in all imaginable ways to the deities, demons, and protective spirits, often in the face of great obstacles. If the priests could not reach a snow-covered mountain shrine, they would force their way up as far as they possibly could and then push the dedicated offering yet a little further up with slings. For they dared not neglect even the smallest *huaca,* certain in the

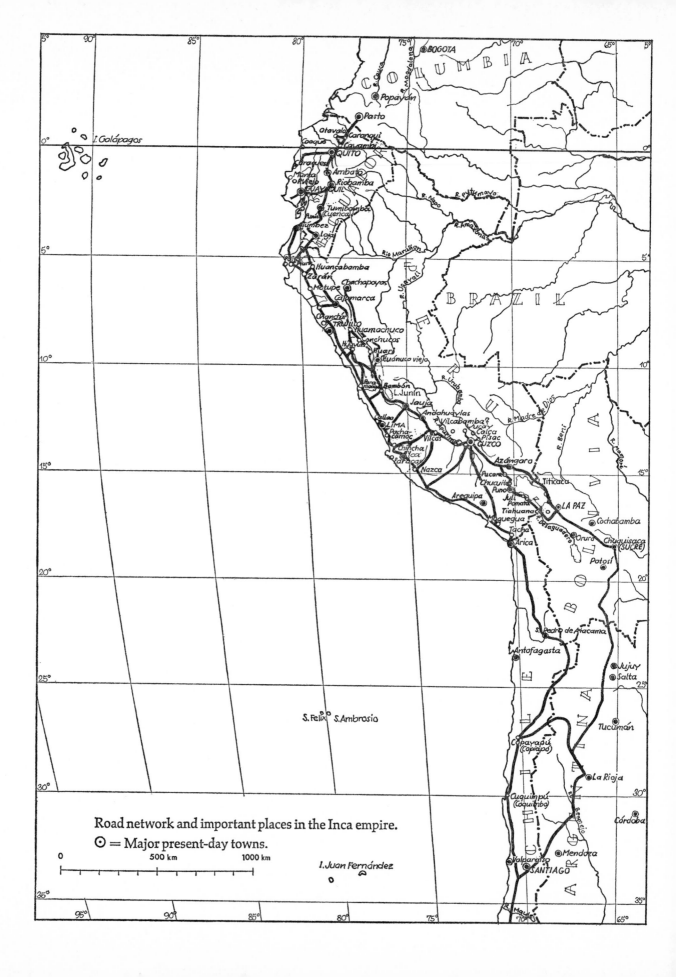

Road network and important places in the Inca empire.

⊙ = Major present-day towns.

0   500 km   1000 km

38

knowledge that if they did, harm might then befall the Inca and the world he ruled.[18]

Huayna Cápac introduced some essential organizational changes at the councils in Cuzco preceding the military campaign. Hitherto the posts of high-ranking officers had been reserved for the *orejones*, the relations of the Inca.[20] Now, however, apart from his brother Auqui Túpac and one *orejón* by the name of Mihac Naca Mayta, Huayna Cápac appointed a number of *curacas* from Contisuyu and Collao as officers and permitted them to have their own litters regardless of their social origin.[21]

He also made changes among the *apucunas*. He recalled his brother Sinchi Roca, responsible for the great building program, and in his place appointed another brother, Lloqui Túpac, and an uncle, Apu Hillaquita. During his long periods of absence, he needed men who could cope with unexpected political difficulties that might arise.

It was more than three months before the last man of the great army that had been encamped outside Cuzco had departed.

The Inca took an immense royal household with him. Cieza says that it included 2000 women alone. The Inca's sister Mama Cusi Rimay, mother of the heir to the throne, accompanied Huayna Cápac to the north. Huáscar's mother Mama Rahua Ocllo was also there. Atahualpa's mother is thought no longer to have been alive by then. He left many of his sons behind in Cuzco, among them Huáscar and Manco, whom the Spaniards proclaimed Inca after the death of Atahualpa. He took Ninan Cuyuchi, his heir, and Atahualpa with him to Ecuador.[22]

It is at this point that the chronicles first mention Atahualpa, the most famous and controversial personality of all the Incas, who may well have received the *mascapaycha*, but was never to enter the city of Cuzco as Inca.

This most magnificent procession in Inca history moved along the "royal mountain road" through the cities of Vilcas, Jauja, Cajamarca, and territories that had long since been subdued, and advanced towards Tumibamba, birthplace of Huayna Cápac and capital of the Cañari in southern Ecuador. We read in Cieza's chronicle that in the course of this march, Huayna Cápac was continually being met by ambassadors bringing him costly gifts and delivering important messages. There were lengthy halts in the major provincial cities. On these occasions the Inca would be attired in the costume of the region.[23]

In Vilcas they were celebrating Cápac-Raymi. The sun temple had just been completed there. Cieza describes how Huayna Cápac ascended a terrace and there performed his devotions and greeted the rising sun.[24] Garcilaso describes this salutation for us:[25]

"In the grey of early morning, the Inca in the company of all the *orejones*, the priests, the *curacas*, and the people, awaited the sunrise, his face turned towards the east. All were barefoot, and immediately the glowing orb appeared, they cowered down on their heels, their arms outstretched and hands raised aloft,

Huayna Cápac with warriors.

39

and blew towards the sun. While all were still cowering thus, the Inca rose, holding a golden vessel filled with *chicha* in either hand. He poured away the contents of the vessel in his right hand as a libation to the sun. The Inca himself took a sip from the other and then gave each of the *orejones* a little in their golden goblets. The intoxicating liquor was also distributed among the *curacas*, the army, and the people."

The next stations along the way were Jauja and Cajamarca. The procession of many thousand souls now faced the long and arduous march from there to Tumibamba. It was approximately the same distance that Pizarro, naturally under more difficult conditions, had to cover from the coast to Cajamarca — about 250—280 miles. From Cuzco to Tumibamba was about three times that distance, and Quito lay about another 220 miles farther north, making a total of about 1000 miles from Cuzco. (The "miles" mentioned in the following passages are Spanish miles — the *legua* — corresponding to 3.5 miles.)

For Huayna Cápac, Tumibamba was rather more than just a military strongpoint for his war against Quito. He loved the land and the city and felt bound to it by destiny, for he was born there and his mother and father had spent many important years of their lives there. In a chamber of the temple of Tumibamba Pachacámac, which his father had built when the young prince came into the world, he placed a golden *huaca* for his mother Mama Ocllo, containing his own placenta in its center, like a reliquary.[26]

Mullucancha (court of pearls) is another name for this temple that appears in the texts, and Balboa mentions walls inlaid with mother of pearl. The walls of the chamber containing the *huaca* of the queen are supposed to have been covered with reliefs of llamas, birds, and plants, executed in fine gold plate, and likewise the interior of the Sun Temple and the Inca palaces belonging to it.

When we think, furthermore, that the entrances to the Tumibamba Pachacámac were painted in bright colors and decorated with emeralds, then we are left with an impression that is completely different from the darkness and heaviness conjured up by the bare stone walls in Cuzco and Machu Picchu.[27]

Tumibamba Pachacámac, or Mullucancha, was not one individual outstanding building, but a complex of temple and palace buildings that was constantly being extended by Huayna Cápac. It is said to have incorporated a temple for Viracocha, one for the sun and one for the thunder god. More than 200 Cañari virgins served there.[28]

Adjacent to the temple area, there were extensive troop quarters and storehouses. In the immediate vicinity, Huayna Cápac also settled *mitmacs* from other parts of the empire, probably the families of his soldiers, who came for the most part from Collasuyu and Contisuyu, the southern regions of the empire.[29]

Tumibamba was the most important center of the Inca empire after Cuzco and came close to surpassing the ancient capital. The struggle for possession of the city led to the civil war between Huáscar and Atahualpa.

The Cañari tribe at all times occupied a rather special position. They probably did not speak Chibcha like their northern neighbors, but Mochica, the language

*III Above: Gold ear plugs.
Below: Small gold
burial gifts.*

11　Terraced pyramid of Etén in the Mocha valley, near Trujillo.

12　One of the ten quarters of the Chimú capital, captured by the Inca about halfway through the 15th century (see p. 15 f.).

13 *Paramonga, the southern frontier fortress of the late Chimú empire in the coastal region.*

14 *Mud brick ruins at Mangomarca, near Lima, with Christian chapel.*

15   Possibly the entry of a returning governor or general, accompanied by music (military bells with trophy heads, and pan pipes). Behind him is a counting board, probably registering the tributes or booty. The Inca Quipucamayos used the same counting boards in addition to the knot records, to help their memories (see drawing by Poma de Ayala, p. 16).

16 Under the sacred palta tree by flowing water (= snake), a priest offers a human
head (?) to the god of war, who is surrounded by radiating snakes' heads.

17 Scenes from the same Mochica vase: warriors (or demons) with animal masks drag
captives along behind them. Even the clubs are portrayed as living combatants. In the
decisive battle between the Inca and the Chanca, too, it was only with the intervention
of inanimate nature and the supernatural powers that victory became a reality.

18 Clay reliefs (heavily reconstructed) on the "El Dragon" building in the outer quarters of the Chimú city of Canchán (above).

19 Detail of an inner chamber at Chanchán (left).

ANDAS DEL INGA PILLCORANPA

guaynacapac

ynga ua ala conquista / delos cayanbis guancabil / ca canari cicho chacha / poya quito latacoga

lleuan los yñs an Jamar cas y / soras lucanas pari na cochas: / alaguerra y batalla de prie / sa lolleuan

batalla del ynga

ESTATVRAS COMO EL YNGA

pelea con suene migo uiencima uelas andas ti ra con
piedras de oro fi no desu pillcoranpa a su cõtrario al apo
pinto guayna pinto y con quista la prouincia de quito
cayanbi cicho latacõga guancabilca canari chaichapo
ya cico chupaycho y lesugeta guaynacapac ynga —

como el ynga ento y leenseñó acomer
coca jun tamente leenseño cõ la ydulatra y dizen q̃ lesus ten
ta. rio creo es un poco de uicio api to uellaca. como unes parol
tauaquero tiene aquel uicio bicio y pertinente. pero el yñs bor ca
cho y eo quero escierto hichesero publico y pontifise del ynga —

como le tray de presentes al ynga ya
la señora coya. los señores prencipales del reyno. acin mismo
alos demas capac apoconas. le presentauan los yñs deste reyno

como el ynga se regalaua de muchos
rre galos. lo mia es cogi do mays. cap ya ut cosara y papis ma
uay. chaucha. y carnero llamado cuyro blanco. y como mi a
chiche. conejo blanco y mucha fruta. y patos. y chicha muy
su aui q̃ madoraua un mes q̃ le llaman yamor aca. y co
mia otras cosas q̃ no tocaua los yñs sopena de la muerte —

el almis que temi y algalia del ynga
y de los señores prencipales deste reyno le llamauan ciya
ya. al mis que. y spinco algalia. cones to se ahumauan y
olian a su mi rio de aquel tienpo q̃ los usarõ los yñs —

perlas del ynga y de sus prencipa
les q̃ son piedras preciosas se llamauan quispe perlas. piedras pre
ciosas. umina. cuychi. uacri. y colares se llama mullo es
tos y has cosas auia en tienpo del ynga en este reyno —

como se banaua el ynga dedos di
as yno se banaua men quan te ni crece iente por q̃ decia q̃
en tal dia yora an daua muy lista las enfer me dades y pe
ligros del cuerpo y muerte q̃ lo ayres el men tos an dan
sueltos de sus natu ra lesas y an dae n cõ tra do cõclue spo—
pill co

of the Chimú empire, and yet they are counted as part of the so-called Chimborazo culture, alongside the Puruhá and other tribes from around Ambato and Riobamba.[30] Though economically strong, on account of their fertile land and their commercially favorable position between the coast and the highlands, they were militarily weak and were continually under pressure from stronger powers.

By changing coalitions, they attempted to preserve their autonomy in the face of Quito, the Chimú, and the Inca. When the territorial expansion of the Inca, led by Túpac, could no longer be halted, they surrendered and paid their tributes and did their enforced military service. Fifteen thousand of their tribe were forcibly resettled as mitmacs in the region of Cuzco, but for the rest they were spared heavy reprisals.[29] The coya, Mama Ocllo won them extensive freedom of worship, and after her death they revered her as a goddess.[31] Huayna Cápac favored the Cañari in particular and entrusted them with duties in the palace interior. The Inca buildings in Tumibamba may very well have had some strong

Huayna Cápac in the Cara war (left).

Facsimiles from the Chronicle of Poma de Ayala, 1587: "... the Inca fights from his litter, and uses his sling to hurl stones of precious gold at the enemy curaca ... and conquers the province of Quito ..." (right).

Orejón.

Mama Ocllo.

Cañari or Chimú-style characteristics. Túpac's palace was, as Montesinos relates, built by the Cañari princes by way of tribute. There is as yet no archaeological evidence supporting this, since Tumibamba was destroyed during the war between the brothers Atahualpa and Huáscar.[32]

Despite the great preparations Huayna Cápac had made for the recapture of northern Ecuador, after some initial territorial gains the war soon met with severe setbacks. The tribespeople banded together against the Inca, and united by iron discipline, they adopted a scorched-earth policy and entrenched themselves in Cayambi, Caranqui, Cochasqui, Otavalo, and other temple cities in the vicinity of Quito.[33] The Incas and their auxiliary troops found themselves in a ravaged land. The organization of their supplies, so highly praised by the Spaniards, broke down completely, the warriors were clothed in rags, and people were dying daily of hunger.[34] The defenseless local population that had remained behind had to endure inhuman reprisals.[35] Military catastrophe was inescapable, and the storming of the military fortress of Caranqui, led by Huayna Cápac himself, misfired. Abandoned by the fleeing *orejones*, the Inca fell to the ground and narrowly escaped death or captivity.[36]

Exhausting forced marches brought the Inca and his army back to Tumibamba. Huayna Cápac did not make his customary entry into the city in his litter, but "on foot, at the head of the army, shield and spear in hand."[37]

The Inca now showed his contempt for the *orejones* in every conceivable way. The court allowances for their food and clothing came to an abrupt halt, so that they literally starved.[38]

For the Inca nobility, who had long resented the way in which their own ancestral rights were passed over in favor of the Colla in the army, and in preference for the Cañari in the palace service, this was the final spur to rebellion. They decided to take all their weapons and possessions and make for Cuzco. At sunrise, the commander-in-chief, Mihac Naca Mayta, assembled them in battle order on the great square in front of the Sun Temple in Tumibamba, and disregarding the attempts of Huayna Cápac's envoys to stop him, he carried the holy stone from Huanacauri out of the Mullucancha. This massive, unhewn, spindleshaped stone was, according to legend, the transformed figure of the brother of the first Inca, Manco. Protected by this *huaca*, to which the Inca chiefly ascribed their victories, they intended to set out on the march back to Cuzco. The *orejones* were not alone, for they were joined by a large part of the war-weary army.

Finally, Huayna Cápac hurried in person to the Sun Temple and attempted to pull General Mihac back by the arm, but to no avail, for the procession moved off. Then he had all the *huacas* brought out of the temple chambers and sent them out, draped in black, to the front of the departing troops. He made the golden *huaca* of his mother, queen Mama Ocllo, address them through the mouth of a Cañari priestess.

This was the one force that still held sway over them. Mihac Naca Mayta carried the Huanacauri stone and the *huaca* of Mama Ocllo back into the temple, followed by the Inca.

The evening brought a sudden change and the pacification of the *orejones*. Now they received all that they had been denied, and Huayna Cápac presented the general and other high-ranking officers with women and costly ornaments.[39]

The great danger of a split between the sovereign and the Inca nobility of Cuzco, which in the next generation of Huáscar and Atahualpa was to become irrevocable, had on this occasion been averted.

Now all forces, even distant garrisons, were mobilized for the ultimate battle. The *orejones* staked everything on being able to regain the Inca's favor and paid for their zeal with a heavy loss of life. The death of his favorite brother, Auqui Túpac, was a painful blow to the Inca.[40] The Cayambi fortress, the key position of the Ecuadorians, fell only after a long siege. Thousands of men, women, and children were driven down to the shore of a lake in the vicinity of Otavalo, and according to old accounts from this region, all were massacred, even children under twelve, contrary to promises of royal clemency. Almost all the sources mention a clump of eight gigantic willows standing in the water as the final refuge sought out by the mass of desperate people. Planks and platforms had been fastened to the tops of these trees, which fell to the copper axes of the beseigers. From then on the lake was known as Yahuaracocha, the Sea of Blood.[41]

A few hundred warriors managed to survive the massacre, and led by a prince named Pinta, they were finally starved out and Pinta was taken captive and brought before Huayna Cápac. The emperor took a liking to him and attempted to raise his spirits. But although the Inca treated him well and offered him rich gifts, Pinta kept his head held low and would not allow him to look into his face.

This was exactly the same gesture of withdrawal and aristocratic pride that the Spaniards found so puzzling in Atahualpa, when they first set eyes on him in the camp outside Cajamarca.

The prince was unable to overcome his anguish at the unsuccessful outcome of the conflict and refused all nourishment until he died.

In order to preserve the power of the dead man for himself, the Inca had a drum made from his skin and had this sent to Cuzco for use in accompaniment to hymns and dances at Sun festivals.[42]

Animal spirits or spirits of the dead.

Ecuador and south Colombia continued to involve the Inca and the Peruvian army in strenuous activity. Inca Túpac had explored only the southern end of the coast, which at that time was rich and densely populated. Large sections of the hinterland were occupied by tribes that were semi-savage. Huayna Cápac mounted a series of expeditions through uncharted jungle, desert, and mountain regions. The chronicler Balboa gives a dramatic portrayal of the arrival at the great white waters of the Angasmayo river and of the laborious journey down river, along the rapids, to the sea. Thereafter the river became the northern frontier of the empire.[43]

These are the regions where the conquistadors had their most interesting and adventurous experiences. Benalcázar and Pedro de Alvarado, the conquerors, endured the most terrible hardships in the heat of the coastland and in the icy heights. It was here that Gonzalo Pizarro set out on his eastward journey to the lowlands of the Amazon.

There were many more of the Incas on the march under Huayna Cápac, and they were accustomed to a rigid hierarchical system. The problems they met with were quite different from those encountered by the Spaniards, who knew from the outset that they would have to fall back on their own resources.

Their strenuous exertions and the climate of alternating rain and heat greatly weakened the Inca troops, who were so far from their base. At first there was little to be seen of the inhabitants of the region, until one morning there came a prolonged, deafening outcry from the throats of thousands of naked warriors. At this point the records are somewhat confused, but they indicate that there was a threat of mass defection by the Peruvian forces, which was halted only at the last minute. Thirst and lack of provisions finally compelled Huayna Cápac to cut short the expeditions.[43]

While the Inca was thus occupied in the north, the Chiriguano tribes invaded the Inca territory in the extreme southeast in what is present day northwest Argentina. There the Inca rule probably relied on no more than a few heavily defended military bases. Consequently, the repercussions of these incursions in the remainder of the empire were slight. One of the texts makes an admittedly disputed claim, which is nevertheless interesting from a historical point of view, stating that among these Chiriguano tribespeople there were a few Spaniards who had come from the Atlantic coast.[44]

There were two subsequent events on the Gulf of Guayaquil that radically influenced the destiny of the Inca and his empire. The first was Huayna Cápac's unsuccessful visit to the island of Puná, and the second was the visit by a Spanish ship to the port of Túmbez.

The island of Puná lies at the entrance to the delta of the Rio Guaya. Both geographically and climatically it belongs to the northern jungle and river basin, and it appears that before the Spanish invasion, the people living on either side of the sound shared many common ethnic and economic features. "The wealth of the coastland in cotton, salt, fish, and the mussels used to make the Chaquira jewelry (pearl jewelry), produced a lively exchange of goods with the highlands"

(Krickeberg), in the main with the hinterland of Ecuador. As with many seafaring and coastal peoples, piracy appears to have been one of the firmly established sources of revenue.

The warlike Puná peoples were extremely skillful sailors and their *balsas* were feared far and wide. The entire island, comprising some 250,000 acres, is supposed to have been surrounded by a stone wall. This exact information about Puná is known to us because Pizarro spent five months there before entering Peru.[45] The population comprised between 6,000 and 7,000 people and included numerous captives taken in the course of raids. Castrated, and with mutilated lips and noses, they are supposed to have lived in the seraglios of the princes.

Puná's counterpart, the city of Túmbez on the southernmost coast of the gulf, traded chiefly with the Chimú peoples, and even appears to have played a part in the organization of the Inca empire for a short while. Cieza's chronicle refers to serveral sporadic attempts on the part of the Inca Túpac to bind that stretch of coast to the Inca empire by sending emissaries there. However, these emissaries perished just as mysteriously as the two Spaniards later left behind by Pizarro, during his first raid on Túmbez. These were supposed to have been brought to Huayna Cápac, but never arrived.[46]

There is only fragmentary evidence to show how deep and lasting was the Inca influence on the coastal region. When the first Spanish ship arrived, Túmbez had an Inca governor, a governor's palace, a sun temple and a house of the *mamacunas*. The Spaniards had wonderful tales of the riches of the Incas, of walls covered with embossed gold plate, and glittering ornaments, such as golden corn cobs on silver-leaved stalks, and gold and silver models of animals and plants. Such splendor intoxicated them.[46]

Huayna Cápac's activities in the Gulf of Guayaquil, aimed at a pacification of his northern coastline, are known to us in some detail, since they were linked with a tragic event, that left an idelible mark on the population.

We have a description of how the sovereign, encamped by the sea with a large number of *orejones*, summoned the local princes of the region, including Tumbalá, the chief prince of the island of Puná, to do him homage and pay tribute. Tumbalá and his followers were well aware that it would not end there, and that what lay in store for them was the loss of the liberties earned by their fathers, and all that this loss implied — compulsory service in the erection of buildings and fortresses, which would need subsequent maintenance, military service, and the obligation to surrender wives and daughters for the houses of the *mamacunas*. In order to avoid having to pay a visit of homage to the Inca camp, they extended a ceremonial invitation of their own to the sovereign to come to the island.

Huayna Cápac accepted the invitation.[47] Before leaving the mainland, the Inca priests offered sacrifices at the ancient maritime shrine of Punta Santa Elena and consulted the *calpa* there. The oracle was unfavorable,[48] but the Inca and the *orejones* nevertheless permitted themselves to be ferried across to Puná by the islanders in their decorated *balsas*, where accommodation for the important visitors was hastily prepared.

Great hunts and feasts were arranged in honor of the Inca.

However, the princes had feigned submission, and the invitation, which Huayna Cápac had accepted with such alacrity in his weariness at the adversities and hardship of the last years, had been a sham in order to lull the Inca into a sense of false security. A surprise attack had been planned in detail with allies on the mainland.

The Inca had already returned to the mainland and the boats were to bring the *orejones* to a certain place on the coast. Despite the large number of *balsas* mustered from the entire surrounding region, there were not enough to transport all the *orejones* in one trip and they had to be taken across in successive groups. As soon as they were out of reach of land, the sailors loosened the fastenings that held the timbers of the great rafts together, thereby condemning the Incas who could not swim to a terrible end. They then returned to take the next equally unsuspecting group. The *orejones* who had remained behind on the island to man a garrison are also supposed to have met with a violent death.[49]

Pizarro was later to be given the same ceremonial reception on Puná and to endure similar horrors on the return to the mainland. It seems miraculous that, in this instance, the Spaniards lost only a few men.

We know that the Incas believed that the dead continued to live on, provided their bodies were preserved,[50] and for this reason, much to the wonder of the Spanish chroniclers, "they devoted more care to the erection and embellishment of the cemeteries in which the dead resided, than to the furnishing of the houses in which they themselves lived."[49] The fact that the unfortunate Puná expedition resulted in the drowning of many members of the highest ranks of the Inca nobility, few of whom could be snatched from the water to be given a proper ritual burial, meant a severe loss in numbers, vitality, and prestige for the hitherto unassailable ruling caste. Huayna Cápac ordered prayers of mourning to be sung in memory of the *orejones*. When Cieza toured those regions many years later, he still heard the death laments.[49] Huayna Cápac exacted a bloody revenge on the coastal tribes, and had thousands of Indians impaled and hanged. He also began building the "Paso de Guaynacapa," a road in the Rio Guaya delta whose unfinished remains made a great impression on the chroniclers. However, Huayna Cápac then abandoned all further plans for that region, leaving the pacification of the Gulf to his governor in Túmbez.[51]

The years in Ecuador had not only resulted in military setbacks for Huayna Cápac, but had also overwhelmed him with supernatural omens, dreams, and visions.

At one point in his campaign against the Pasto in the far north "lightning flashes sprang from his feet; taking this as an evil omen, he returned to Quito . . . just as the news came from Cuzco of an outbreak of bubonic plague there."[52] It is not mere chance that in the passage quoted from the chronicle of S. C. Pachacuti about the appearance of lightning flashes should have coincided with an outbreak of disease, for in Peruvian mythology the snake and lightning symbolized forces that could bring sickness and decay.[53]

We are also told: "While on the march to the coast, at the midnight hour the sovereign suddenly saw himself and his line encircled by thousands upon thousands of human figures. No one knew who they were, nor did they ever find out. The Inca is supposed to have said that they were the souls of living persons, and God had shown them to him in order to make it plain that they would all die of the plague. The souls, it is said, moved ever closer to the Inca, until he suddenly became aware that he himself was their enemy. Then he sounded the alarm and ordered the return to Quito, where they prepared for Cápac-Raymi."[52]

In Cuzco the plague spread rapidly. Its victims included close relatives and trusted advisers of the sovereign, such as the governor Apu Hillaquita, Auqui Túpac, and his sister Mama Coca.[54] This was the third in a series of catastrophes whose cumulative effect over seven years was to bring the framework of the Inca state, supposedly founded on the unshakeable basis of religious tradition and subtle political organization, to the point of total collapse.

Spirits of the dead with rattles.

The chronicles are highly contradictory in their references to the activities of Huayna Cápac's last years, following the expedition to the coast. It is reported that he intended to go to Cuzco in order to reorganize everything afresh there. However, it seems to emerge fairly certainly from the texts that, after some hesitation, he set off in an entirely different direction and death overtook him when he was far from Cuzco.

At all events, we next see him at his residence at Tumibamba. The shadow of the plague followed him even here. The sinister prophecies and visions came more frequently.

Garcilaso writes: "As they were celebrating Inti-Raymi in Cuzco, the people saw an eagle flying in the air pursued by a flock of smaller birds of prey, which repeatedly attacked it with their beaks. Since he could no longer defend himself, the eagle dropped down into the center of the square in front of the Sun Temple. The Incas rushed towards it and, on picking it up, they saw that it was sick and that its whole body was covered with scabs and lacked most of its feathers. They cared for it, but within a few days it had died." The Inca and his followers were utterly dismayed by this terrible portent. And it was not an isolated omen. Earthquakes shook the land, there were floods along the coast, comets appeared in the skies, and the moon had three great haloes, one blood-red, another shading from black to green, and another ashen.

This combination of extraordinary phenomena strengthened the general fear, already aroused by older prophecies, that fate had further evil in store for the Inca dynasty and empire. According to the numerous allusions in the Spanish texts, an ancient oracle distinctly referred to the coming of "strange peoples, of a kind that has never been seen before; these would rob the Inca of his empire and destroy its state and religion."

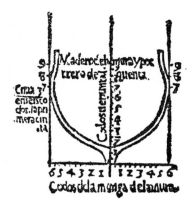

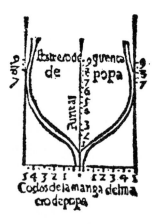

Designs for a Spanish ship (woodcuts from the *Instrucción náutica para navegar* (16th century).

Great sacrifices were offered by the Inca, and he ordered the priests to question their gods, each in his own province.[55] He was particularly concerned with what the oracle at the ancient shrine of Pachacámac had to say. Its reputation, power, and wealth had grown immensely during his reign. He himself visited it repeatedly at decisive stages of his life, as for example during his expedition from Cuzco to Tumibamba and again after the painful discomfiture at Gulf of Guayaquil. Time and again, this ruler, who must have had a rare quality of foreseeing what was to come, reveals his fear of the sea and of a disaster that was to come from there and overwhelm his empire. It was for this reason that he sought advice and protection against these dangers at the ancient coastal shrine.[56]

These presentiments, omens, oracles, and natural phenomena, which these people associated with evil times to come and with the invasion by strangers, all occurred at a time when news of sea voyages, landings, and assaults by the strange white men could already have reached the Inca.

Between 1500 and 1527, the years of Huayna Cápac's reign over the Inca empire, the white conquistadors were engaged in fierce activity along the northern coasts of South America.

On the twenty-sixth of September, 1513, from the top of a high mountain (far east of the Isthmus of Panama, which was not discovered until later), Vasco Núñez de Balboa, the Spanish adventurer, was the first European to set eyes on the Pacific Ocean. He thereupon claimed this part of the world for the Castilian crown. One of his companions was Francisco Pizarro. Vasco Núñez is thought to have heard something about the Inca empire, its fabulous treasures, its ocean traffic in *balsas,* and about the llamas used as transport animals, from the Chibcha peoples who lived on the Isthmus. He dismantled his ships with the utmost care and painstakingly brought them across the Isthmus. But others were to profit from his discoveries. In 1519, at the age of forty-two he himself was condemned at a sham trial, mounted by those who envied him.

It was still in Balboa's time, in 1514, that Francisco Becerra, the seafarer, set out on a voyage along the west coast of Colombia. Almagro and Pizarro followed with their protracted and initially unsuccessful attempts to penetrate farther southward involving heavy loss of life. In 1527 Pizarro took thirteen men in a small boat — the pathetic remainder of his second expedition, which had already been taken for lost — and crossed the Gulf of Guayaquil, swarming with *balsa* traffic and overlooked by densely populated shores. He sent the Greek, Pedro de Candía, ashore with a few companions.[57] This event caused alarm in the Inca empire. The communications, which Huayna Cápac's governor in Túmbez sent to the sovereign in the highlands, by means of Chasqui messengers, have been preserved for us by Cieza, Sarmiento, Balboa, Cobo, and Garcilaso, the later Spanish chroniclers, and so we are able to follow this meeting both from the Indian and Spanish sides.

In Cobo's chronicle we read how Huayna Cápac received the news of the thirteen Spaniards:[58]

"Huayna Cápac had been recovering at his palaces in Tumibamba, and celebrating the festivals, when a message from his governor in Túmbez was brought to him by runners. Breathless and terrified at the things that had happened, they told the Inca that curious strangers, such as no one had ever seen before, had landed on the beach at Túmbez. Their faces were white and they had beards and were covered from head to foot in clothing, and they were altogether quite wild in their appearance. They recounted many other things besides, which amazed the Inca. The strangers had crossed the sea in great wooden houses. They were able to steer and turn these and move them here and there, and could come and go with them wherever they pleased. At night they would return to the sea and sleep in the house, whence they would then come back to land again. The Inca was speechless at what he had heard and was overcome by such melancholy and dismay that he retired to his chamber and did not emerge until darkness had begun to fall."

The Indians at Túmbez must have been really panic-stricken when they saw the Spaniards unload their horses, which looked to them like four-legged monsters.

The Spaniards describe very vividly how their ship was encircled by canoes containing many armed men, who did not, however, make any move against them. Pedro de Candía and the other adventurers were allowed to walk through the town unhindered and enter every house. The Spaniards even inspected the town garrison and looked at the governor's palace and the temples and hurriedly helped themselves to as much of the costly gold and silver ornaments as they could. After five days, the small company boarded their ship once more and sailed on.[59]

There is also the story of a pair of wild animals — a lion and a tiger — with which Pedro de Candía suddenly found himself face to face as he prowled through the state buildings. The fact that these trained pumas did not instantaneously tear the Spaniards to pieces, but held themselves back, must have robbed the Inca governor of his last shred of courage to resist. Criminals and enemies of the state used to be thrown to the animals, and the reaction of the beasts was regarded as a kind of divine judgment in Peru. This procedure was simply part of

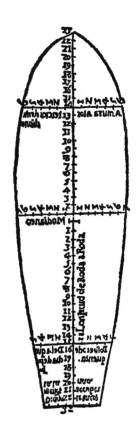

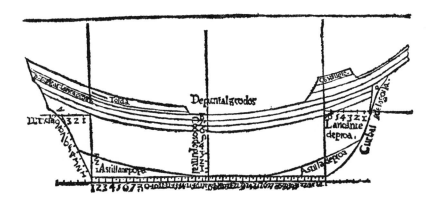

Wild cat.

Inca justice, and the prisons of Hurinsaca and Sancay near Cuzco are supposed to have been full of the most dangerous beasts of prey and poisonous snakes. We are reminded of the Babylonian king's lions' den, into which the Prophet Daniel was thrown.

The messengers are even alleged to have told the Inca Huayna Cápac that the pumas "cowered on the ground (before the Spaniards) and wagged their tails ingratiatingly at them."[60]

Let us follow the course of events at the Inca court: "The Inca was beside himself at the latest reports of the plunderers in Túmbez. He made the messengers tell him once again what had happened and then he jumped up in a state of great agitation and, shaking his cloak, called out, 'Out, out, you lords and soothsayers! Is it your wish to shatter my might and bring the state into confusion?!' But the next moment, he had sat down once again . . . and ordered the messengers repeatedly to start afresh, since he seemed not to have taken in what he had heard."[60]

Two of the bearded men — several of the chronicles give their names as Molina and Ginés — had at their own request remained behind on land. Huayna Cápac was determined to see them and was continually asking where they were. They never appeared before him and no trace was ever found of them. Pizarro's ship had meanwhile sailed on farther south.[61]

Pedro de Candía wrote a report of his visit to Túmbez, together with his own first "Relación" of the western coast of South America. Pedro de Candía is also supposed to have made a drawing of the town and fortress of Túmbez on a piece of cloth. The report by the Greek (now unfortunately lost) and the valuable pieces of booty finally convinced the Spanish throne of the value of the Peruvian ventures, and led Pizarro and Almagro to return four years later, when a new man, Atahualpa, was making a bid for the rule of the Inca empire.

Ever since that Inti-Raymi, when the eagle had crashed down in front of the Sun Temple, Huayna Cápac kept himself surrounded, as Garcilaso tells us, by a heavy guard made up of the most trusted men in his army. The priests, those "petty magicians" against whom his father Túpac had fought so bitterly, were always at hand. Throughout the land, countless priests listened for the oracular decrees of the ancient gods, whose cults had long since been neglected in favor of the worship of the sun god.[62]

In all the texts there is not a single mention of a favorable omen that might have revived the Inca's flagging spirits.

Huayna Cápac continued to absent himself from the capital of the empire and remained in Quito, where he held his court. This city, too, was now struck by the plague, and many of his people died of it.[63]

The most important accounts of this period were written by Cobo and the Aymará chieftain Santa Cruz, and even these give only the scantest, fragmentary, and conflicting versions of the dark weeks and days preceding the death of the ruler in the remote provincial city of Quito. They list the names of high-ranking persons who fell victim to the plague and in this connection there is further reference to Huayna Cápac's visions. Santa Cruz describes how:

"At the hour of the repast, a messenger with black mantle comes (to Huayna Cápac), embraces the Inca with great respect, and hands him a *putti*, a covered casket with a key. The Inca bids him open it, but the messenger declines — the divine creator had directed him to allow no one but the Inca in person to open the *putti*. The Inca agrees, and as he opens it, he lets out something like a cloud of butterflies or little bits of paper that fly away or scatter, until they disappear from sight. With this the plague had struck, and within two days General Mihac Naca Mayta and many other leading personalities were dead, their faces disfigured by boils."

It is said, furthermore, that Huayna Cápac had a house built of stone blocks in which to hide himself, and that he had had himself completely walled in, and had died inside it.[64] There is frequent reference to the way in which the Indians locked themselves away in rooms to fast. Cobo describes a *zaziz* such as this in connection with a vision at the outbreak of the plague in Quito: "... In a room containing no one but him (Huayna Cápac), there entered three Indians such as no one had ever seen, very small, almost dwarfs, and they addressed him, saying: 'Inca, we have come to call Thee!' Terrified by the vision, Huayna Cápac cried out for his attendants. As people entered the room, the dwarfs disappeared without anyone having seen them, apart from the king. He then asked his men: 'What happened to the dwarfs who were here just now to call me?' They replied that they had seen nothing. Then the Inca said that he was going to die, and soon after he caught the plague."[65]

This "house of stone blocks" is reminiscent of the custom of Peruvian magicians to put people who were very sick into locked-up rooms. "The floors and walls of these rooms were first scrupulously cleaned ... then rubbed down with black and white maize, which was subsequently burned, and finally sprinkled with a mixture of maize flour and water. The sick person was then laid on his back on the floor of this room, thus 'purified of all harmful influences.' The medicine men then put him into a deep trance and he would then witness his body being cut open with crystal knives, so that snakes, toads, and other impure creatures could be removed from it and destroyed in the maize fire that was burning in the room ... This purification of the sick body would be accompanied by prayers and incantations."[66]

Cieza reports that when Huayna Cápac was struck down by the plague, he had sacrifices made in all the shrines of the land for his recovery.[67] He sent messengers to the temple of Pachacámac to ask what could be done to save him.[65] But whatever the priests and sages may have divined, it was too late to bring hope. The house in which the Inca was living was struck by lightning, and comets again appeared in the sky, one of them deep green in color.[62]

Counsel arrived from Pachacámac, advising that the Inca should be brought out into the open, into the sun. This advice was no longer of any help, but simply served to accelerate the course of the sickness.[65]

The last hours and days were spent waiting for an omen that would indicate who was to be the next Inca. Huayna Cápac's sons, the military leaders, and the governors who were in the vicinity, hurried to the sickbed. Atahualpa was among them, while Ninan Cuyuchi was in Tumibamba and Huáscar in Cuzco. Balboa tells us how Huayna Cápac made a will by using the *quipu*, the colored knotted strings, which was interpreted after his death by the *quipucamayos* in favor of Ninan Cuyuchi. According to Sarmiento, Huayna Cápac is supposed to have told the leading figures of the empire that Ninan Cuyuchi should be his successor, provided the *calpa* proved favorable towards him, and if not, it was to be Huáscar.[68] Atahualpa, whom Pizarro saw as Inca a few years later, was not even mentioned as a candidate.

The importance of the *calpa* in the succession has already been described.

This time the sacrifice was performed by the *orejón* Cusi Túpac Yupanqui, whom Sarmiento describes as "Mayordomo Mayor del Sol." This shows that there was a *villac-humu* once again and we assume from this that Huayna Cápac must have relinquished the office of high priest before his death.

The first *calpa* for Ninan Cuyuchi was unfavorable.

Cusi Túpac Yupanqui then performed a second sacrifice for the second son, Huáscar, but once again evil omens appeared in certain arteries and elsewhere.

He rushed to Huayna Cápac with this news, so that he could name another successor. But the king was no longer alive. The *orejones* were undecided as to what should be done. At this Cusi Túpac Yupanqui is said to have called out, "You see to the dead! I am going to Tumibamba to bring the *borla* to Ninan Cuyuchi." But when he arrived there, Ninan Cuyuchi had meanwhile also died of the plague.[69]

In trying to understand the character of a person like Huayna Cápac, we are made aware of the shortcomings of the texts at our disposal, which were compiled either by foreigners or enemies, or at best by *mestizos* or Indians. We do not possess a single account dating from the time prior to the Spanish arrival, written by a friend or even an *amauta* at the court. The descriptions of the Spanish chroniclers provide us with scarcely any indication of how this great man must have appeared to the people around him, and in order to form our own judgment we must examine all the facts and descriptions that can be found scattered throughout the texts.

The unbroken power of Huayna Cápac's predecessors Pachacútec and Túpac emerges quite plainly from the historical facts alone, from the successful military campaigns, from the enumerations of booty, and from accounts of fundamental religious reforms.

In Pachacútec we see a man at the height of his power, strong-willed in thought and deed. He showed moderation in balancing the claims of the wide variety of conflicting tasks that faced him and in dealing with threats to the unity of the empire. His harmonious personality expressed itself in his death hymn, which has been recorded in Spanish: "I grew and unfolded like the lilies in the garden, and when my time came, I aged, and when it was time to die, I withered and died."[70] In the characters of Túpac Inca and his sister Mama Ocllo, creative imagination seems to have been curbed by supra-individual dispositions.

Huayna Cápac seems to have been completely different. It is impossible to form a consistent picture of him and his reign, for halfway through his life there is a great division — his early years still belong to the expanding era of Pachacútec and Túpac, whereas in the second half of his life he was already under the shadow of decline, as were his sons Huáscar, Atahualpa, and Manco Inca, and his grandsons.

During the initial period of tranquility, before the great expeditions and campaigns took him to the periphery of the empire, the economy, architecture, and art flourished.

The northern campaign brought Huayna Cápac to Tumibamba, his birthplace, which had been of major importance as a base for his father Túpac's conquests in the north. There the young ruler found the freedom to establish his own individual style of life more fully than he could have done in Cuzco.

Thus Cuzco became almost a city of the past and of the priests. His son Huáscar remained there together with a few of the governors, whereas the younger princes, among them Atahualpa and Ninan Cuyuchi, the heir to the throne, flocked to the ruler in the new royal residence in Ecuador.

Huayna Cápac was no upstart surrounding himself with barbarian splendor. The tradition of several dynasties and ancient cultures provided the necessary framework for the development of his personality. He drew upon this tradition with all the sovereignty and assurance of a confident heir to power. His life was largely free from the restrictions that had hampered his fathers. Yet there is almost a hint of pessimism and a yearning for the primitive.

There are lively accounts of the young monarch's delight in the pleasures of life and of great hunts and drinking bouts. He appears to have been much given to drink, and according to the overwhelming evidence of the chronicles, to women.[71] Garcilaso maintains that he was never able to "deny a woman anything, no matter what her rank or appearance." In Father Oliva's little book, it is even written that the two Inca roads from Cuzco to Quito, the "royal mountain road" and the "royal coast road," one of the greatest civilizing achievements of the Peruvians, are supposed to owe their existence to an "amour" of the ruler's. Consumed with love for Vayara, the daughter of the ruler of Quito, Huayna Cápac allegedly had the two great highways constructed "in order to be able to visit the princess more easily." This is just one of the many fanciful and sometimes horrible stories that circulated about the Inca's amorous exploits, and that have little literary or historical value.

Cieza writes that Huayna Cápac readily listened to flatterers, "of whom there was no shortage in the Inca's entourage, and gave ear to slanderers," which resulted in the death of many innocent people. This defect was the other side to the otherwise appealing nature of this Inca, who was inclined to disregard the demands of etiquette and to select the people he wished to have about him by merit and whim.

The king loved individuality in people, and extreme courage, even in defeated enemies, attracted his attention. One instance of this is the way in which Huayna Cápac tried to win over the captured Cara prince Pinta to him.

The Inca had a warm and easy manner in his dealings with simple people, in direct contrast to the marked melancholy, gruffness, and imbalance of his character.

Cieza's chronicle tells us: "As he was passing through the beautiful valley of Chayanta in the Chimú territory, at the place where Trujillo stands today, an old Indian at work in his field heard that the Inca was close by. Thereupon the little peasant quickly pulled up three or four cucumbers, ran with them to the Inca, and handing them up to him as they were, still covered in earth and dirt, he said to him: 'Great Lord, eat this!,' and in front of all the courtiers round about him, Huayna Cápac took the cucumbers, and to please the old man he bit into one of them and said, 'Truly, they are very sweet.'"[72] There is a deeper significance to this charming story, if we remember that in Peru, as in ancient China, it was customary for the emperor to cut the first furrow in the land as a ceremonial inauguration of the cultivation of the fields.

"When the Inca, or his viceroy, or one of his captains, was present, he would cut the first sod with a golden spade that was brought to him. All the lords and nobles in his entourage then followed suit. The Inca would soon stop work and the other lords and nobles would also stop, and they and the Inca would sit down to a banquet, which was said to have been very festive." (Cobo)

But relations deteriorated between the Inca, his family, and the Inca caste, who together had controlled political and religious life and had appointed the military hierarchy.

The provincial nobility, the *curacas*, who had previously been considered inferior to the *orejones*, were now the favored group. Social regroupings now occurred in many areas of life. We recall how the officer posts were filled on Huayna Cápac's departure from Cuzco, and the role played by the Cañari in the temple duties at Tumbibamba.

As a young man, Huayna Cápac also played an active part in the organization of the sun cult. He was the only Inca to combine his secular office with the office of high priest, and to be worshipped as a deity.[72] This brought him one step farther than his father and grandfather along the road to manipulating the religion as a doctrine to uphold the state. These innovations were met with such opposition that he was compelled to give way on some points. Shortly before his death, we learn that there was once again a "Mayordomo del Sol," a principal priest, who performed the *calpa* in Quito.[73]

The war in Ecuador, which occupied Huayna Cápac's full attention, became a trial of strength for the Inca and his ruling class. Many of the best men fell. The Cara uprising was the most dangerous resistance to the imperialist expansion of the Inca. It required the utmost effort to counter the threatening, retrograde trend. The dwindling trust between the Inca and the *orejones* almost developed into an open rift. But the sovereign and his army became reconciled, not least as a result of the personal bravery of the Inca and his endurance in the face of hunger, cold, and fatigue.

The annihilation of the Ecuadorians on the Yahuarcocha was probably the last great success scored by Huayna Cápac and the Inca empire. It is here that we come to the turning point in the life of this ruler.

His father Túpac's legacy, which had brought the light-hearted young Inca to great eminence, now began to make demands on him, demands which he found himself increasingly powerless to meet. Although the alliance of the Ecuadorian tribes had been defeated, the power of the Inca and his sons and the proven organization of the Incas were no longer adequate to prevail against and restore the conquered lands. Ecuador remained an area of unrest and misery.

The south's attempt to conquer the ethnically and climatically different north reached no permanent conclusions. Unification and total integration was never achieved. The two great highways which Huayna Cápac constructed as far as Quito fulfilled their task of linking the different peoples, but only for a short time. They served their purpose through years of protracted wars and were ultimately the means of conveying the European cavalry, soldiers, traders, and colonizers through Peru.

Huayna Cápac's dangerous expeditions into the mountains, jungles, and coastal regions of Ecuador, some following the trail of Túpac, and others covering entirely fresh ground, never met with the success of his predecessors, for all the great risks and energy involved. The unfortunate outcome of the visit to the island of Puná leaves an air of uncertainty hovering over the whole chapter of Peruvian expansionist policies.

There is scarcely any part of the Tahuantinsuyu which Huayna Cápac, this most restless of all the Inca rulers, did not visit at some time, either in a warlike or peaceful role. At one point we see him in the Chimú region, the next moment he is back in Pachacámac. But the destiny of the empire follows its own course and he is apparently much grieved at his inability to exert adequate influence over it. In dreams and visions he sees imminent catastrophe. The silent armies of people that were to perish as a result haunt him in his visions.

In this tense situation, the news of the appearance of the thirteen Spaniards, the "sea monsters" in "wooden houses" on the water, must have had a most alarming effect on the people. For the old prophecies had forecast that disaster would befall the Inca and his empire from the ocean, and it was thought that the hour of destruction for the Inca empire was at hand, though in fact it was not to come for another six years.

We know that in the latter period the sovereign was making very strenuous bids for the powerful non-Inca oracle shrines, such as those at Pachacámac and on the coast of Ecuador, to which he had been laying claim for some considerable time. The array of offerings to great and minor *huacas* far exceeded the customary amount.[74] In the latter period, the sun cult may well have been overshadowed by more powerful deities.

Now, as those about him — the priests, the oracle diviners, and the Chasqui — could bring nothing but evil omens and predictions, while the terrors of the plague afflicted the land, the king, once so carefree, now became a stranger in a world from which he could not escape any more than from the terrifying images of his darkening spirits.

In those weeks, when the great plague struck part of Peru and raged through the entire Tahuantinsuyu from south to north, leaving a graveyard of some 200,000 dead in its wake, the Tahuantinsuyu experienced unrest, misery, and pain, which persisted for decades.

The Colla who lived in the area of the ancient Tiahuanaco culture around Lake Titicaca were for the most part spared the bloody chaos that followed Huayna Cápac's death. The Spanish seizure of the area was much less damaging than, for example, in Ecuador. The national strength of the Aymará tribes is still very powerful today, and they are now the foremost champions of Indian self-determination.

The national disaster of the plague and the war of succession that followed Huayna Cápac's death prepared the way for the foreign conquistadors and created the necessary climate for the conquest of any people, no matter what their traditions, culture, and religion were.

IV   Mummy from the Paracas Necropolis.

20   *Huayna Cápac, the last great Inca, portrayed in a colonial oil painting. He reigned from approximately 1493 to 1527.*

21   Ruins of the Sun Temple of Vilcas, or Vilcas-huaman ("sanctuary of the sun hawk"),
in the heart of the Inca empire.

22   Intihuatana (sun seat) in the holy sector of the mountain city of Machu Picchu,
carved out of the living rock.

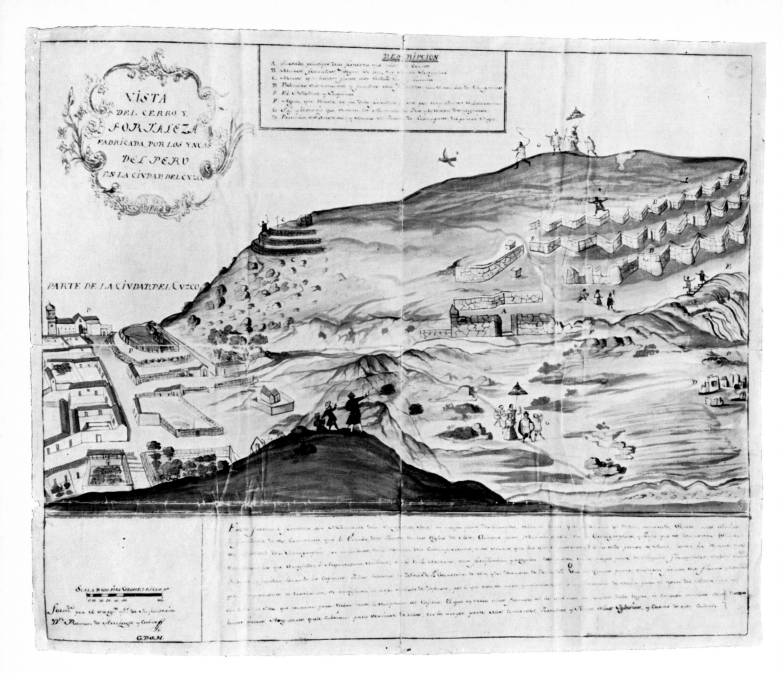

23 Bird's-eye view of the mountain fortress of Sacsayhuaman, with a part of Spanish
Cuzco. Water-color dating from 1778 with pastoral figures in Inca dress.

24 Dance games, with the participation of the Inca and coya (left, below, with the sun
emblem and the sickle moon) and animal masks, in an 18th-century drawing.

25 *Group of thirty-nine turquoise figures, the largest about 2" high, wearing diverse costumes and head coverings. They could represent different tribes or hierarchical levels.*

26 *Gold-and-copper alloy sacrificial knife (17" long) with turquoise and mother of pearl inlays.*

27 Stone seat from the province of Manabi (Ecuador coast).

28 Sandstone relief (approximately life-size) from the coast of Ecuador with impressive head adornment in the form of a sun.

29   *"Counting board" from Tumibamba.*

30   *Small wooden box with lid from Paramonga.*

31 *Dead spirit blowing pan pipes. Since the Incas also had similar concepts about the realm of the dead, the stories of Huayna Cápac's visions of armies of dead souls are entirely credible.*

32 *Dead spirits dancing and playing musical instruments — warriors, women, and children, with jugs of intoxicating maize beer between their feet — on a Mochica vase.*

33 *Detail from a similar vessel.*

◁ *34 and 35   Embroidered figures on burial cloths from Paracas; typical pan-Peruvian symbolism: trophy heads in the hands, on the hips, and as earrings, sacrificial knife, snake-like tongue, birds or other animal forms on the back.*

36   Heavily stylized god or demon figure, also from Paracas. Transition to the geometric forms that later predominated with the Incas. Inca art itself was almost entirely nonpictorial.

37 *Breast adornment of embossed plate of gold, possibly from colonial Peru (palm-leaf motif).*

38 *Head band of thin plate of gold (Inca).*

39 *Mummy of a noblewoman from the Paracas Necropolis (detail from color plate IV). It gives a strong impression of the majesty of the cult of the dead in ancient Peru. The mummies of the Inca kings were seen by the Spaniards, who described them in detail but subsequently burned every one of them.*

40 and 41   Colonial portraits of Huayna Cápac's successors, Atahualpa, the victor and (right) Huáscar, the defeated.

CHAPTER III

Strife over the succession to Huayna Cápac between his sons Huáscar and Ata-hualpa (ca. 1527–1532) — Restoration and priestly rule in Cuzco — Growing influence of the hitherto neglected great and minor oracle shrines — Civil war and victory of the usurpers led by Atahualpa.

Huayna Cápac was the last Inca whose death was celebrated with full ceremonial honors, as in the time of his fathers, receiving the veneration of all sections and peoples of the Tahuantinsuyu. After ten days of mourning in Quito, his body was taken first to Tumibamba. There the body was embalmed, prepared, and adorned as a seated mummy, a gold mask over its face, and attired in the robes and insignia of the "Sapa (all-powerful) Inca," with *llautu, borla,* and scepter. This was how the first Spaniards saw it a few years later, when they came on a reconnaissance expedition to Cuzco.

The mourning ceremonies in the Cañari capital lasted for a month, and then began the 1250 mile journey to Cuzco. Atahualpa had accompanied the body of his father as far as Tumibamba. At this point he took leave of the mourners and is supposed to have stated that "it was his firm intention not to leave the land in which his father had begun and ended his life and work."[1]

The greater part of the nobility accompanied the dead king. The high priest Cusi Túpac Yupanqui may be regarded as their leader and the executor of Huayna Cápac's testament. The Inca's widow Mama Rahua Ocllo, the mother of Huáscar, must also have played an important role. The *orejones* are supposed to have taken captives, women, and booty along with them, as they wanted to compensate for the triumphal entry into Cuzco that Huayna Cápac had not lived to celebrate. Huáscar is later said to have missed these military spoils of Huayna Cápac's, and his women, and ordered them to be brought to Cuzco.

Huayna Cápac's funeral procession was still an exemplary display of Inca royal dignity, veneration of the dead, and religious restraint. Together with the mummy, the most revered *huacas*, among them the famous egg-shaped stone of Huanacauri, were brought to Cuzco. In the most distant villages the death of the Inca was still being mourned. Men and women climbed hills, prayed aloud, and pulled out their eyelashes and eyebrows and blew them into the air.

The funeral celebrations were continued in Cuzco itself in the greatest style; the chronicles suggest they lasted between three and four months. In all the streets of the city, the houses were hung with the finest colored cloths and decked with silver and gold. The deeds of the late Inca were celebrated in song and were portrayed as they had been at the triumphal processions in his lifetime.

The provincial deputies praised his kindness. Gigantic offerings were made and the texts report that large numbers of women and servants followed the ruler to his death.[2]

The arrival of the funeral procession and the celebrations in the capital were, however, overshadowed by considerable tension and intrigue, and it is even said that Huáscar expressed criticism of the excessive display and participated in the festivities only with extreme misgivings. Since his father had left Cuzco as a young ruler, Huáscar had grown up at the old court in Cuzco, away from all the developments and vicissitudes of war. The conduct of government lay in the hands of the governors. The plague had brought about a fundamental change of circumstances. It had killed not only Huayna Cápac and his successor to the throne Ninan Cuyachi, but also the leading *orejones*.

Huáscar, and all who had reason to hope for his favor, now faced unexpected possibilities. He and a group of *orejones* — Titu Atauchi, Túpac Atauchi, Inca Roca, Urco Huaranhua, and Titu Conte Mayta, who are described as his advisers — had no dangerous rivals to fear in Cuzco, for his many brothers and relatives accepted his precedence. He continually widened the circle of his supporters by conferring offices and distributing gifts of gold, ornaments, garments, and women from the sun "convents."[3]

When the *orejones* and priests arrived from Quito and Tumibamba with the dead king, Huáscar was virtually lord of Cuzco. The knowledge that he had the whole of Cuzco behind him and that he had been accorded all the honors to which he was now entitled could not, however, have blinded him to the fact that without the army, which Atahualpa had detained in Quito, his power rested on an insecure footing.[4]

His indignation at the failure of Atahualpa and the generals to come to Cuzco to do him homage was unbounded. One after another, Cusi Túpac Yupanqui and the other intimates of Huayna Cápac were unobtrusively seized and questioned under torture, why they had left Atahualpa behind in Quito. The prisons of Arauay and Sancay became full of the trusted friends of the late Inca.

Huáscar publicly disowned the *ayllus* of Hanancuzco, to which those concerned had belonged. The whole of Cuzco was horrified at the actions of the new ruler, and all the people from the provinces and a large proportion of the Cuzco-born *orejones* who had accompanied the body of Huayna Cápac from Ecuador, fled back to where they had come from.

In this way Huáscar lost a large proportion of his old and new supporters right at the beginning of his reign, and the position of Atahualpa, which until then had been very much open to criticism, now consolidated itself.[5]

Húascar could also no longer trust the bodyguard that he had inherited from his father, and now formed a new, strong guard composed of *mitmacs*, Cañari, and Chachapoya who had been forcibly settled in Cuzco by Túpac.[6]

The sources do not make it clear whether Huáscar had taken the *borla* immediately on hearing the news of his father's death. There is no doubt that he did, in fact, wear the insignia of the Sapa Inca, the *mascapaycha*, and the *sunturpaucar* (*borla* and scepter). The chroniclers give detailed descriptions of the coronation rites and report that he received the *borla* from the hands of the high priest Chalco Yupanqui, who was descended from the line of Inca Viracocha.[7] We are struck by the fact that there are suddenly two high priests: first, the "Mayordomo del Sol," Cusi Túpac Yupanqui, ordained as *villac-humu* under Huayna Cápac and entrusted in Quito with the *calpa* that was to determine the succession. Then there was the high priest Chalco Yupanqui in Cuzco, of similarly eminent descent, but we know nothing of when and in what circumstances he assumed office.

It was Chalco Yupanqui who subsequently earned the most violent hostility from Atahualpa's party.

The writings of an anonymous Spanish cleric from the early colonial period convey most plainly how fluid and changeable the hierarchical structure of the Inca empire was. He points out how closely interwoven were the secular and priestly powers and how intense was the antagonism between the two, so that at one stage one might refer to a theocracy and at another to a suppression of the priesthood: "In ancient times all servants of the cult were held in high respect by the Peruvians, for they were rich and powerful, descended from ancient nobility, and strong through their family connections." The numerous, huge temple cities in the immediate vicinity of Cuzco and farther afield are evidence of their power and cultural importance.

"The great *villac-humu* was rather like a pope and was chosen from the great array of priests. He gave the final judicial decision in all things that concerned religion and the temples, and even the kings and the nobility acknowledged him and honored him just as much as the people and the servants of the cult did . . .

In ancient times even the king was subject to the judgment of the high priest, and on special occasions would confess to him . . . But at the time of the Inca Viracocha, there was ferment and open rebellion by the people, incited principally by the priesthood. This led to real wars and led almost to the destruction of Inca rule. Prince Titu Yupanqui," who later became Inca Pachacútec, "attacked and seized the temple cities and led numerous *huacas* and captive priests back to Cuzco in triumph and stripped the latter of their office and their livelihood forever."[8]

From then on, the above-mentioned fortified shrines (Ollantaytambo and Yucay in the Urubamba valley, and Calca and Chincheros are well known to archaeology) were used by the Inca kings as places of religious retreat and assembly or as summer residences.

Pachacútec's son Túpac fought against the oracle priests and those responsible for sacrifices, namely the inferior representatives of the local cults called *layca* and *humu*. He "burned numerous shrines and *huacas* and had salt strewn on the places where they had stood."[9]

Gold headdress decorated with jewels and feathers, possibly the tiara of the *villac-humu*.

Inca sling thrower.

Inca general.

Under Huayna Cápac the provincial shrines gained renewed importance at the cost of the priesthood in Cuzco. After Huayna Cápac's death, the latter became the ruling power and Huáscar's best support, and the high priest was now more powerful than the Inca himself.

The final destruction of the resurgent Peruvian theocracy was brought about shortly afterwards by Atahualpa, his generals Quizquiz and Chalcochima, and by Cusi Túpac Yupanqui, in shameful betrayal of his priestly office.

When the mourning ceremonies for Huayna Cápac were over, Huáscar and his advisers tried to consolidate his position as Inca by marriage to his own sister, Mama Chuqui Uzpai. The texts report unusually strong resistance to this marriage, not least on the part of the mother, Mama Rahua Ocllo. The oracles, too, were unfavorable to this project. Not until exceptional sacrifices and entreaties had been made to win over the priests of the sun and thunder temples and the *ayllus* of Túpac and Huayna Cápac, could the marriage take place; it was then held with even greater pomp and splendor than usual.[10]

In the first year of Huáscar's rule his position appeared to be gaining strength. He sent troops to quell some insurgent Chachapoyas in the Andes, southeast of Tumibamba, and met with reasonable success.[11] However, Atahualpa's army in Quito continued to be a constant threat.

Huáscar repeatedly sent emissaries to Atahualpa to induce him to come to Cuzco and acknowledge his supremacy. Atahualpa's reply was that he willingly regarded himself as Huáscar's vassal, but he asked to be allowed to retain his own position as governor in Quito and the neighboring provinces, as befitted an Inca.[12]

Urcos Colla, the *curaca* of the Cañari in Tumibamba, seized upon this word "Inca" and secretly sent word to Huáscar asking whether he knew of and consented to his brother Atahualpa's assuming honors in Quito to which only the reigning Inca was entitled. At this, Huáscar held a council with his relatives and followers. His reply was that, if Atahualpa came to Cuzco and handed over the army to him, he would live a life appropriate to his rank. He was unable to grant Atahualpa's request for the province of Quito, and furthermore, in addition to the army, he insisted on the return of the women, servants, and treasures that Huayna Cápac had left behind in Quito.

Atahualpa's reply was once again evasive, but accompanied by rich gifts. Huáscar burned the gifts and had four of the emissaries put to death, while the remainder had their noses cut off and their garments shortened to their belts.

He then sent them back to Atahualpa with the message that if he did not come to Cuzco, he would have him brought there by force.

Urcos Colla used the manner of Huáscar's reply to his brother as a way of provoking Atahualpa. He reminded him that he too was a son of Huayna Cápac and that he should therefore insist on his rights and defend them, by force if no other way were possible. In this, he could rely upon the support of himself, Urcos Colla, the *curaca* of the Cañari, and his followers.[13]

With matters coming to a head in this way, it was now unthinkable for Atahualpa and Quizquiz, Chalcochima and Rumiñahui, the generals who had risen to power under Huayna Cápac, to comply with Huáscar's command to come to Cuzco. It was all too plain what fate awaited them there. In Quito, on the other hand, they had attained a position, since the death of Huayna Cápac, previously unheard of for any subject of the son of the sun, and did not wish to surrender it. Ideally, however, they needed an Inca prince as a leader to support this power.

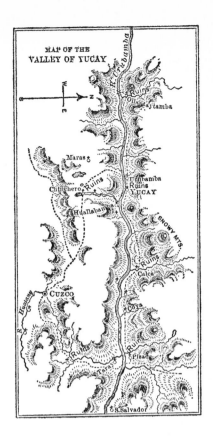

Cuzco had refused to agree to Atahualpa's governorship of Ecuador, and so, inevitably, matters reached the point where Atahualpa was pronounced lord of Quito. This, in effect, produced a *de facto* division of the empire created by Pachacútec, Túpac, and Huayna Cápac.[14]

Modern scholars give little credence to the theory that Huayna Cápac himself had already decreed a division of his inheritance and of the empire between his sons Huáscar and Atahualpa, as a result of which Atahualpa was to continue the tradition of an ancient Quito kingdom. This thesis is based largely on passages in the ninth book of the Garcilaso chronicle and has been much disputed by 19th-century American and Ecuadorian authors.

The political intrigues immediately preceding the outbreak of war between the two brothers were too complex to examine here. Cieza himself admits that "these Indians describe it in many different ways."

The main objective of both Atahualpa and Huáscar was to gain a firm foothold in Tumibamba, the most important administrative center in the empire after Cuzco. When his father's body was being brought back to Cuzco, Atahualpa had stayed in Tumibamba; after that we see him again in Quito.[15]

One chronicler describes a military campaign led by Atahualpa against the Huancavilca[16] in the coastal region of the Gulf of Guayaquil, where his father had previously been heavily engaged. The Spaniards who marched in with Pizarro saw the terrible devastation caused by Atahualpa in those regions.

It was at this point that Huáscar sent Atoc, one of his military leaders (and probably a brother), to Tumibamba with 2,000 men so that, with the aid of the Cañari, Atahualpa, whom he now regarded as a rebel, could be delivered into his hands.[17]

Atahualpa, for his part, tried to win the Cañari over to his side — the leading figures among the *mitmacs* as well as the old local inhabitants. He even intended to erect his own palace in Tumibamba next to the palaces of his forefathers.[18] But now, as Atoc approached, while Atahualpa's generals were 200 miles away in Quito, the Cañari decided to opt openly for Huáscar. Atahualpa was taken captive in a street battle. While the allies were holding banquets in the city to celebrate the capture of Huáscar's most dangerous rival, he managed to escape with the help of a palace maidservant, who had brought him a bar which he used to break through the wall. He is later said to have boasted to his soldiers that his father, the sun, had changed him into a snake and that in this guise he had escaped from the prison by crawling through a narrow hole.[19]

Battle scene.

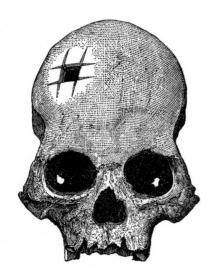

Trephined skull.

The news of Atahualpa's escape to join his troops in Quito spread like wildfire throughout the whole empire. War between the two brothers could no longer be averted.

With Cañari auxiliary forces, Atoc marched toward Quito. He had first sent emissaries to Atahualpa, still hoping to persuade him to negotiate. Atahualpa, carried aloft in a sumptuous litter on the shoulders of his favorites, at the center of his marching army, laughed at this entreaty and had the messengers put to death, although they were *orejones*.[20]

The first battle between the two parties took place at Ambato, roughly halfway between Quito and Tumibamba. After an initial setback, Atahualpa handed over command to the leaders of his army, Quizquiz and Chalcochima. The Quito party killed nearly all its captives, including Atoc and Urcos Colla. In accordance with military custom, Atahualpa had a drum made out of his brother Atoc's skin.[21] The skin from the belly was stretched and used for the drum skin, which was struck by the dried boneless arms as they swung in the wind. To complete the trophy this was topped by the shrunken head, with its original hair. The skull, covered in gold, was used by Atahualpa as a drinking vessel, much to the horror of the Spaniards.[22]

Atoc's defeat and death took Huáscar by surprise. Many llamas were sacrificed in Cuzco and the oracles consulted. Huáscar's advisers now urged him to recall the provincial *curacas* back to Cuzco. This time, the *curacas* from almost the whole of Chinchaysuyu, the northern part of the empire, which subsequently became the main area of conflict, still rallied to his call. Apart from the Quito region under Atahualpa's rule, the whole empire stood by Huáscar and everywhere troops were held ready.[23]

Whereas Atoc had been supplied with only 2,000 men, Huanca Auqui, Huáscar's brother, now set out from Cuzco with 12,000 men. By the time they reached the main base of Tumibamba, their numbers had swollen to 80,000. In spite of this, the city and province were lost immediately, and although Huáscar's general was able to replace and even increase his army, he was relentlessly driven back southwards by Atahualpa's generals.

Quizquiz and Chalcochima were soon in control of a vast hinterland area, from which they ruthlessly recruited troops.

In addition, deserters from Huáscar's ranks were continuously augmenting the size of their army.[24]

The Cañari and Chachapoya fought on with the courage of desperation, for they could hope for no pardon if they were defeated and Huáscar was their only hope.[25]

Far in the south on Lake Junín, 100,000 men fighting at the side of Huáscar held fast against an equally large army of the Quito party for three days, but then even this resistance fell apart.[26]

Since his victory over Atoc and Urcos Colla, Atahualpa had been regarded as Inca,[27] and he now approached the besieged capital city of Tumibamba with an immense following.

A host of wailing people, men, women, and children of all ages, approached the glittering procession of the victor with green branches in their hands, imploring him to forget the past and show them mercy. At the Inca's command, all but a few small children and the *mamacunas* were pitilessly cut down.[28] He then assembled the leaders of the Cañari in the city and ceremoniously received the *borla* and the other insignia of Inca dignity. These festivities provided only a short respite for Tumibamba, which had already endured much suffering. By the time Cieza traveled through Peru, he found the once flourishing capital of Túpac and Huayna Cápac reduced to ruins. The male population of the province was almost completely exterminated. The texts are not clear as to when and for what reason the final destruction took place.[29] The devastation extended well beyond the immediate battle area and over vast stretches of the hinterland.

Atahualpa's next objective was Cuzco, the capital. But he was not to reach further south than Huamachuco.

It was probably the news of the Spaniards' arrival in Túmbez, and the fear that they might support Huáscar, that made him decide to remain there and await developments.[30] He set up camp in Huamachuco with vast forces and an extensive courtly household. According to Spanish eyewitnesses his court had all the fabulous splendor of a reigning Inca, even though his position had not yet been acknowledged in Cuzco.

Atahualpa's numerous successes had strengthened his belief that the gods were on his side and fighting on his behalf.[30]

Huamachuco was also the home of the ancient Catequil *huaca*, which had been greatly revered in the time of Huayna Cápac and taken into battle many times.

"When he arrived in Huamachuco, Atahualpa sent two *orejones* to the shrine to make sacrifice there and to consult the *huaca*. They went there, made their offerings, and waited for the oracle to speak. The answer they were given was that Atahualpa would come to a bad end." The Catequil image had once before made a similar prediction about an Inca. At that time it had been that Huayna Cápac would not return alive from his expedition to Quito, and this had come true. If we are to go by the account of an anonymous Augustine monk, which says that the Huamachuco oracle declared Huáscar to be the rightful sovereign, then we can appreciate how Atahualpa was overcome by unbounded rage. "Atahualpa called his warriors and surrounded the shrine. He himself picked up a halberd and rushed into the sanctuary with the two *orejones*. He was met by a hundred-year old man, attired in a garment completely covered in seashells. This was the priest who had made the prediction. When Atahualpa heard who he was, he raised the halberd and with one blow he cut off the priest's head. Then he rushed into the chamber, and also dashed the holy image, which was made of stone, into fragments. He had the house, the *huaca*, and the priest's body set alight and scattered the ashes to the winds." As a member of a race who preserved the dead with such anxious care, where even the body of a defeated enemy was preserved as a precious trophy, Atahualpa must have believed that in utterly eradicating the Catequil image he could guard himself against any influences that might be threatening him from this direction. "He even had the hillock on which the house had stood flattened", as he wanted to remove any trace of the shrine.

Atahualpa had the fragments of the Catequil image thrown in a nearby river. But it appears that the priests had secretly removed the broken pieces and installed them in a new temple in Porcón and later hid them from the Christians in a mountain cave, where they were finally discovered after lengthy searching. Atahualpa is said to have removed the gold and silver treasure of the *huaca*, and it is thought to have been among the valuables handed over to the Spaniards in Cajamarca.[31]

Apart from this occasion when he consulted the Huamachuco oracle, there is little reference in the texts to Atahualpa fasting or making any major sacrifices.

The unfortunate Huáscar, on the other hand, repeatedly held great fasts at all the shrines in the land, just as his father had done during the time of the plague. He had sacrifices made and awaited the pronouncements of the oracle. He fasted for several days in Huanacauri, the important shrine near Cuzco. At Pachacámac he was promised victory, provided that he could concentrate his forces; Huanacauri prophesied victory, if he placed himself at the head of his army, and the remaining oracles prophesied a victory at Vilcas. The soothsayers predicted that everything depended on not allowing the enemy to cross the Angoyaco River. If he were able to stop them there, Huáscar would no longer be in any danger. In Sarmiento's chronicle, however, it says that the priests predicted disaster and that only the soothsayers and fortune-tellers gave the Inca hope for a happy outcome.[32]

The achievements of a new commander-in-chief, who replaced Huanca Auqui, brought one month's breathing space, but then the positions along the Angoyaco River had to be abandoned.[33] Worn down by the exertion of endless battles in the difficult ravines and mountains, Huáscar's men were driven further up the Apurímac. The Quito generals appeared to be invincible.

But Cuzco was not without defense and had not yet been surrendered to the enemy. In the Huatanay valley a great throng of warriors were assembling before the ancient walls of the fortress of Sacsayhuaman, near Cuzco, and their numbers increased daily. Urgently awaited contingents rallied to Huáscar from the Chiriguano, from Chile, from Tucumán, from the Andes, and from the coast.

After all his hopes had been dashed at the Angoyaco, despite the favorable predictions, he decided to enter the war himself.[34] He now did his utmost to raise a new army by extracting the remaining male population from the exhausted land. The vast encampment that had been erected in front of Sacsayhuaman was no longer big enough to house the great numbers that arrived.[35] For the first time, Huáscar now found himself at the head of an army.

The great suspension bridge across the Apurímac, which was maintained and used until the 19th century.

89

Accompanied by the *orejones* and his heavy bodyguard consisting of Cañari and Chachapoya, the Inca set out in a festive procession and led the army down into the Apurímac valley. The many tribes, each in their own different colored costumes, were spread out above and below and densely filled the narrow ground of the ravine of the Apurímac River. Santa Cruz Pachacuti, the Indian, tells us how Huáscar Inca now "mounted a hill, and surveying the scene in the valley below, rejoiced to see men numerous as grains of sand by the sea, and away over the mountains and ravines, the glitter and shimmer of gold and silver and feathers of a thousand bright colors. And there was not a patch of earth over a length of twelve miles and a breadth of six to seven miles that was not covered by moving men. Voices and a confused din wafted up to the Inca from all sides. All the tribes sang their war songs and beat their drums and sounded their various different instruments. The noise and color was enough to make one take leave of one's senses."[36]

The first engagements with the Chinchaysuyos, as Santa Cruz Pachacuti always calls Atahualpa's troops, now began as these moved down from the mountains and led the attack. On the first day of fighting, neither side was able to gain the upper hand, although thousands of men died. There were five further engagements each time beginning in the early hours and continuing until sundown, and with each day the situation became increasingly desperate for Quizquiz and Chalcochima, who despite their large army, were still outnumbered and in enemy territory.

On the second day, fighting broke out in the ravine of the Cotabamba river, where the Colla succeeded in isolating a division of Chalcochima's men and cut them to pieces.[37]

Huáscar was almost beside himself with joy at this success and said, "Pachacámac has accepted my fasting and my sacrifice."[38]

When, on the fourth day, Quizquiz and Chalcochima saw that they could no longer hold their positions, they retreated and sought shelter on three mountain peaks. At first light on the following day, Huáscar's armies surrounded them. When they had driven the enemy on to the highest of the three mountains, they set fire to the dry, man-high grass that covered the entire mountain above the forest line. A strong wind came up, and in no time the whole area was a sea of flames. A large proportion of the Chinchaysuyos perished in the fire, and the remainder rushed out, straight into the arms of the enemy, and were killed almost to a man.

Quizquiz and Chalcochima escaped and fled with scarcely more than 2,000 men. Huáscar's generals now urged the Inca to follow them and annihilate the remainder. But as it was dark and he believed total victory to be theirs, Huáscar would not undertake anything further and postponed the decision until the next day.[39]

When Quizquiz and Chalcochima realized that no one was following them, they reassembled their troops by sounding war horns. At midnight, Quizquiz and Chalcochima each lit a wax taper which they held in their left hands, one for Huáscar and the other for Atahualpa. Huáscar's flame burned bright and strong, while that of Atahualpa was very feeble. And then, so the story goes, Huáscar's bright flame suddenly went out, while that of Atahualpa began to burn fiercely. The Quizquiz and Chalcochima struck up the "Haylli de quichu" — the victory hymn — and thereby gave the soldiers to understand that all would end well.[40]

Both now gave their undivided attention to the person of the Inca. They learned from spies that the Cuzco army was now pursuing them, but that the Inca Huáscar together with a smaller group was advancing separately. He had sent his brother Túpac Atoc on ahead in the early hours of the morning to make sure that the way was free. The scout patrol had fallen into the hands of the enemy. Heavily wounded, Túpac was taken prisoner. His warriors shared his fate or were killed. In this way Quizquiz and Chalcochima learned that Huáscar would soon follow, and they prepared a trap for him.

Visible in his litter above the heads of the warriors, the Inca was cheerful and unsuspecting as he advanced rapidly towards the narrow neck of the gorge. It was at the upper exit to the gorge that Huáscar came across the first of the dead. Sensing something untoward, he ordered his men to turn back immediately. He soon found himself face to face with Chalcochima, and when he tried to reach the upper end of the gorge once more, the warriors of Quizquiz fell upon him. Desperately searching for a way out, the litter-bearing troop moved backward and forward. Heavy fighting broke out, and Huáscar's men grew ever fewer. Chalcochima, whom Huáscar had not let out of sight, finally pushed his way alongside the litter, caught hold of the Inca, and brought him down. The course of events is highly reminiscent of the manner of Atahualpa's subsequent capture by the Spaniards.[41]

When Huáscar had been brought into safe custody, General Chalcochima got into the Inca's litter and had himself carried to Huáscar's army, followed by Quizquiz and his soldiers. This diversion, unprecedented in Inca history, met with complete success. The enormous army at first greeted the supposed Inca with great jubilation, but within seconds this turned to dismay and confusion as Chalcochima revealed the truth by sending a heavily wounded Cuzco warrior among them. Retreat across the Cotamba River was now no longer possible, as the narrow bridge could not take such a massive load.[42]

So the war which had raged for years between the brothers was brought to an entirely unexpected conclusion. Fortune had favored not the greater army, but Atahualpa's two desperate generals, the mere mention of whose name, like some demonic force, struck terror into the heart of any opponent.

Without bothering about Huáscar's army, which was now in a state of dissolution, the victors now crossed over the Apurímac and moved on toward Cuzco. They still hesitated to enter the city itself, however, and called a halt at Quiuipay, a small town nearby. They had brought Huáscar there with them.[43]

On a hill, from which they could look down over Cuzco, some of Chalcochima's soldiers heard the crying and wailing of the desperate inhabitants.

Quizquiz and Chalcochima let it be known to the people in Cuzco that they had nothing to fear, since they were in no way to blame for this war, which had been

Mourning *orejón.*

a conflict between the two brothers.[44] But the *orejones* and all those in high office were commanded to present themselves at the camp in order to pay homage to the *huaoqui* of Atahualpa.

Shrinking at this ominous demand, the *orejones* requested three days in which to reflect. Quizquiz consented, certain that they would not attempt any further resistance as long as Huáscar was in his hands. There were violent discussions among the Cuzco nobility as to whether they should surrender to the enemy or try to resist. But when the time was up, the *orejones* appeared in Quiuipay, ranged in order of rank.

As they prostrated themselves before Atahualpa's *huaoqui*, Quizquiz had them surrounded with warriors, who seized Huanca Auqui and Huáscar's other military leaders, as well as the high priest Chalco Yupanqui and the other priests who had participated in Huáscar's enthronement.

In Atahualpa's name he graciously forgave them, but had them beaten across the back with stone clubs, from which a number of them died.

Then he ordered everyone to crouch down, their faces turned towards Cajamarca, where Atahualpa was, and to pray to their new lord. In mortal dread, the *orejones* did everything Quizquiz asked of them. They plucked out their eyelashes and eyebrows and blew them to the wind as a sign of prayer and called out loud, "Long live Atahualpa, our Inca! May the sun, his father, preserve his life!"[45]

The Inca, too, and his wife and mother were now made to face the *orejones*, who did not dare to look at their king in his humiliation. Huáscar, "his hands and feet tied to a bier made of bundles of straw," was now subjected to a torrent of abuse by the Quito generals. Pointing their fingers at him, they taunted him, saying, "Look at your master, now, who said that he would be fire and water to his enemies in battle!"

The high priest Chalco Yupanqui now unabashedly confessed his guilt to Huáscar, while Mama Rahua Ocllo joined in the abuse. Both later shared the same fate as Huáscar.

The general permitted part of the *orejones* to return to Cuzco. On their way back to the city, they are supposed to have addressed the following prayer of desperation to Viracocha; "O creator, you who have given life and grace to the Incas, where are you? Why do you permit such persecution to befall them? Why have you raised them so high, if they are to meet such an end?" And as they spoke, they shook their *mantas* as a curse that should afflict one and all.[46]

Now that all the leaders of the opposition were in the hands of Atahualpa's generals, the city was at the mercy of Quizquiz and Chalcochima and exposed to all the terrors that a savage army brings with it.

"And this came to pass, even though Cuzco was the holy city for all the people of the Tahuantinsuyu. Only the Sun Temple, and the house of the *mamacunas* that served it, were spared from plunder."[47]

The reckless butchery that followed in Cuzco is the darkest chapter in the whole of Inca history.

"At the news of the fall of the capital, Atahualpa had sent his relative Cusi Túpac Yupanqui to Cuzco with instructions to leave no relation or follower of Huáscar alive." In this way the former high priest was able to get his own revenge for the shame which he had suffered through Huáscar. Cusi Túpac Yupanqui had stakes erected on either side of the road leading up from the city to the fortress of Sacsayhuaman. Here, before Huáscar's eyes, all his wives who had borne him children were hung together with their children, and those who were pregnant had their bellies slit open. But it was not only Huáscar's family and all his friends that could be found who met with this fate, but almost all the *ayllus* of the Hurincuzco tribe, so that the chronicler Sarmiento thought it significant to enumerate the survivors of these *ayllus* individually by name.[48]

The *ayllu* descended from Túpac Inca was singled out for especial hatred. Chalcochima is supposed not to have shrunk from burning the mummy of this great Inca. Cobo, Murúa, Sarmiento, and Balboa all record this, whereas in the *Informaciones* it is stated that Juan Pizarro perpetrated this act in the hunt for treasure.[49] "Among those Cusi Túpac Yupanqui seized and condemned to death was a son of Huayna Cápac, by the name of Paullu. Protesting vehemently, he alleged that he had been put in prison for being a supporter of Atahualpa, and appealed to Chalcochima, who had set him free. Chalcochima confirmed this, and Paullu escaped."

However, Paullu Inca was apparently in prison for personal rather than political differences with Huáscar. He is supposed to have seduced one of Huáscar's wives.[50]

The massacre continued; many Cañari and Chachapoya were put to death. The remaining warriors of Huáscar's army, who came mainly from the southern provinces, were released to return to their homes.

What happened to Huáscar and his closest relatives, Mama Rahua Ocllo, the *coya*, Huanca Auqui, and others, remains obscure. We know only that Atahualpa ordered them to be brought to Cajamarca.

Alone in their immeasurable distress, the people of Cuzco turned to the god Viracocha and, with a great *capacocha*, implored him to send men to their aid to deliver their Inca out of the hands of those who held him captive in Atahualpa's name. They themselves no longer had the power to do so. Not long after, when the news of the coming of unknown strangers and of the capture of the much-feared Atahualpa reached Cuzco, Huáscar's supporters were convinced that their sacrifices had been accepted and must have believed that Viracocha himself had sent these strangers to their aid.

Whereas all the coastal Indians and the followers of Atahualpa simply called the Spaniards the "hombres barbudos," the bearded men, for the defeated in Cuzco and for all who stood by Huáscar, they were the "Viracochas," and this name persisted for a considerable time.[51]

With the capture of his brother Huáscar, Atahualpa had in fact become lord of the empire, and there seemed no longer to be anything standing in the way of his receiving the *borla* in Cuzco and reigning there.

Young *coya*.

93

But residents of Cuzco were never to lay eyes on the new ruler. For Atahualpa remained in Huamachuco — if we are to believe the Spanish texts — because of the news he is thought to have received from the *curacas* of Túmbez and Paita about the ventures of Pizarro.

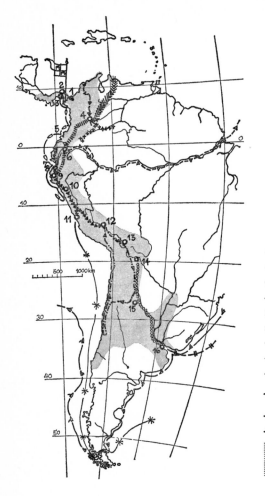

CONQUISTADOR EXPEDITIONS

V. Nuñez de Balboa	1513
J. Díaz de Solís	1516
Magalhães	1519—20
A. García	1524—25
F. Pizarro	1524—27
F. Pizarro	1531—33
Benalcázar	1533—39
Almagro	1535—37
Federmann	1535—39
Quesada	1536—38
Gonzalo Pizarro and F. Orellana	1541—42
Philipp von Hutten	1541—44
Sarmiento de Gamboa	1580
The Spanish viceroyalty of Peru (ca. 1650)	

DISCOVERY and ESTABLISHMENT of TOWNS

1	Santa María de la Antigua	1510
2	Nombre de Dios	1502
3	Panama	1519
4	Bogotá	1538
5	Isla del Gallo	1526
6	Quito	1534
7	Isla Puná	1531
8	Túmbez	1526
9	San Miguel	1531/34
10	Cajamarca	1532
11	Ciudad de los Reyes (Lima)	1535
12	Cuzco	1533/34
13	La Paz	1548
14	Potosí	1547
15	Tucumán	1565
16	Buenos Aires	1536/80

CHAPTER IV

Pizarro's march to Cajamarca — Capture of Atahualpa (1532) — Spaniards' diffi-
culty in orienting themselves to the numerous power factions in the land —
Cult objects among the gold treasure melted down at Cajamarca — Atahualpa
garroted (1533).

It was the conquistador Pizarro's third expedition in the southern seas that caused the downfall of the enormous Inca empire. It had been preceded by a first and second voyage of discovery that had already had certain repercussions on events within the Inca empire.

The men who organized these ventures were Francisco Pizarro, Diego de Almagro, and Hernando de Luque. "They made a contract, swearing on the Host, whereby Pizarro was to lead the expedition, Almagro was to secure the supplies, and Hernando de Luque was to provide certain additional funds."[1] Francisco Pizarro was born in 1475 in Trujillo in the province of Estremadura, Diego de Almagro in 1463 in the province of Cuenca. Thus by 1533, the former was fifty-three and the latter seventy. Pizarro was the illegitimate son of a Spanish nobleman. Some kind of offence when he was a young man is supposed to have made him leave Spain and set sail for the West Indies. Almagro, too, is supposed to have come to America as a young man, but little is known of his origins and his early life.

The financial backer, Luque — a priest who may well have been an intermediary for someone more important, namely Espinosa, the cleric — is not mentioned again in the account of the venture, and so we really have only two men to consider.

The first expedition left Panama in 1524. For three years their ventures met with no success. The crews assembled by Pizarro and Almagro were small. On one occasion 112 Spaniards embarked at Panama, on another 110, and again 160, and of these nearly 300 died, some of fever, a considerable number in battles with the savages, but the great majority from hunger, damp, and cold, without ever having caught the merest glimpse of Peru. Even today the Pacific coast of Colombia is hostile to man's survival; Negroes are the only people who can tolerate the climate, and advanced cultures have never developed there. Several times Pizarro failed to meet Almagro, who was supposed to bring him supplies. Francisco Pizarro was once severely wounded, as was Almagro, who lost an eye. Both fell ever more heavily in debt and it beame increasingly difficult to find companions who would go with them. Even the authorities refused them support, so that each departure and each return was accompanied by untold difficulties. But the two leaders were no novices; they knew the New World and had taken many setbacks in their stride. Pizarro had preceded Nuñez de Balboa in the Gulf of Darién in northern Colombia.

The perseverance and obsessive tenacity of purpose of Pizarro emerges most plainly from the incident when, in 1526, he held out for five months with only twelve men on a coastal island, the Isla del Gallo, after many other members of the expedition had obeyed an order by the governor of Panama to return. It was this second expedition that brought the first foretaste of success. The Spaniards found a good harbor in the bay of San Mateo in Ecuador and, leaving their boats there for a longer period, they went inland and came to fertile and densely populated territories. The one circumstance not to their liking was the model cultural and military organization of these communities, which did not permit them to plunder. At one time the Spaniards numbering no more than ninety men are said to have seen a battle formation of 1,000 Indians ranged before them.

They finally decided to retreat to the sea and return to the safety of the island.

It was from the Isla del Gallo that the helmsman Ruiz set out on his famous reconnaissance voyage, in the course of which he captured a large trading *balsa* from Túmbez and, in addition to gold and textiles brought six natives back with him. After waiting out the five months, the thirteen Spaniards set off on their pirates' quest in the Gulf of Guayaquil to Túmbez and still further south along the coast to *Santatol*, where they discovered Peru, which proved to them that their travels had been worthwhile and spurred them on to the subsequent conquest of the Inca empire.

Pizarro now hurried back to Panama with the captured treasures, having already overstayed the time granted him by the governor. "As the two leaders were now completely without resources and owed such great sums of money that they could no longer help themselves, Francisco Pizarro went to Castile with just over 1,000 Castellanos, lent to him by his friends, and made a report to his Majesty."[2]

Pizarro returned from the court with numerous titles and powers. He was made great *alguacil*, knight of the Order of St. James, and was granted in advance the governorship and absolute jurisdiction over the territories to be conquered. With this, the relationship between the two partners Almagro and Pizarro ceased to be on an equal footing. When Pizarro's four brothers followed him out from Spain, Almagro was increasingly thrust into the background.

On his return to Panama, Pizarro now prepared himself for his third journey to the south. The imperial papers and privileges did not have the desired effect here. Now, as before, the governor placed obstacles in his way.

In January, 1531, Pizarro left the port of Panama with as many men as he could muster, namely 180 men and 37 horses.[3]

V   *Anthropomorphic figures with animal heads (stylized masked dancer).*

Painted wooden goblet (quero), probably Inca style.

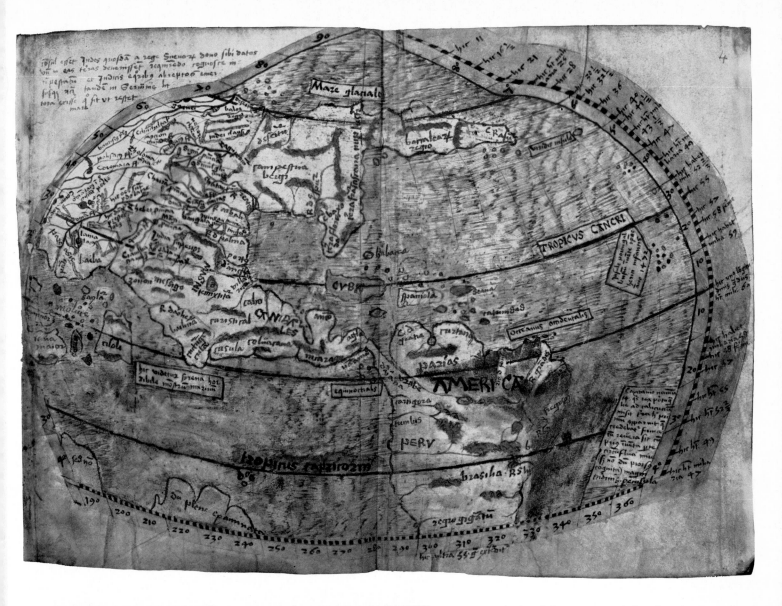

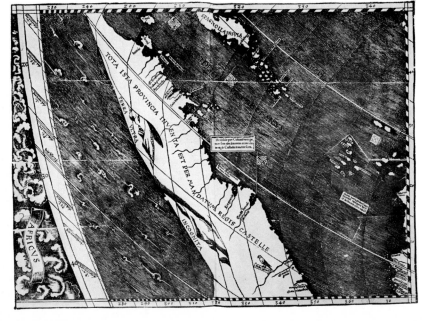

42 Early hand-drawn map of the American continent (above).

43 Part of Waldeseemüller's woodcut map of the world of 1507. West of the mountains lies the TERRA ULTRA INCOGNITA.

44 "COLUMBUS LYGUR NOVI ORBIS REPTOR."
Oil painting in the Museo Naval, Madrid.

45 16th-century model of a nao.

46 *Columbus stayed at the monastery of La Rábida on the Rio Tinto, facing Huelva,*
before setting out on the 3d of August, 1492, from the nearby port of Palos de la Frontera
on his first voyage to the West Indies, which led to his discovery of America.

ATAHVALL PA INGA XIV

El Vencido, Hijo de Mama Chachapoya Reyna de Quito Aclamado por R-
ey de Cuzco Fue vencido y preso del
Conquistador D.ⁿ Fra.ᶜᵒ Pizarro y despues degollado en Caxamarca, hallase que
fue bautizado y se llamo D.ⁿ Juan Año 1533

47   *Inca Atahualpa. Colonial oil painting.*

48a and b   *Two pieces of woven fabric, Inca style. Above: the garment of a nobleman. Below: a simpler black and white piece belonging to an Inca warrior (right).*

49   *Inca granite sculpture of a captive (below).*

50 Detail from a woven fabric from the Paracas Necropolis.

51 Ritual container in the form of a terraced temple. The drinking vessel brought to Pizarro by Atahualpa's emissary may well have looked like this.

52 "Pacha" (vessel in the form of a richly decorated model of a house).

53 View of the city and harbor of Seville. This was the quay where the treasures from Mexico and Peru were unloaded.

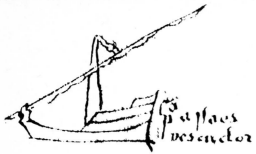

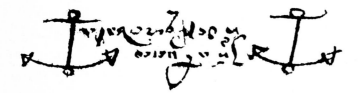

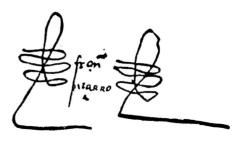

54 and 55 Signatures of 15th-century Spanish fishermen from Puerto de Santa María (Cádiz). They could not write, but were able to draw very realistic sketches of their boats. Their names were then added by a scribe. Francisco Pizarro (right) did the same as "Gobernador" of Peru. His "signature" consisted of the two flourishes framing the name (see text p. 140).

⊲ 56 Baroque church portal in Cochabamba, Bolivia. Evidence of Indian tradition can be seen in the small figures.

57 Fray Vicente de Valverde, Pizarro's field preacher and first bishop in Peru, according to a later portrait.

58 Pocket-sized catechism of Pedro de Gante, a cousin of Charles V. It is drawn in the manner of the Maya Codices and is in color (below).

59 *Magnificent portal of the colonial church of Santa Cruz in Julí on Lake Titicaca. Greek, Christian, and Indian tradition are blended here to form a highly individual style. In among the abundant grapevine sit the parasitic birds, familiar to us from ancient Peruvian art; the Peruvian bell-shaped flower Kantu also appears as part of the decoration.*

VI Left: figures with sprouting branches
           and trophy heads.
    Center: swaying figures with a chain of
           trophy heads and tumi (knife) in
           their hands.
    Right: two-headed snake — symbol of
           fertility, disease, and decay.

Once again they landed in the bay of San Mateo and worked their way inland with indescribable hardship through the marshy jungle, swimming across the wide rivers, and pulling the sick after them on rafts. At the equator they came to a civilized settlement called Coaque "with 300 large houses."[4] Starving and at the limit of their endurance, they did not attempt to make contact with the residents, but attacked the place, seizing not only ample provisions, but also much gold and silver and a large quantity of emeralds. They were not familiar with these and after testing them with a hammer, threw them away when, unlike diamonds, they were found to shatter.[5]

After a long detour inland, they reached the Bay of Caraques. Here, Pizarro ordered the greater part of the force to proceed by boat, while he continued on

Woodcut map of America by Sebastian Münster (1550). Japan (Zipangri) was still thought to be near Mexico. The banner of Castile on the Antilles and the Portuguese flag in the south Atlantic mark the areas of power and influence at that time.

109

foot with twenty-six horsemen and thirty foot soldiers through jungle, mountains, and deserts. The inhabitants of the province had presumably been warned by the attack on Coaque, and so the party found neither booty nor provisions. Three Spaniards ate a snake, as a result of which two of them died.[6] They rejoined their ship once more on the northern bank of the Guayaquil. Their next goal was the island of Puná.

By this time rumors about the white men, their ships, and their horses had spread through the country.[7] For some time after the *curaca* of Túmbez had sent his emissaries to Huamachuco, Atahualpa had heard nothing more about the white men. It was assumed that they had disappeared, just as their predecessors had done five years earlier, shortly before the death of Huayna Cápac. At that time, the prophecies had proclaimed that they were bringing disaster from another world, but they had turned out to be nothing more than miserable coastal pirates.[8]

It was not to be long before Atahualpa and Pizarro saw each other face to face. From the time of their arrival on the island of Puná, more than a year had passed before they finally decided to leave the coast and cut themselves off from the sea, their link with Panama and home. The overland journey from Coaque north of the equator to the island had already taken more than half a year. Pizarro's famous march of just under two months from the coast to Cajamarca, was thus comparatively fast[9] — it took the Inca's runners twelve to fifteen days to cover this stretch[10] — and it was accomplished virtually in full view of the Inca, as from there on messengers kept him informed of every detail of the Spaniards' movements.

The Spaniards were received in friendly fashion on the island of Puná, which is said to have had more than 12,000 inhabitants at the time. Tumbalá, the chief, and a crowd of people across the "Paso de Huayna Cápac" went to meet them in *balsas*, since the shallow water prevented the European ships from coming in to land. In accordance with the custom of the land, he brought them food and invited them to complete the crossing in their boats.[11] Warned by their interpreter Felipillo, the Spaniards were on their guard on the *balsas* and compelled the Indians, who had already started to loosen the fastenings of the rafts, to take them safely across. The Spaniards remained for quite a long time on the island — some chroniclers say two months, others five — and are said to have lived very well there. But when they began to plunder and to violate the women, the Indians became angry and decided to kill several Christians.

Pizarro, who had meanwhile received reinforcements of two brigantines, immediately took the chief prisoner, but forfeited his advantage by releasing him in exchange for gold and silver.[12] He now placed all his hopes on the people of Túmbez, 600 of whom he had liberated from slavery in Puná and had sent back home in the charge of three Spaniards.[13] He sent the remainder of his men back to the mainland on *balsas* with Túmbez helmsmen, expecting a dazzling reception from the city, which had become a legend to the Spaniards, since Pedro de Candía's visit five years earlier.

Reality proved quite different. Shortly before they were ready to land, the Túmbez men jumped into the sea, leaving the Spaniards to be washed ashore, where armed Indians were waiting to slaughter them "like seals," while the rafts holding most of their equipment drifted away.[14] Having survived the danger, they finally forced their way into the legendary Túmbez, which proved to be a sore disappointment. The flourishing city of five years ago was in ruins, burnt down and plundered in an attack by the Puná warriors, and still suffering from the effects of the plague.[15] The war between the island and Túmbez was related to the war between Huáscar and Atahualpa. The three Spaniards, who had accompanied the 600 liberated prisoners, disappeared without trace, and it was thought that they had been sacrificed.[16] Having spent a month or more in the barely pacified town, in the continued hope of discovering something about the fate of their three companions, they left Túmbez once more. Pizarro advanced southwards with most of his force, and the remainder followed later.[17]

They were now entering the area of the former Chimú state, which, like the province of Cajamarca, had been part of the Inca empire for only a few decades. They had to march across long stretches of desert before they reached inhabited regions once more. After 25 days they came to Puecho, a large town, 30 Spanish miles from Túmbez. There they were given a friendly welcome and hospitably entertained.

As night began to fall, the Indians led the Spaniards to a fortified enclosure, providing very comfortable quarters.[18] This fortress must have been one of the many *tampus* along the Inca roads, intended as accommodation for troops and the nobility. For by now, as we learn from Xerez and other chroniclers, the Spaniards were advancing along a broad road, lined with walls on either side, and more of these fortresses were to be found at regular intervals along the route.

Every day Indians from the surrounding countryside would bring food for the strangers and fodder for the horses and were generally helpful to the Spaniards in every way.[19]

As on all their voyages of discovery and conquest, the Spaniards used interpreters to tell the inhabitants of the land about God, the Catholic faith, and about the Apostolic Church in Rome, which they were to obey, and that in earthly matters they were subjects of His Majesty of Castile and León.[20]

This was the so-called "Requerimiento," a tract that had been drawn up in 1513 by Palacio Rubios, legal officer of the Crown, when the King and the Council for the Indians had been unable to agree whether a certain heavily armed expedition could be considered as a real war or not. This was the expedition planned by Pedrarius Dávila against the Indian tribes on the Isthmus of Darién and against Vasco Núñez de Balboa, who had fallen into disgrace. Since that time, rejection of this "offer" to the natives gave conquistadors grounds for the most rigorous action, and at first they even went so far as to sell the defeated natives into slavery. Despite the protests of Las Casas and his circle, the recital of the Requerimiento continued to be enforced during subsequent missions of conquest.[21] Apart from the cynical way in which it was often interpreted, it gave many conquistadors a religious strength in critical situations.

A few *curacas* in the nearby mountains remained rebellious and were finally compelled to make peace by Hernando de Soto's cavalry. The *curaca* of a tribe settled by the mouth of the River Chira, who had attacked a Spanish ship's crew as they were landing, was burnt at the stake by Pizarro.[22] The conquerors were now in a position to establish a settlement by this river called San Miguel, once their supply routes had been secured.

The Spaniards remained here, close to the coast, for several months more, trying to find out what was going on in the country. Pizarro heard a great deal about "rich settlements along the road to Chincha and Cuzco" — this is the first time, the name "Cuzco" is mentioned in the chronicle of Xerez. He learned, furthermore, that in a valley called Cajamarca, about twelve to fifteen days' journey inland, was the army camp of the most important ruler of all the surrounding territories. Zárate asserts that Pizarro received a message from Huáscar at this point: "In this place (in the port of Paita), the governor received a messenger from Cuzco, sent by Huáscar, who had not yet been taken prisoner, informing him of his brother Atahualpa's insurrection, seeking his help, and asking him to defend the justice of his cause."[23]

Months of fear, doubt, and hesitation preceded Pizarro's decision to march inland with 62 horsemen and 106 foot soldiers in search of the great king himself.[24]

The plan in itself was nothing new for Conquest methods — we have only to think of Mexico. Ever since their arrival in Inca territory, the Spaniards had always first tried to win the *curacas* over, or had taken them in custody, as in Puná. Where they encountered resistance, as in the case of the *curaca* of Amotape, they did not hesitate to torture and burn alive. While Pizarro was still in San Miguel, a spy sent by Atahualpa appeared in his camp. The chronicler Mena, who was an eye witness, reports the event as follows: "When Atahualpa learned that the Spaniards were coming, he sent a captain to ascertain what kind of people we were. This captain, disguised as a humble Indian, made his way into our camp, and despite the size of his force, he did not dare attack us. He then returned to report to his lord, and asked him to give him more men, saying that he would return to attack the Christians. The Kazik (Atahualpa) replied (as he later told us himself) that he would be in a far better position to attack the Christians if they came to him."[24a] In the course of the seven weeks' march[25] to Cajamarca, the Inca kept a watch on the Spaniards from his camp, while Pizarro with his small body of men groped their way slowly forward and were able to enlist the help of only a few individual Indians of the local population, so that they never gained a clear picture of the situation in the highlands or of the intentions of the Inca. Moreover, the Spaniards could not know whether they were being given reliable information by their interpreters. The best known of these intermediaries, Felipillo, has also gone down in the history of the Conquest as an extremely dubious character.

By the time they reached Piura, before the conquistador finally left the coast and turned inland, the first nine Spaniards had already turned back for San Miguel. All the *curacas* of the region warned them of Atahualpa and made them afraid. Pizarro, too, on asking the way, heard nothing favorable — whole areas of land had been depopulated; the route across the cold heights of the Cordillera took five days, two of which had to be endured without water. Nevertheless, the diminished band of Spaniards continued on its way. They now discovered that the Inca's troops were not far ahead of them, in Caxas, a settlement between the mountains, which they could skirt on their route. This place was said to house rich provisions of every kind.[26]

A group of fifty to sixty men under De Soto now left the main party to make their way there. Although they made a difficult detour across the mountains, in order to escape attention, they repeatedly saw that they were being observed by Indians. When they arrived in the small valley of Caxas, they found distinct signs that troops had been there. The attitude of the natives towards these new armed arrivals was evasive, even hostile, and they relaxed only gradually as they realized that the Spaniards were anxious to be on good terms with them.

The people had been thoroughly frightened. Caxas had very recently been the scene of one of Atahualpa's actions, and his warriors had left the place only a few days before. The *curaca* of the place told the Spaniards of the horrors they had had to endure on account of their support for Huáscar. The former population of between 10,000 to 12,000 had been reduced to scarcely 3,000. Outside the town, the Spaniards saw men strung up by their feet, the first gruesome evidence they had met of the war in the interior.[26]

Hernando de Soto appears to have either reassured the town *curaca* or intimidated him to such an extent that, as Mena records, he "opened one of the closed houses (women's 'convents') and removed four or five women and gave them to the captain so that they might serve the Christians on their march and prepare food for them."

The chronicler Trujillo is more direct than Mena and speaks of savage attacks and the danger of a clash with one of Atahualpa's captains and his 2,000 warriors.

Mena describes the sudden appearance of one of Atahualpa's emissaries in Caxas in the following scene: ". . . the *curaca* of the town sprang up, as he did not dare remain seated in the presence of one higher ranking than himself. But Hernando de Soto bade him to be seated once more at his side."

The messenger had brought gifts for the *Gobernador* (as the chroniclers call Pizarro), and De Soto now accompanied him to Carán, where he was awaited by Pizarro, who had had some misgivings about letting him go in the first place.

The gifts were very curious — a pair of stuffed ducks and two pottery models of what looked like fortresses. The Spaniards did not know what to make of them. In answer to their questions, the messenger is supposed to have said that they could tell from the ducks what the Inca intended to do with them. This presumably referred to the shrunken heads and drums made of human skin

Aclla (temple virgin).

113

displayed at the Inca court. The model fortresses that Xerez describes as drinking vessels, may well have also been intended as a threat.

In return the *Gobernador* sent gifts of "a very fine shirt and two glass goblets," and instructed the messenger to tell his lord, that he "was coming to Atahualpa as a friend and that he was looking forward to seeing him,"[26] and of his own accord he sent an Indian of rank to Atahualpa's camp in order to discover the strength of his army.

On the 20th of October, Pizarro left Çarán.[27] He found nearly all the places through which he passed had been destroyed. All the villages had had to provide troops; their original *curacas* were now in Atahualpa's camp and had been replaced by trusted followers of the new ruler.[28] As the Spaniards were still advancing along the wellbuilt Inca road, they always found comfortable quarters and ample food in the fully equipped *tampus* that had been constructed at regular intervals of two Spanish miles along the route. However they sensed danger on all sides and were prepared for enemy attacks at every hour, for they simply could not understand why Atahualpa allowed them to continue to advance without making any move to stop them. Pizarro resorted to every measure to try and find out from the Indians whether the Inca had any designs on him. One of the Indians finally submitted under torture that Inca troops were awaiting the Christian with hostile intent at three places," at the foot of the mountains, on the pass at the top, and finally at Cajamarca." Pizarro wanted to have confirmation of this, and asked an Indian nobleman from San Miguel, who had attached himself to the Spanish column, to cross the mountains and enter Cajamarca as a spy. His reply was, "I dare not go there as a spy, but I will go as your emissary and speak with Atahualpa and thereby I shall discover whether there are warriors in the Cordillera and what they intend to do."[27]

The Spaniards were now in a dreadful state of uncertainty and the men were continually urging their leader to abandon the march to Cajamarca and not to press on to the mountains, where the enemy was lying in wait, but to take the southern road towards Chincha. But Pizarro pointed out to them that "since their departure from San Miguel, Atahualpa was aware of the Christians' every movement . . . He considered that it would be most dangerous if the Inca sensed they were afraid.[27] Then they commended themselves to God and set out on the strenuous march."[28]

They ascended the heavily fortified pass with the utmost care. A handful of warriors would have been enough to repel a whole army. But to the Spaniards' surprise they found this stronghold abandoned just as other fortified places on the way had been. This surprising development was possibly another result of the war between Huáscar and Atahualpa, since between them they had mustered all the available troops in the land. Not even token garrisons had been maintained. Later they were surprised to find that even the citadels in Cajamarca were left unmanned, being so close to the Inca camp. Exhausted by the continuing uncertainty, the hardship of the march — they had to drag the horses up steps for part of the way — and by the icy cold, the Spaniards stopped to rest.

Two acllas are presented as a gift to the Spanish leaders, in accordance with Inca custom.

A little later they were met by emissaries, who, on Atahualpa's instructions, again invited them to come to their ruler in Cajamarca. The Christians were even brought llamas, provisions, and other things.[27] Someone gave Pizarro colored shoes to wear when he appeared before the Inca.[29] The emissaries also confirmed what he had already learned from the local population, that Atahualpa had arrived in Cajamarca from Huamachaco only a few days before. But they said that their king had only very few men with him, which contradicted what the inhabitants of the nearby villages had told them about Atahualpa's camp. Pizarro recognized one of the emissaries as the same aristocratic Indian who had delivered the curious gifts in Carán, and the Spaniard was highly delighted to see a familiar face. The emissary assured him that his sovereign would receive the white men "in peace and friendship."[27]

Thus everything appeared to be working out well, and many a simple soldier once more dared to dream that he would after all have his share of gold and end his days in a distant land.

Suddenly there was a great commotion in the camp — Pizarro's own emissary had just returned from his visit to Atahualpa and, on seeing the Inca's messenger, fell upon him and pulled him by the ears, shouting at him angrily that Atahualpa had not come from Huamachaco with only a few men, but with a vast army. He, the governor's emissary, had not even been allowed to see the Inca; they had not given him food and had even tried to kill him, and it was only by threatening that Pizarro would retaliate by immediately killing Atahualpa's emissaries that he succeeded in leaving the camp alive. A relative of Atahualpa's had been the only one to speak with him, and had questioned him as to "what kind of people these Christians were and what weapons they had." He, the ambassador of the Christians, had told him of the firearms and "of the horses, that could run like the wind and kill people with their mouths and their hooves."

But the reply to this had been that all that was unimportant, for the Christians were few in number and had only two cannon, and they were only biding their time to slaughter the invaders.

Pizarro rebuked the excited Indian abruptly and appeared to take the side of the powerful ruler in Cajamarca, whereas he was secretly convinced that what his own messenger had seen and heard was all perfectly true.[27]

In the virtually desperate situation in which the Spaniards had continually found themselves ever since landing, there seemed no alternative but to press on to the encounter with the most powerful ruler in the land.

At last the mountains were behind them, and they now found themselves before a broad and fertile valley with a series of hills jutting up like islands. The city of Cajamarca was on one of these. Heavily armed, they continued on their way, sending a messenger on ahead to the Inca, inviting him to come and meet them.

When they reached the city, they saw Atahualpa's camp at some distance in the plain. It must have been a shock to them to realize that the excited messenger of a few days earlier had been right when he told of the vast assembly of troops. The number of white tents was impressive and they were all grouped around a central house, sheltered by a few trees.[30] Hesitantly Pizarro and his small band of Christians entered the city. It was the 15th of November, 1532. They reached the center, a broad square, without seeing a soul. All around were heavy walls and fortified houses, concealing no one knew what. The white men did not dare to stir from the spot, and the riders remained on their horses. They must have been utterly perplexed; Pizarro had no alternative but, once again, to send an Indian to Atahualpa to inform him "that he had now arrived and was waiting for him to come and show him where they should go."[27] He wanted at all cost to make contact with the other party, for the deathly silence was undermining the spirits of his men. He gradually built up a picture of the layout of the city from his Indian spy — the Spaniards did not dare to move away from the open square. There were only two ways of entering the square in the center of which they had remained in serried ranks, and both these entrances were guarded. Access from the valley was only by means of a stairway, and the mountain side was covered by a fortification constructed on three levels — like a spiral, according to Xerez — and partially cut out of the rock. To right and left there stretched endless walls, behind which were buildings almost 500 feet long, apparently troop quarters, which in turn were again enclosed by walls. There were fountains in the courtyards, fed by water that was brought over great distances through pipes. A second, smaller square lay slightly higher up, where the *mamacunas* were kept with their guards, who were the only people left in the deserted city.[27]

It was getting late and still no answer came from Atahualpa's camp. Then Hernando Pizarro and Hernando de Soto urged their leader to let them go with a few Spanish horsemen to Atahualpa. Hesitantly, Francisco Pizarro agreed, and initially gave De Soto only twenty horsemen to take with him. Watching the little group from the tower of the fortress, he was dismayed to see in the distance that in the Inca's camp more and more warriors were streaming out of their tents, and so he sent his brother to follow up with reinforcements. Soon after, the sky darkened, it began to rain and hail, and it became cold. The Spaniards had to shelter in the houses for the night. With a couple of marksmen and the two cannon, Pedro de Candía, the engineer, occupied the tower. They had scarcely completed this operation when the awaited messenger from the Inca arrived and announced that they could settle down wherever they liked, but that they were not to enter the upper fortress.[31] This confirmed Pizarro's belief that the occupation of this point was of great strategic value, and that he had thereby done something that ran counter to the Inca's plans. The experiences of Hernando de Soto and Hernando Pizarro in the Inca camp are related in greatly differing versions. According to Mena and Xerez, De Soto left his comrades behind at the edge of the camp and rode entirely alone through the rows of tents, past the archers, sword bearers, and halberdiers in their brilliant clothing and their war paint, without being stopped by the bodyguard, until he stood before the

Inca. "Atahualpa sat in the open, on a low seat in front of his house, arrayed in the costly insignia and apparel of the Inca. The *curacas* and counselors stood by him and a number of women were busying themselves around him."

The Inca took no notice whatsoever of the stranger, but remained completely motionless, his head hung low, so that the wide *borla* hanging from his forehead entirely covered his eyes.[32] Mena continues:

"De Soto moved his horse so close to the Inca ... that the beast's breath stirred the *borla* on his forehead." But even this did not induce the Inca to alter his position. "De Soto now took a ring from his finger and offered it as a token of friendship. Atahualpa accepted it with indifference."[32]

Whatever the Spaniard now said to the Inca, through the interpreter he had brought with him on the crupper of his horse, was answered only by a representative who spoke in his name.

It was only when the second Spaniard, the brother of the governor, who had pushed his way through the crowd in his haste to catch up with Captain De Soto, addressed the Inca, that he began to speak. He was well aware of "how badly the Spaniards had treated the *curacas*," and that Christians and horses alike had already been killed by the Indians. Nevertheless, he proposed to come to the Christians on the following morning. Hernando Pizarro now began to speak grandly about the invincibility of the Spaniards, how justly they behaved towards the local inhabitants, and how very useful they could be to the Inca, if he would be their friend. The interpreter must have translated all this very accurately, "for the Inca laughed and said that they should drink with him" (Xerez). Thereupon, the women appeared with golden goblets of *chicha* beer. When Atahualpa saw how impressed the Spaniards were with the heavy gold, he immediately called for vessels twice the size. Although they were afraid, the Spaniards could no longer refuse to drink, but they then rapidly took their leave.[33] They were scarcely able to pass through the closely-ranked Indians, but when Hernando de Soto's horse brushed against a few of the Indians, they fell back several paces. However, as soon as the riders had disappeared and the camp returned to life, these had to pay a terrible price for their cowardice; Atahualpa had them put to death there and then.[34] But the subsequent catastrophe of Cajamarca shows how very mistaken the Inca was in his belief that he could banish the Indians' elemental fear of the white man by such Draconian measures.

The Spaniards continued to wait, and on the following day their fears increased hourly, for they guessed that the Inca must be making colossal preparations for the impending meeting, and they had so little with which to oppose him. They established themselves in the fortress as best they could, but all the time the Pizarro brothers had to go from man to man and boost their courage. All that remained to them was their trust in God's help.[27]

Finally, the time came, and an eyewitness reports:[35]

"On the same day, Atahualpa set out for the city of Cajamarca and arrived there towards evening. He was carried by several kaziks in a litter covered with the finest gold. He was preceded by many Indians, who cleaned the roadway, although it seemed neat enough and there was not actually anything to clean. These were followed by a crowd of other Indians, some of whom sang while others danced around the Inca. In addition to these, the procession included a great number of Indians, who were called "gaudules" and formed his personal bodyguard. Some of these carried battle-axes and others had halberds of silver or clubs hanging from their belts. A further "batallion" of these gaudules were armed with spears, bows and arrows . . . This was the manner of Atahualpa's entry into the city; he left a great multitude on the field outside, amounting as I was later told, to some 40,000 gaudules armed with lances 20 feet long, not to mention axes, halberds, clubs, and slings. He had ordered the men, who had remained in the field outside," as it later transpired, "to lie in ambush in the different quarters of the city of Cajamarca, so that, when he entered the city and the Spaniards took flight, they would be hemmed in on all sides. And it seemed as if victory was already his."

The great mass of Indians who entered the city with Atahualpa to meet the Spaniards were, therefore, only lightly armed. Mena, Hernando Pizarro, and Xerez say that they carried their weapons hidden under their clothing. The heavily armed forces remained posted outside the city, and it was intended that the big weapons were to be carried in and handed over to the warriors who had already gone before.[36] Pedro Pizarro says that Atahualpa's general, Rumiñahui, had already surrounded the city the night before with 20,000 men with slings and *bolas* to prevent the Spaniards from escaping.

Later, after he had been taken prisoner, Atahualpa is supposed to have mentioned casually, that the situation in which he now found himself, was what he had destined for the Spaniards.

The fabulous splendor of Atahualpa's entry into Cajamarca, the array of warriors, at once awe-inspiring and festive, Atahualpa's own decision, and the sacrifice that had hastily been made beforehand, indicate that there was more to this scene than just a routine military action. It was a combination of sober calculation, unrealistic gambling, and curious inspiration. It is reminiscent of Huáscar's failure as a military general, and of the preparations for great tournaments and sacrifices, where the Inca would always be present as the central figure. It seems that this band of foreigners, who had been met with such remarkable honors, had been chosen as a rare and special human sacrifice.

Pizarro, too, was no mere desperado, exploiting circumstances to his advantage. Strengthened by his faith in the Virgin Mary, in the saints of his homeland, and by his command from the king, he calmed his companions who were half-crazed with fear and, following the example of Cortés in Mexico, he made use of every advantage offered by the unfamiliar surroundings to further his aim of capturing the sovereign of the Inca empire alive.

"The sun was already very low" when Atahualpa finally arrived in Cajamarca. Carpets were spread out in his path and, high above the heads of the bodyguard and the singers and dancers, a magnificent litter decorated with gold and parrots' feathers appeared in the central square of the city. Close behind him, there followed other high-ranking persons, similarly carried in litters and hammocks.

"He stopped in the center of the square, without descending from his litter, and all the while more and more men crowded into the square, until it could not hold another person.[37]

"There was no sign of the Christians, and Atahualpa asked in surprise where 'the bearded men' were. At this the Spanish chaplain Vicente de Valverde emerged, cross and breviary in hand, and walked right up to the Inca's litter. On Pizarro's instructions he addressed him through the interpreter saying that the governor requested him to come into the house. Atahualpa replied curtly, "that he would not move from this place until the Christians restored to him everything that they had stolen throughout the country, and then he would still do whatever he chose."[28]

Thereupon, the chaplain began to launch into the previously mentioned "Requerimiento," and spoke to the Inca ruler of the creation of the world, of the fall of Adam and Eve, of Jesus Christ, of His birth, His death, His Resurrection and Ascension, and how He had appointed St. Peter as His representative on earth, and of His successors, the popes in Rome; that the Pope had divided the world among the Christian kings and had granted this land of Peru to His Majesty, Emperor Charles. Francisco Pizarro represented the person of His Majesty, and if the Inca would permit himself to be baptized and obeyed the Emperor, as did the great majority of Christianity, then he would enjoy his protection and friendship. "If not, the governor would fight him lance in hand with blood and fire."[38]

The Inca Atahualpa's response to this speech was immediate. According to Velasco, he found it "most surprising that the Pope was able to give away something, that did not in fact belong to him . . . Nor did he understand how the god of the Spaniards could have died so ignominiously . . . The sun, which he and his people worshiped, never died and was never in danger of falling into the hands of enemies."

The manner in which the chronicler Zárate quotes the text is unmistakably controversial, and shows how this "Requerimiento" had become a vexed question among the clergy. Their contemporaries obviously felt that this conscientiousness on the part of Pizarro and Valverde in such a situation was grotesque.

The Inca demanded to know how the monk knew all this. The monk handed the breviary up to him; this, he said, contained the truth.[39] The sovereign tried in vain to open the clasp, and eagerly Valverde reached up and tried to help him. Indignantly, Atahualpa struck him on the arm. Finally he broke open the clasp, but after the briefest glance at the book threw it angrily into the crowd.[40]

This provoked and expected rejection of Christian truth and Imperial grace was the signal for the attack. The monk ran back to Pizarro, shouting loudly.[41] Atahualpa stood up in his litter and called out to all sides, and the Indians answered with their battle cry.[42] Thereupon, Pizarro rushed headlong right through the dense crowd up to the Inca's litter, without so much as a backward glance to see if any of his men were following, and catching the Inca by the arm, he shouted, "Saint James," the ancient battle cry of the Spaniards. In the same instant, the two cannon thundered, the trumpets sounded, and the Spanish cavalry and foot soldiers stormed out of hiding.

And now the utterly incomprehensible happened — the marvel of Cajamarca. Not one of these many thousands of Indians offered any resistance; instead they threw themselves into headlong flight. As the square was so crammed with people, their immense numbers proved their undoing; all the exits were blocked, and with men falling over one another and the horses crushing them, the Spaniards created an appalling bloodbath.[43]

The Inca's litter still rested on the shoulders of its bearers, for as one after the other they sank to the ground, bleeding, others quickly stepped in to take their places. All this while, Pizarro had kept hold of Atahualpa's arm, but it was not until several bearers had sacrificed their lives, and the litter collapsed to the ground, that Pizarro tore the sovereign out of it, and in so doing reduced his gorgeous apparel to rags and shreds. Only by the greatest effort did Pizarro succeed in getting the Inca out of the tumult alive. The high-ranking princes in the other litters, and the *curacas* from the various provinces, who had been surrounding the Inca, had died before his own eyes.[44] Thus Atahualpa met with a similar fate as had befallen Huáscar a few months earlier, as a result of an even more cunning trick on the part of the Quito generals.

When, on the following day, the Spaniards scoured the neighbourhood of Cajamarca, they found vast quantities of abandoned lances and other weapons.[27] General Rumiñahui and his troops, who had been gathered outside the city, had left for Quito.[36]

With Atahualpa, the Spaniards had captured the head of the Incas, but the really dangerous men, Generals Quizquiz and Rumiñahui, were still at large and in command of great armies.

The months of Atahualpa's captivity were a time of great expectancy and tension. No one did anything.

Every one of Pizarro's observations and actions (Xerez, Zárate, and other texts confirms this) make it plain how disquieting the Spaniards found this inactivity. On the coast they had had to deal either with friends or with enemies. Conditions in the Yunca valleys had suggested that tribal princes there had not been entirely robbed of their autonomy either under Chimú rule or under the Incas. They had ventured to take their own decisions and had had their own political aims and disputes.[45] However, only a few miles further inland, where the mountains began, it became obvious that the hand of Atahualpa ruled.

Although they stayed in Cajamarca for months, with the captured Atahualpa sleeping in the same room as Pizarro, the Spaniards were unable to establish any clear picture of what was going on around them.

The presence of Atahualpa in Cajamarca attracted hundreds of *curacas*. They brought the prisoner gifts and women, as if nothing in his position had altered. The Spaniards were unable to communicate with them, and constantly fearing an uprising, they lent a ready ear to any whisperings. They were not to know that these *kaziks* were politically insignificant and that they were utterly dependent on the person of Atahualpa. They had little support in their own areas, as they were not descended from long-established local families, but had only recently been installed in preparation for the arrival of Atahualpa.[27]

The real danger came from quite a different direction, in the form of the two victors of the civil war, Quizquiz and Chalcochima, who were far off in the south, one in Cuzco and the other in Jauja. The obscure figure of the third general, Rumiñahui, in Quito, was to play a serious role only after the death of Atahualpa.

For the time being, however, the Spaniards' greed for gold dominated all other thoughts, cares, and doubts, and in this Atahualpa was of inestimable value to them alive. For by threatening him with death, they were able to extort as much gold from him as they desired. The monarch promised Pizarro that he would fill the room in which they were — it is supposed to have been some 21 feet by 15 feet — with gold as high as his arm could stretch.

As things were not moving fast enough for the Spaniards, in order to save his life, he divulged the whereabouts of the most venerated sanctuaries in the country and enabled them to travel unmolested and in comfort through the land, like great *curacas* and Incas. He placed litters, traveling hammocks, and numerous attendants at their disposal. He himself acted as a hostage for their safety. With a brother of Atahualpa's for a guide, three Spanish captains set themselves no less a goal than the capital, Cuzco, more than 600 miles away. These travels gradually gave the Spaniards an inkling of what was taking place in the country, outside Cajamarca.

The defeated Huáscar was now on the sad march to Atahualpa, together with his wife Mama Uzpai, his son, his mother Mama Rahua Ocllo, the high priest Chalco Yupanqui, and other survivors of his party. South of Huamachaco, they encountered the Spaniards. Huáscar apparently managed to speak with the foreigners and is supposed to have promised them even more gold than Atahualpa. But the Spaniards continued on their way; either they had not fully understood the significance of the encounter or they considered it unwise to interfere, in view of the superiority of Atahualpa's forces.[46]

The chronicler Mena records their visit to the holy city, as follows:

"They arrived in the city of Cuzco and there met one of Atahualpa's generals by the name of Quizquiz, which in their language means 'barber'. He was not very impressed with the Spaniards, although their appearance amazed him. One of the Christians wanted to attack him with a dagger, but was discouraged by the large number of people the warrior had around him. He gave them to understand that they could not expect too much gold from him; if there were not enough to meet the ransom required for the *kazik* (Atahualpa), then he himself would come to liberate him. Then he sent them to several 'Bohios del Sol' (cham-

Orejones.

bers) used in the sun worship. On each of them, the wall facing the rising sun was covered with great sheets of gold ... The Christians entered the Bohios and started to tear down the gold sheets with copper rods. The Indians would not under any circumstances help them, for according to their belief this would have resulted in instant death for them. Instead, they went through the city collecting a mass of gold vessels which they brought for the Spaniards to take back as ransom for their king ... It is scarcely credible how much gold there was in the various buildings ... They entered another house, where they found a sacrificial bench made of gold, that was big enough for two men to lie down on. "In another house they came upon some pottery vessels, thinly clad with gold, which were very heavy. The Spaniards did not dare to break them for fear of antagonizing the Indians. In the house inhabited by many women, they found two embalmed bodies with gold masks over their faces and richly adorned gold staffs in their hands. A woman was flicking dust and flies from the bodies with a whisk and would not permit them to enter without removing their shoes. They obeyed and drew near to observe the shriveled forms, and removed many costly objects from them. But they did not rob it of everything, for the *kazik* (Atahualpa) had requested them not to take anything as it was the mummy of his father Cuzco (Huayna Capác) ...

"Finally, they started to load all their gold. The general helped them as best he could. The Christians also found much silver in the city, and they told the governor (Pizarro) that there was a large house there full of jugs and large vessels, goblets, and other objects, and they could have brought much more back with them. But they had been anxious not to spend too much time there, as they were alone and more than 250 miles away from the other Christians ...

"They locked the doors of the house and put the seal of His Majesty the Emperor and of Governor Francisco Pizarro on it, left a guard of Indians to watch over it, and installed a city governor, as they had been ordered to do. Taking the gold, they set off on their way."

Of the precious objects that were brought to Atahualpa's famous room and were subsequently melted down, we shall mention only a few special pieces — silver tableware, golden fountains, silver models of lizards and corn cobs, a medallion with the picture of an Inca and his Coya, and a male and female figure, the height of a ten-year old child, all of solid gold.[47]

The golden sun bird Inti-Illapa, the huaoqui, or symbolic brother, of Pachacútec Inca Yupanqui, is also said to have been hacked to pieces and brought to Cajamarca.[48]

"In all my life I have never seen anything that so delighted my heart, for in them I saw things of wonderful artistry and was amazed at the subtle ingenuity of these people in foreign lands." These words of Albrecht Dürer referred to the Mexican cult treasures, which the German artist saw exhibited in Antwerp in 1520. He was virtually the only person in Europe to appreciate the artistic and spiritual content of the Indian cult objects. The authors are not familiar with any similar contemporary assessment of the Peruvian works of art, with the exception of the chroniclers writing in America. It is hard for us to understand today how Charles V, a sensitive member of the house of Habsburg and heir to the tradition of Burgundy, and his entourage had no eye for the Indian works of art, and appear to have been interested solely in how much gold they would yield when melted down to fill the eternally empty war coffers.

Francisco Pizarro appears to have behaved with scrupulous honesty in the protection of His Majesty the Emperor's interests. The chronicler Zárate writes: "He would often rise from his seat while watching the melting down of the gold and silver to retrieve a small piece of the king's share, which had fallen to one side as it was being broken down, and in so doing he remarked that he would pick up the king's property with his mouth if need be."

Before the adventurers had returned from Cuzco, a group of Spaniards arrived in Cajamarca, who, led by Hernando Pizarro, had been to Pachacámac. Not only did they bring back gold with them, but they had also taken prisoner one of Atahualpa's great military generals, Chalcochima. Pizarro was delighted at this success and received the general with great courtesy. But Atahualpa was dismayed to see Chalcochima, on whom he had presumably been relying, in the occupied city.[49]

Before entering the room where Atahualpa held court under Spanish guard, the general removed his sandals and placed the symbolic burden on his shoulder, which ritual demanded of every Inca subject. Why Chalcochima, who as Quizquiz's right-hand man had overcome the most desperate situations, should now have left his troops behind in Jauja defies explanation. In vain the Spaniards used torture to try to learn of any secret arrangements between him and Atahualpa. Chalcochima survived his king for only a short time; Pizarro is said to have handed him over to the reviving forces of Huáscar's party, by whom he was burned alive.[50]

Xerez reports how Atahualpa, who normally talked in a very lively fashion, behaved quite differently towards his subjects. "He spoke with dignity and calm, like a great lord. He was eloquent and had a quick mind. When the Spaniards understood what he was saying, they thought he had a sensible outlook, and considered him an intelligent man. He was by nature cheerful, but when he spoke with his leaders or with other countrymen, he was melancholy and showed no sign of pleasure . . .

"When they appeared before him, his subjects displayed great respect and kissed his hands and feet; and he, for his part, would not raise his eyes and look at them."

The Inca was, incidentally, still fairly young — Xerez says between thirty and thirty-two years of age and describes his figure as "handsome but rather fat." His face was "large, handsome, and wild" and his eyes "slightly red-rimmed and inflamed."

His daily life followed much the same pattern as it had when he had been at liberty. The conquistadors allowed him for the most part to live according to his own morals and customs, even though they did at times disturb Pizarro.[27]

The curiosity with which the Spaniards observed the Inca's mode of life is known to us from a vivid description by Cobo:

"The Inca was waited upon in his rooms by one of his sisters and a large number of the daughters of the nobility of the land. They would perform this honorable office for only one week, and then it would be taken over by another sister and her ladies in waiting. While he ate, the king would sit on a low stool, only about two hands high, which was made of delicate, red wood and was always covered by a cloth. The right to sit on such a *duho* was reserved for the nobility and counted as a special privilege. On the floor, strewn with fresh green rushes, the dishes were set out at his feet in earthenware, silver, and gold vessels.

One of his women would offer him the dish and hold it in her hands while he ate. He would change his clothing very frequently, never wearing one and the same garment for any length of time, and would discard it immediately if it had the tiniest stain. One day in Cajamarca, Atahualpa was dining in the presence of the Spanish guards. As he was about to take a mouthful of food, a small drop fell on the garment which he had just put on. Angrily pushing aside the woman who was holding the food, he stood up and went into his room to change his clothing. He returned wearing a fresh undergarment and a dark brown cloak. One of the Spaniards went up to him and felt the cloak. It was softer than silk and he asked what it was made of. The Inca replied, 'Of birds that fly by night in Puerto Viejo and Túmbez and bite human beings.' They finally deduced that it must be bats' skins. And when the Spaniard then asked how it was possible to collect such a quantity of bats, Atahualpa answered, 'Those dogs in Túmbez and Puerto Viejo, what else did they have to do apart from catch birds for my father, Huayna Capác's clothing?' Even as a prisoner, he still acted the great lord."

His haughty manner was very much in evidence when the high priest of Pachacámac visited him in Cajamarca.

He had special reasons for harboring resentment against the shrine of Pachacámac. Twice the oracle there had made predictions in favor of the Inca, and on both occasions the reverse had come to pass. The first time it had promised that Huayna Cápac would recover, and he had died of the plague; the second time it had prophesied that he, Atahualpa, would kill the Spaniards.

He abused the high priest loudly for being a liar and requested Pizarro to provide him with a chain so that he himself could tie him up. Pizarro was only too willing to comply, for this meant that he could now send his brother Hernando to Pachacámac to plunder the temple unhindered. However, loyal servants of the sanctuary had meanwhile carried off everything of value to safety.[51]

In his present precarious situation, the Inca continued to be preoccupied with the past events of the civil war and with the destruction of his enemies in the interior. It was for this reason that Pizarro was most eager to see Huáscar and his followers in Cajamarca, and he is supposed repeatedly to have harassed Atahualpa with this demand.

VII   Woven cloth
from the Peruvian coast,
Tiahuanaco style.
Transition from naturalistic
to abstract geometric forms.

As we know, Huáscar and his entourage was supposed to have been brought before Atahualpa. At first they were under the care of Chalcochima's section of the army. Later, as the situation became confused and Atahualpa himself was taken captive, the escort party and their distinguished prisoner went ahead on their own and had the brief encounter with the Spaniards, who were unaware that they could have turned the situation to their own advantage.

Thirty Spanish miles from Cajamarca, the death sentence was meted out to Huáscar and all those with him. The name of the place where Huáscar died was Andamarca, near Lake Conchucos in one of the Rio Santa valleys. His executioners are said to have thrown Huáscar's dismembered body into the Yanamayo River, along whose banks Atahualpa had years before "erected boundary stones to indicate to his rival Huáscar that he acknowledged his right to all the land south of this river, but that he himself claimed the territory to the north."[52]
Huáscar's last words are supposed to have been, "I have been master and king of this land for only a short time, but my brother, at whose command I die, will not endure any longer than I have."[46]
One cannot be certain how long each of them wore the *borla*. Very little time elapsed between Huáscar's death and the garroting of Atahualpa, so that Atahualpa's reign, which began only during the war with his brother, was of even shorter duration than that of his brother.

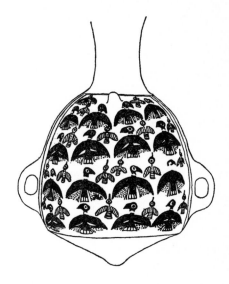

Inca vase painting with birds.

Atahualpa was constantly aware of what was going on in the country, as messengers from all the provinces came and went every day.[27] The Spaniards had to allow him this exceptional privilege, since they would otherwise not have gained any information themselves. This was however, of little use to the Inca; he knew perfectly well that the Spaniards would counter any attempt to liberate him by immediately killing him.
His generals were condemned to inactivity. There was a grand plan for his escape, which never came to anything. Plans were presumably prepared, but at the decisive moment Atahualpa himself is supposed to have put a stop to it. Such rumors continually put the Spaniards on the alert, but whenever they looked into them, they always drew a blank.[27]
But apart from a fear of attack, the Spaniards' chief concern was, now as ever, gold. Atahualpa's position took a turn for the worse with the arrival of Almagro, accompanied by officials of the Spanish emperor and fresh troops. Since Pizarro's companions, who had been present at the capture of the Inca, laid claim to the entire gold booty, with the exception of the royal fifth share, and did not wish to concede anything to the new arrivals, the latter had no interest in keeping alive this monarch, with his uncanny resources of gold; for to them he served as a daily remainder that even as a prisoner he was still obeyed by the people of Peru, who took little notice of anyone else except his closest friends.
When Hernando Pizarro, whom the Inca trusted most, was about to set sail back to Europe, he said to him, "So you are going away, and I am most down-

hearted. For I have no doubt that Potbelly and the One-Eyed one will have me put to death, when you are gone." He was referring to the royal treasurer Riquel and to Almagro, who had lost an eye.[53]

Atahualpa may now have seriously been intent on rallying the Indians to liberate him.

In order to put an end to all doubts, five men of the original guard — Hernando de Soto, Rodrigo Orgóñez, Pedro Ortiz, Miguel Estete, and Lope Vélez — volunteered to search the country themselves for any sign of hostile troops on the march. They wished to remove any grounds which would justify a precipitate condemnation of Atahualpa. But during their absence, their opponents talked Pizarro into bringing Atahualpa to a hasty trial and having him garroted.[54]

Ancient Peruvian transport of captives.

"Twenty days before this happened and before there had been any suspicion of hostile activity, while Atahualpa was engaged in lively conversation with a few Spaniards one evening, a sign like a fiery comet appeared in the sky in the vicinity of Cuzco and did not disappear until well into the night. Atahualpa knew this to be a sign that a great lord was soon to die in the land."[27]

This had now come about.

When De Soto and his companions returned from their reconnaissance and reported to the governor in Cajamarca, they found Pizarro "in mourning with a great felt hat on his head and deep rings under his eyes." They reproached him severely with Atahualpa's death, for there had been no truth whatsoever in the allegations of an imminent uprising. They had not seen one armed Indian anywhere and had been well received everywhere. Then Pizarro said, "Now I see that I have been deceived . . ."

Some days later, after the actual state of affairs had been made known, and several voices publicly expressed the opinion that this prince had been too harshly dealt with, Pizarro, Brother Vicente de Valverde, and the treasurer Riquel exchanged hard words. Each laid the blame on the others and there were many accusations of lying. Their dispute was witnessed by many. Finally, when it came to sharing out the gold they decided to let the matter rest.[54]

The execution of this prince, who had by now become famous, caused a great sensation outside Peru too, and gave rise to years of moral and legal debate.

Official opinion in Central America and in Spain dissociated itself strongly from the bloody measures adopted by the Conquest and was very sensitive in its reactions to trials whose moral tone resembled the procedures of the Inquisition, which had as yet scarcely been applied in Spain and had otherwise not been permitted against the natives of the New World.[55]

The comments of Oviedo, the "Historiador de las Indias," on this trial are as follows:

"In gratitude (to Atahualpa for having procured them masses of gold) they held burning straw under his feet to make him confess that he had intended treachery against the Christians, and by making false assertions against him, they declared it as proven that he had wanted to kill them . . .

"And all this was the work of evil tongues. It came about because the *Gobernador* did not see clearly and because he had been badly advised. And they set about putting Atahualpa on trial, a trial that was badly conducted and ineptly recorded. Of those who spoke against Atahualpa, one was a turbulent, excited, and squalid cleric, another an unscrupulous and uncouth writer, and the remainder were no better." Included in the indictment were the horrors that Atahualpa had perpetrated against his own people, as well as the murder of Huáscar.

The Spaniards were certainly not entitled to tax him with these things, but the thought that Atahualpa might once be in a position to wreak vengeance on them in a similar way was probably the strongest argument in favor of the death sentence, which was incidentally passed with only thirteen in favor and twelve against.

The Pizarro coat of arms redesigned in 1578 to include Peruvian attributes. The rope around the necks of the Indians is also included (see p. 179).

In the end, the Inca allowed himself to be baptized by Valverde. This saved him from death by fire and the total destruction of the body, which struck the imagination of this people with the utmost horror. For them, life after death "depended on the preservation of the outward form of the body ... if it were possible to arrest its decomposition, then the continued existence of the dead person was assured. If the corpse decayed, the existence of the dead person was thereby terminated — a "'second death' extinguished his 'life' for ever."[56]

Pizarro and Inca Manco enter Cuzco together (1534) — Destruction of the wandering army of the Quito generals Quizquiz and Rumiñahui — Insurrection of Inca Manco with European weapons and retreat to Vilcabamba — Beginnings of Spanish colonization — Death of Almagro (1538), Francisco Pizarro (1541) and Inca Manco (1544).

It was not until after Atahualpa's death that the Spaniards fully realized the security that this hostage had given them. The Inca's brothers had willingly brought them gold to Cajamarca. Under their protection, De Soto and Hernando Pizarro had been able to travel through the land in safety. Most of the Indians, who had served the Spaniards in Atahualpa's name, now abandoned Cajamarca, and the Spaniards were left without porters.

A well-known anecdote tells how some influential *orejones* showed the Spaniards how little of his gold Atahualpa had given away and how much more still remained. They brought a bucket of corn from the granary and emptied it into a heap on the ground. Taking one grain, they said, "This is how much he has given you and," pointing to the heap on the ground, "this much he has kept back."[1]

The early Spanish accounts all make the same fundamental mistake of assuming that the gold of Cajamarca belonged to Atahualpa, whereas the ransom was made up of the cult treasures of the entire land.

From his administrative seat in Central America, the scholarly Oviedo assembled all the facts for a comprehensive history and description of the discoveries and conquests in the New World. He had little to say in favor of Pizarro and his companions in Peru.

Using awkward phrases, supported by Latin quotations, he affirms the Emperor's innocence of all the shameful deeds and injustices perpetrated in his name, since he had known nothing of them, and he judges them as follows:

"All the Spaniards want is to return to Castile laden with gold. Thinking of nothing but their spoils of gold, these brutal men die, and if they are spared death and some of them survive, only few will rejoice in their ill-gotten gains."

Bernal Díaz, on the other hand, writing of Mexico, describes how many veterans — some maimed — were placated with titles and laudations, and how "even at the time there were pen-pushers who disparaged the way in which the conquistadors were honored." Many stayed behind in the newly conquered desolate lands, engaging in incessant fighting, until both young and old alike died. They had little benefit from their gold in the new colonies for it fell in value day by day. All the commodities which the soldiers traded amongst themselves soared to exorbitant prices. In Peru, a horse cost over 3,000 pesos, a bottle of wine 60, a pair of stockings between 30 and 40 pesos. Even garlic became expensive.

Debtors went from house to house with their Indians laden with gold, attempting to pay their creditors. But the latter did not want to accept anything. Some of them would hide and others, when tracked down, would say that payment was not yet due and that they preferred the debtor to keep his gold for the time being.[2]

Until the gold was on the ship and safely in Spain the creditors prepared an outstanding debt, for they scarcely knew how these great burdens of gold would reach the coast.

"Many of the Spaniards who had conquered the land, especially those who had already been there for a long time, as well as others who had either fallen sick or been wounded, went to the governor and requested permission to return to Spain with their share of gold, silver, gems, and other valuable items . . . The governor provided the Spaniards to whom permission had been granted with llamas and Indians to carry their gold and silver as far as San Miguel . . . Some of them lost over 25,000 castellanos in gold and silver on the way, as a result of animals bolting and Indians running away . . . On the 200 mile journey from Cuzco to the port, all of them had to endure hunger, thirst, and fatigue because there were insufficient porters for their possessions. From San Miguel they went overland to Nombre de Dios, where they embarked for Panama. The Almighty brought them safely back to Seville, where to date four ships have arrived . . . The first of these ships arrived in Seville harbor on the 5th of December, 1533. On it were Captain Cristóbal de Mena, who brought with him 8,000 gold pesos and 950 silver marks as his share, and then there was Juan de Losa, a respected clergyman, who possessed 6,000 pesos in gold and 80 marks in silver. In addition to these sums, the ship had another 38,946 pesos in gold on board. In 1534, on the 9th of January, the second ship, carrying on board Hernando Pizarro, sailed up the river to Seville. The ship carried 153,000 pesos in gold and 13,500 marks in silver for His Majesty. This sum consisted of bars, sheets, and pieces of gold and silver and was packed in great chests. In addition to this wealth, the ship had also brought the king thirty-eight golden vessels and forty-eight silver ones, including a silver eagle whose body could hold two buckets of water; two huge pots, one gold and one silver, each big enough to hold a cow cut up into pieces; two two-*fanege* (200 pound) corn sacks filled with gold; a golden idol the size of a four-year old child; and two small drums . . . The treasure was unloaded onto the quayside and taken to the storehouses of the *Casa de Contratación*. Large numbers of vessels were transported loose and the remainder was packed in twenty-seven chests, and wagons drawn by a pair of oxen would take these away two at a time . . .

"On the 3rd of June of the same year, the remaining two ships arrived. One was piloted by Francisco Rodriguez and the other by Francisco Pavón. They had 146,518 gold pesos and 30,511 silver marks in private possessions on board . . . "Excluding the vessels and pieces of gold and silver mentioned above, the four ships carried altogether 708,580 gold pesos. Therefore, if we add up all the gold listed in the cargo, not counting the vessels and other objects, we arrive at the sum of 318,861,000 maravedi . . .

"All the silver amounted to 49,008 marks. Allowing 8 ounces to the mark at 2,210 maravedi, this comes to a total of 108,307,680 maravedi for all the silver."[3]

The deserted city of Cajamarca was no longer of any importance to the Spaniards and most of the veterans and newly-arrived conquistadors were anxious to move on to Cuzco, the center of the old empire, which for them was enveloped in mystery. However, Pizarro did not dare to go there without the authority of a new Inca, and he now commanded Prince Túpac Hualpa, who was scarcely more than a child, to take up the *borla*. Túpac Hualpa was one of the few surviving sons of Huayna Cápac.[4]

It was during the preparations for the Inca's consecration that the Spaniards first learned something of the practices of *zaziz*, when, to their amazement, the prince withdrew to fast and did not reappear until several days later for the beginning of the ceremonies. Túpac Hualpa did not see Cuzco again.

He died mysteriously on the way, in Jauja, allegedly poisoned by Chalcochima.[5]

Spaniards and Indians do homage to the Inca (*wood engraving from the first edition of the chronicle of Cieza de Leon, 1553*).

After the nine months inactivity during Atahualpa's captivity, things suddenly began to happen.

Quizquiz set out with a large army in the direction of Cajamarca, in order to avenge his ruler. A brother of Atahualpa's, Titu Atauchi, was on his way there with a large quantity of gold for the ransom of the captured Inca, whom he still presumed to be alive. On hearing of his death, he abandoned the treasures, assembled 6,000 Indian warriors and set off in pursuit of the Spaniards. A few unprotected Spaniards fell into his hands in a small town in the province of Huaylas. Among them was the Spanish writer Sancho Cuéllar, who had drafted Atahualpa's death sentence.[6] According to Garcilaso, they were all taken to Cajamarca, where they were tried and sentenced. The chronicler maintains that Cuéllar (like Atahualpa in his time) was garroted, while the remainder of the accused were allowed to go free.[7]

Oviedo reports that the Indians destroyed the town, "leaving no stone standing," and that they exhumed the body of Atahualpa and brought it to Quito.[8]. Pizarro's small fighting force encountered the first of Quizquiz's divisions deep in the south, at Jauja, without getting involved in heavy combat. The *Gobernador* established a colony there and stayed behind for some time to await reinforcements, while Hernando de Soto, with Almagro hard on his heels, hurried ahead to Cuzco in forced marches across innumerable passes and rivers, for each of them wanted to be the first to reach the city.

De Soto and his horsemen very nearly perished in the Cordillera, quite close to Cuzco. Trapped in a narrow gorge by a massive force of Indian warriors, he was rescued at the last moment by his friends and rivals, Almagro and Pizarro. The contradictory accounts of the chroniclers do not make it clear whether the attacking Indian troops belonged to Quizquiz or to the opposing party, supporting the young Inca Manco, whom De Soto had provoked into action against him by his thoughtless cruelty.[9]

According to one unauthenticated version, Quizquiz is also supposed to have set up his own Inca in the person of Paullu Túpac,[10] whom he had liberated from his brother Huáscar's prison.[11] Zárate records that Paullu, who later became known as the Inca of Vilcabamba and Manco's opponent, had already offered his services to the Spaniards at that time, assuring them of a peaceful reception in Cuzco.

The same chronicler, however, goes on to tell of fierce combat outside the capital and of pillaging and looting by the retreating Quito men.[12]

Diego de Trujillo and a notary by the name of Sancho both record an encounter between Pizarro and prince Manco on the way to Cuzco, when the young prince asked the Spaniards for help against the hated men of Quito.

Though somewhat inaccurate in terms of dates and places, by far the most colorful account of the arrival of Pizarro and Manco in Cuzco has come down to us from the pen of the Indian chronicler Juan Santa Cruz Pachacuti. Written about a hundred years later, its lively style preserves all the great splendor of the Tahuantinsuyu within the context of the eagerly adopted new faith:

"With his sixty or seventy men, Pizarro arrived at the bridge over the Apurímac, where the Inca Manco and all the *orejones* and *curacas* had assembled to acknowledge him as their lord and to be baptized . . . Later Pizarro and all the others set out for Cuzco, with the Spaniards and the *curacas* in excellent trim and the Inca Manco in his litter alongside the father and captain Francisco Pizarro, who much later called himself Don Francisco Pizarro.

"And so they arrived outside Cuzco . . . and the Marqués and the Inca, together with the 'Holy Gospel of Jesus Christ Our Lord,' staged their entry with royal magnificence and majestic pomp. The Marqués, with his grey hair and long beard, representing the Emperor Charles V; Father Vicente with his miter, representing St. Peter and the pope in Rome; the Inca, in his litter lined with a carpet of feathers and attired in the richest apparel, bearing the *santurpaucar* (the scepter) and the insignia of Cápac Unancha; as well as the many Spaniards, aroused the inhabitants of the city to great jubilation."

The style of the passage almost leads one to believe that the writer was describing a great event, which is how for centuries it was presented to the Incas and presumably to the many other tribes, one of which Santa Cruz Pachacuti came from. As the description continues, Valverde, the monk, emerges as the central figure:

"Finally Father Vicente went straight up to the Coricancha, the house built for the creator by the first Incas. Thus the Law of God and the long awaited Holy Gospel finally came to take possession of the new vineyard that had for so long been in the hands of the ancient enemies. There, at the Coricancha, the father preached continuously like a second Thomas the Apostle — the patron saint of this kingdom — without pausing for rest in his zeal to win souls and convert them. They baptized the *curacas* merely by sprinkling them with holy water, as they could not pour holy water over every one of them. Had he been able to speak the language, he would have had an even greater effect, but he was compelled to speak through an interpreter . . .

"When Rumiñahui had been with the Inca in the camp outside Cajamarca, he had seen for himself that the Spaniards were not so intent on profit and gain as they are today (in Pachacuti's lifetime); at that time they had been very sincere in their worship of God and the Indians were encouraged by their good example."

In this early period, Manco emerges solely as a puppet king of Pizarro, a tool of Spanish power. It was only later that he grew to historical greatness as a champion of the liberation of Peru from the foreign yoke.

Apart from the Spaniards and Manco, and the roving Quizquiz, Rumiñahui ("the stony eye") was the major force in the former Inca empire. Until then, this general had attracted little attention, and right from the start, even during the civil war, had kept in the background. Rumiñahui must have been Atahualpa's political adviser. He had always been at the king's side when Quizquiz and Chalcochima would leave Atahualpa and his camp far behind, when they set out on their military exploits.

Together Rumiñahui and Atahualpa had waited for the Spaniards in the camp at Cajamarca, where the general had witnessed the exchange between the prince and the two intrepid Spaniards De Soto and Hernando Pizarro.

Whereas the other leading figures accompanied Atahualpa into the city and perished there, Rumiñahui escaped this fate. He had taken over the command of the troops stationed at the ready outside the city and had thereby been able to await the outcome of the encounter. That very same night he and his troops retreated in the direction of Quito. There he remained until the death of his king.

Taking advantage of the geographic isolation of the province, with sober political calculation he endeavored to establish autonomy in Quito. Although he had worked to this end for the sake of Atahualpa, after the death of Huayna Cápac and Ninan Cuyuchi, he now refused to install another Inca, and did not waste time in dreaming of a revival of the empire of Huayna Cápac.

He made an alliance with several *curacas* in Ecuador and took charge of the treasure and allegedly also those of Atahualpa's children who had remained in

Quito.[13] It is untrue that they were all killed by him (as Zárate says), for three of them later turned to the Crown for protection and revenue.[13a] Furthermore, following the (historically unauthenticated) transfer and burial of Atahualpa's body, Rumiñahui is supposed to have made the Cajamarca leaders (including a brother of Atahualpa's) drunk and then disposed of them.[13]

From the outset, the shadowy figure of this Inca general fascinated the Spaniards, for he was the first unyielding opponent they encountered on the soil of the Tahuantinsuyu. Besides, the stories of internal strife and palace murders in Quito were useful in distracting attention from the horrors and devastation of which they themselves were guilty in Ecuador. The conquest of this "ever green land" became one of the bloodiest episodes of the Conquest.

Led by Benalcázar, 280 Spaniards, who had just arrived by boat from Panama, Guatemala, and Nicaragua, pushed their way toward the mountains. They received active help from the Cañari, for these old enemies of Atahualpa's were not interested in Rumiñahui's tyrannical rule either, and they were being hard pressed by Quito.

One chronicler maintains that the Spaniards could never have got the better of Rumiñahui if the Cañari had not provided them with porters, taken charge of supplies, and fought for them.

They were indispensable as scouts, for they were continually detecting obstacles and traps cunningly laid by Rumiñahui, "similar to those which Caesar used at Alesia during the Gallic Wars."[14]

This war once more involved the Cañari in heavy loss of life. This tribe had already been decimated as a result of Atahualpa's vengeance. Cieza describes with unmistakable compassion how in many instances, women and girls carried the Spaniards' loads, saying that he had seen it himself. He also said that some of them were very beautiful, fiery, and affectionate to the Spaniards.

The Cañari were appropriately rewarded by the Spaniards for their secession from the Indian cause. The King of Spain gave them titles, awarded them certain residences in the Santa Ana quarter of Cuzco, which had previously belonged to Inca dignitaries, and granted them the privilege of leading the processions on All Saints Day.[15]

Rumiñahui appeared quite unruffled, but then had to relinquish one position after another, until he was finally compelled to leave Quito itself. Before doing so, he brought all the treasures to safety, had Huayna Cápac's magnificent state garments burned, and also set fire to the palace.

A few days earlier he is supposed to have said to the *mamacunas* and the women of the royal harem, "The Spaniards will shortly be arriving here and then you can enjoy yourselves with them." Some of them laughed innocently at this, but Rumiñahui had already given the order to kill them.[16]

He established himself in a mountain fortress in the vicinity of Quito and devastated the land. It is possible that he was finally killed by his own people,[17] as later happened to Quizquiz.

Despite the use of torture, the conquistador Benalcázar was unable to learn the whereabouts of Atahualpa's gold, which Rumiñahui was supposed to have carried off.

Meanwhile, Quizquiz had also arrived in Ecuador. He had apparently quite deliberately refrained from going to Rumiñahui's aid, but had held back in the *tampus* of Huancabamba to await the outcome of the battle with the Spaniards, thus sparing his own resources.

Similar rivalries were hampering the activities of the Spaniards. In addition to Benalcázar and Hernando de Soto, who had followed the army of Quizquiz on its way from the south, Almagro now arrived in Ecuador. The famous conquistador Pedro de Alvardo had also landed in Puerto Viejo with a large army from Guatemala. Almagro had intended to stop Alvarado from landing, but once the latter had arrived in the mountain valleys of Ecuador by a devious route, they found themselves compelled to take up the common cause against Quizquiz.

This decade of fighting, disease, devastation, and conscription meant much the same for Ecuador as the Thirty Years War did to Central Europe. An appalling reduction in the population was the result.

Indians taking stores to the *tampus*.

The misery of the people emerges pathetically from a few lines by Zárate, describing how, following a great defeat of Quizquiz, the battlefield was full of women and poor people who had been dragged along in the general's line and had now been abandoned without food, many hundreds of miles from their homes.[18]

In the villages, as yet untouched by war, the Indians continued to bring the harvest into the *tampus* as before, so that they would be able to give account to the departed Inca if he returned from the beyond. Thus the opposing parties were continually able to replenish their stores.[19]

Pedro de Alvarado's expedition turned out to be one of the greatest tragedies for the natives of America. Disregarding the warnings of Panama officials — in a letter to Charles V, its governor outlined in detail the inevitability of catastrophe — the voracious conquistador crammed 4,000 Guatemalan Indians together with 500 Spaniards, including women and girls, and 200 horses into twelve ships, some of them quite ridiculously small. Following the ancient sea routes of the Indian voyagers, he sailed with them to Ecuador, which had already spelled disaster for so many. His enforced recruiting measures violated the laws protecting Indian rights, which the Spanish governor of Guatemala had unrelentingly compelled his fellow countrymen to observe. These stated that Indians must not be called away to other work during the sowing season, that work without payment and slavery were prohibited, and that the penalty for carrying Indians off outside their own country was death.

Of the 4,000 Indians from Guatemala, who were intended to help take Quito, not one saw his homeland again. Nearly all these tropical people perished in the dense blizzards of the icy Andean passes in Ecuador, following the seven long months of exhausting progress through the jungle of the coastal plain.

Sixty Spaniards also died of cold and hunger in the Andes. "... One Spaniard had his wife and two small daughters with him; they were so exhausted that they sat down in the snow, and he could neither help them nor carry them, so he remained with them and all four froze to death. He could have saved himself, but he preferred to die together with them."[20]

However, Alvarado's dream of an independent, self-governing Ecuador came to nothing. Benalcázar had forestalled him and had already founded the Spanish city of Quito. After a series of long wanderings through Ecuador, Pedro de Alvarado came to an agreement with Francisco Pizarro in Pachacámac, whereby he handed over the remnants of his army and his fleet in exchange for an indemnity of 100,000 pesos and sailed back to Central America with one single ship. Pizarro paid him in silver bars. Later it turned out that half of these were copper.

The accounts of the battles between Quizquiz and the Spaniards tell of severe hardship and the crossing of raging mountain rivers, since the Indians had burned the suspension bridges. This was true mountain warfare.

Quizquiz's army line stretched for miles, and it would be attacked sometimes in the front, and sometimes the rear, or the main force would be engaged. More often than not he was able to repulse the Spaniards. His best military leader was Inca Huayna Palcon, who caused Pizarro, De Soto, Alvarado, and Almagro a great deal of trouble. Quizquiz himself was no longer the intrepid fighter he had been in the challenging circumstances of the civil war and he now spent most of his time with the women, behind the front line.

The old Inca general's army was extremely unwieldy, since it took with it an enormous train of followers. Apart from the recruits, there were many women moving with the army, and the number of livestock for consumption is said to have amounted to 15,000. The Spaniards maintained that his camp extended over a radius of fifteen miles.

Rope bridge across the Rio Pampas.

He approached all subsequent military engagements with caution and retreated ever farther north. It was the time factor that ultimately played into the hands of the white conquerors. For the disorganized land could scarcely supply Quizquiz with provisions any longer and the number of deserters increased.

"His officers advised him to make peace with Benalcázar, but this suggestion drove him into such a fury that he threatened to put to death anyone who dared to speak of peace. Then Huayna Palcon hatched a plot and together with several other leaders he went to Quizquiz and pointed out to him that they were being destroyed by hunger in this desolate land. When the general refused to listen to their suggestions, Huayna thrust his lance into his chest; the rest of the conspirators beat him to the ground with their clubs and cut up his body with axes. Then they disbanded the army and allowed everyone to disperse."[21]

The last battles of Atahualpa's generals against the conquistadors took place where the civil war between Atahualpa and Huáscar had begun years before.

Rumiñahui's power had ended not far from Quito, and it was at Riobamba, close to where the first battle had been fought against Huáscar's brother Atoc, that the army of Quizquiz dispersed "like smoke"[21a] after his death.

All the well-known figures after Huayna Cápac — Huáscar, Atahualpa, Chalcochima, Rumiñahui, Quizquiz, and finally even Manco Inca, treacherously murdered by some Spaniards — all of them met a violent death. It was the same for the Spaniards who had tried Atahualpa: Almagro was executed after a sham trial; Francisco Pizarro was assassinated; and Valverde, the preacher, was slaughtered by natives on the island of Puná.

The Spanish town of Riobamba, founded 1534.

Throughout the former Inca empire, the Spaniards had emerged victorious over Atahualpa's generals, and for the time being there was no longer any organized power for them to fear in this newly-conquered part of the world. The time appeared to be ripe for peaceful colonization. The first attempt was at Lima, which had been founded by Francisco Pizarro in 1535 and had been named "La Ciudad de los Reyes" in honor of the three Holy Kings. (The very first Spanish colony with the same name at Jauja had had to be relinquished.)

The interior and Cuzco itself still remained a hunting ground for adventurers. The ancient Inca city was just the place to unleash the conquerors' passions — their greed for gold, lust for women, quest for revenge, and their envy.

Today Lima — it retained its Indian name — has a population of two million inhabitants. But from the time of its foundation, the city was more than just a part of Peru and derived many of its characteristic features from different areas in the Old World.

The Indian population of the Rimac Valley were driven out and replaced largely by Negroes.[22] The valley was fertile, and besides the indigenous crops, many things that had been introduced from Spain and elsewhere were soon flourishing there — Cieza mentions vines, figs, bananas, pomegranates, sugar cane, melons, oranges, lemons, and many vegetables.

The city was planned on a large scale in the approved chessboard pattern to accommodate future growth. In the early days, however, there were only about a hundred "vecinos" (citizens) living in strawcovered mud houses in the immediate vicinity of the central Plaza de Armas, which covered an entire map square. All the remaining squares were initially taken up with gardens and Indian and Negro quarters. They were more or less arbitrarily handed out to the landowners as a bonus, and later, under the viceroys, when Lima became the foremost trading and administrative center in the Pacific, they were profitable reserves for property speculation.[23]

The founder, Francisco Pizarro, concerned himself with the smallest details, showing just the same enthusiasm that he had applied to military undertakings. He supervised the construction of the first buildings, laid the foundation stone of the cathedral, planted the first orange and fig trees in his garden, and assisted in the casting of the first bell.[24]

Pizarro particularly loved the feast of Epiphany, which is still the climax of the year in the Latin American countries today, and he stipulated how it should be celebrated even after his death — with great Vespers and responses at his own grave.

"And the unpretentious conquistador, who probably knew nothing about the 'escandalo luterano,' volunteered to obtain papal bulls from Rome and secure indulgences for all future participants at this festival in Lima."[25] He endowed a fund for weekly masses to be said for the salvation of conquistadors who had died penniless, as well as for Negro slaves and Indians who had assisted the Conquest.

The fate of the poor souls in purgatory was a particular preoccupation of Pizarro. He wished "that every evening in Trujillo, his birthplace, one of the four sacristans who served in the church there should run through the neighboring streets with a small bell summoning people to pray for the souls in purgatory and calling out in a loud voice to which pious believers in Jesus Christ would listen, 'Think of the souls in purgatory and recite a few Ave Marias and Paternosters, so that there shall be no dearth of persons to pray for you in turn!'

. . . And so for years and centuries this urgent plea for peace by the most adventurous and audacious of its sons was to echo through the steep alleyways of the ancient town of Trujillo."[25]

What the restless conquistador most wanted was not the bliss of paradise, but to be laid to rest in the cathedral at Lima with something akin to full Inca honors. He insisted on a magnificent sarcophagus, covered with a purple velvet cloth, in the central aisle of the church. The instructions he left for Mass and its attendant rituals cover even the minutest details — how many wax candles to be lit, the choice of times of worhip, and all manner of items, such as chalice, wine cruet, candlesticks, holy-water sprinkler, Mass vestments, adornments, altarcloths, etc., are all listed in his will.[25]

In everyday life, Pizarro was very modest: "The Marqués always appeared dressed in a long coat of black cloth that reached down to the ankles and fastened over the hips, boots of pale suede, a white hat, and a sword and dagger in the old style. Sometimes on feast days his men would persuade him to wear a garment of marten skin, sent to him by Hernando Cortés from New Spain — as Mexico was then called — but he would take it off again as soon as he came out of Mass and would remain in his undergarments. He usually wore a kerchief around his neck to mop up the perspiration from his face, for in peacetime he spent most of the day at the ball game."[26]

The elderly Pizarro is supposed to have played this swift and strenuous game with such enthusiasm and stamina that he left even the youngsters panting. He would play with anyone he happened to find at the striking wall. "A horse belonging to one of the soldiers died; Pizarro made his way to the pitch, where he had arranged to meet the soldier, with a sheet of gold weighing 500 pesos stuffed in his doublet, so that he could hand it over in person. On not finding him there, he began to play, without taking off his doublet, because he did not want to remove the gold, nor let it be seen. He played for more than three hours in this way, until the soldier came. Pizarro drew him aside and handed over the gold, remarking that he would willingly have given him three times as much, if he had not had to endure such pain as a result of his absence. It was hard for any business to drag him away from a game, especially when he was losing. Only if he were notified of some Indian disturbance, would he hurry off, put on his armor, seize his shield and spear, and rush through the city to the scene of the disturbance with such speed that his men had difficulty in following him." Brief allusions such as these indicate that the pacification of Peru was not such a straightforward affair as the sources would have us believe. "One day, as he was crossing the river La Barranca, one of his Indian servants was swept away by the raging torrent. The Marqués immediately swam after him, and seizing him by the hair, dragged him to safety. He had endangered his own life with this act, for the waters raced with such ferocity that not even the bravest of his men would have lightly attempted this feat. When a few of his leaders criticized his rashness, he retorted that none of them knew how attached one could become to a servant."[26]

In his will, Pizarro made ample provision for his children, relatives, and various impecunious people, but there was virtually nothing in it to provide for the political future of the new country. In this, Pizarro and his contemporary and rival Almagro both displayed a striking lack of statesmanship. These resourceful commanders, who showed such presence of mind during the period of discovery and conquest, were simply not adequate to the ever increasing problems of administration. Like most of the conquistadors, their achievement ended with the conquest. The task of subduing the chaos fell to others.

The major cause of their difficulties may well have been that neither Pizarro or Almagro could read or write. As a result they were always dependent on their current clerk. Pizarro would sign every document, whether it concerned his governorship or the tributes of the Indians, by drawing two great flourishes, executed with painstaking, calligraphic strokes, and between the two the secretary would then insert the letters of the name Pizarro. His last secretary, Antonio Picado, knew how to do this clearly and particularly well. It is striking that between 1533 and 1535 Pizarro changed secretaries four times, until finally one García Díaz Arias and this same Antonio Picado shared the post. The first, according to the sources, was a sensible man, who, if he thought the occasion warranted it, would even venture to submit his own view and counsel discretion. But the latter was the worst kind of minion, to whom current personal interests were of greater importance than the general good and the future.

Picado had come to the country with Alvardo, had then joined up with Almagro, and finally moved on to Francisco Pizarro. This was at a time when there was great tension between the three men. Many of the most disastrous decrees, and the very ones that provoked hatred against Pizarro and caused the regime of this family to be so short-lived, probably stem from Picado. Pedro Pizarro, a cousin of Francisco and a remarkably non-partisan chronicler of the period, said that he had not occupied the position any time at all before everything was being done the way he wanted it.

By 1535 he was already in a position to dismiss important people from office. His love affairs, his shameless ostentation, and his corruptibility were common knowledge. He had soon become the key figure for obtaining certain posts and revenues.

Various important additions and deletions of entire sections of Pizarro's will were probably made without his knowledge. His brother Hernando Pizarro, and Picado, are thought to have been equally responsible in this. Picado ultimately emerged as successor to the governorship, after a number of different candidates had been put forward. He was never to take up the office.

Pizarro had a weakness for new faces, and trusted men would often cease to mean anything to him, if they were far away at some important post. The governor's illiteracy made private contact by letter impossible without the agency of a third person.

His cousin Pedro Pizarro, for example, was awarded an "encomienda" (an immense estate), extending from Cuzco right down to Arica, in the far south on

VIII   Dancer with condor mask and sprouting branch.

the Chilean coast. No sooner had this award been made, than Francisco Pizarro in Lima realized that it was technically impossible to implement, since it interfered with other people's interests. The award was countermanded and Pedro Pizarro had to content himself with a very small area of a mere 900 souls. Pizarro had a habit of making grandiloquent pledges to many Spaniards. The Inca empire he had conquered was by no means small, but it would have had to be four times its actual size if he had wanted to meet all the promises of land he had made.[25] The control of Cuzco changed hands four times. De Soto and Almagro were first put in charge; then the young Juan Pizarro was given command. Finally, when Hernando Pizarro returned from Spain in 1535, he was appointed as the governor's representative in the city. He had brought the emperor the fifth share of Atahualpa's treasure, the greatest riches to have reached Europe so far. Charles V had rewarded him with the Order of St. James and had revised the land demarcations by extending New Castile, the area controlled by Francisco Pizarro, to include Cuzco, at the expense of the territory of New Toledo, which had been promised to Almagro, thereby weakening the private agreement between Almagro and Francisco Pizarro. Pizarro managed to bring about a reconciliation with Almagro, who emerged the loser. The old oath of allegiance was restored and they again consumed a Host together. After this Almagro and his followers set out for the south again, in the hope of finding a second Eldorado there, where he could extend himself, undisturbed by the countless relations and Estremaduran friends of Pizarro.

The Chilean expedition was, as we know, a total disaster. The vast salt and saltpeter wastes, extending across almost one degree of latitude, and the arid high plateaus of the Atacama, presented the inexperienced Spaniards with insuperable transport and supply problems. Many froze to death in the Andes, where the temperature veers between 30° C (86° F) in the daytime and −30° C (−22° F) at night.

What thorough preparation and what a vast complement of men and material must have been needed when the great Inca Túpac decided to add these regions to the Inca empire! We have a detailed account by Garcilaso el Inca:

"He sent spies with runners, who were to find a route to Chile and report on the conditions. The scouts were Incas, for the kings would entrust missions of such importance only to blood relations. He already had some information about an empire in Chile, but the spies were to establish a marching route and every two miles they were to send back reports of what they had encountered, so that all the necessary equipment could be assembled. The spies advanced with the utmost vigilance amidst indescribable hardship and exertion. They left a trail of markings in order to make the return journey easier and to point the way for those following behind. There was a constant coming and going like ants, some reporting back on what they had encountered, while others brought up supplies. In this way they covered the 80 (Spanish) miles to Copayupú, a small but densely populated province surrounded by desert. After Cuquimpú, they had another 80 miles of desert to cross. When the spies had reached Copaypú and inspected it, they returned to report to the Inca on what they had found. Acting on their information, he sent 10,000 soldiers led by a general. In addition, he arranged for adequate provisions and supplies to go with them on llamas, which themselves provided additional food, since their flesh is very tasty." This first contingent of troops was followed by another 10,000 soldiers as reinforcements, so that after Chile had been opened up, "more than 50,000 men were under arms and were as well provided for and equipped as if they had been living in their garrison at Cuzco." Almagro's party, however, lacked a number of these advantages. They are supposed to have returned so weakened in bodily health by lack of food and equipment, that Almagro's followers, or the "Chile party," were henceforth known as the "rotos," or "ragged ones."

Those familiar with the historical pattern of development of newly-established colonies will have often discerned the same phenomenon — initial success is achieved only by finding sufficient people, who can be induced to settle there and take on the risk of colonization for the Crown by the incentive of acquiring vast areas of land and exceptional privileges.

In no time at all land becomes scarce and later arrivals feel themselves at a disadvantage.

These apportionments of land (*mercedes de tierra*) are not to be confused with the *repartimientos* or *encomiendas* (tribute areas).

Pedro Pizarro describes the foundation and settlement of Cuzco and the distribution of the *repartimientos* in the country: ". . . in order to induce people to remain and settle in Cuzco, which involved great risk and danger to life, because there were so few Spaniards and so many natives there, he (Francisco Pizarro) distributed immense *repartimientos* — as big as entire provinces — and as many as anyone wanted."

Estates, lands, and tribute areas in which no one was interested were held back in "deposito" (reserve), so that they could be freely disposed of at a later stage.[27]

The Pizarro brothers and their friends used this method of rewarding fellow soldiers to create a power structure of medieval feudalism with vassals and sub-vassals.

Francisco Pizarro, himself, "owned" about 100,000 Indians. *Encomiendas* of this size, however, were no longer what the king and the Council for Indian Affairs imagined them to be.

Repartimiento initially meant allotting Indians to conquistadors in reward for their services. The classic *encomienda* entitled the owner to levy tribute from a given area in the form of natural resources, textiles, jewelry, or gold and silver. There were numerous special privileges associated with the economic resources of the different areas and with the system of tribute current before the Spanish Conquest, which were more or less arbitrarily exploited by the Spaniards.[28]

Since 1512, the number of Indians obliged to render service or tribute had been limited by law to 150. The *encomiendas*, too, had not originally been heredi-

On visits to his villages, the *encomendero* had himself carried in a litter like an Inca. If the Indians did not greet him appropriately with singing and dancing, he would have them beaten and severely punished.

tary.[29] What happened in Peru shows that these restrictions were scarcely observed.

In most cases, however, the extension of privileges to individuals, which caused so much confusion, was expressly granted by the Crown in reward for vast assignments of gold sent back to Spain, which were urgently needed to finance the European wars against the Protestants, the pope, and the Turks. In the course of time, speculation and the amalgamation of these areas of land, apportioned by the king, which were subsequently combined with the *repartimientos* of Indians, gave rise to the great latifundia, which to this day inhibit the social development of the Latin American countries.[30]

The activities of the young Pizarros and a group of unscrupulous, immature hotheads in Cuzco, the so-called "pages of the Marqués", became increasingly unrestrained. Juan Pizarro was then twenty-four years old, and Gonzalo Pizarro, who was later to be the uncrowned king of Peru, was only twenty-two.

Every week they demanded vast quantities of gold, as if "it was to be found like pebbles, and even so they could never get enough, because they would immediately gamble it all away amongst themselves."[31] On his return from Spain, the thirty-four year old Hernando Pizarro's savagery against the powerless inhabitants and the Inca rose to a peak. Manco Inca was taken prisoner in order to extort more gold from the people. With an iron chain around his neck and manacles on his feet, he was made to endure the most unspeakable treatment. The young soldiers soiled the vessels from which he drank, urinated on him, spat in his face, ill-treated him with kicks and blows in the face, and violated his women and serving maids in his presence.

On his return from Chile, Almagro received a message from the captive Manco in Cuzco, asking him for help. "It seemed certain to him," it said, "that he would have to die, since he could not possibly succeed in assembling the quantities of gold and jewelry demanded of him by Hernando and Juan Pizarro. Manco sent further secret messages to various Christians, who he thought were favorably disposed towards him, imploring them at least to try and stop him being burned alive or being thrown to dogs and dismembered and see to it that he should only be hanged."[32]

Once again, the pattern of events on the island of Puná was repeated. Hernando Pizarro released Manco in exchange for a promise of even greater quantities of gold. The Inca mobilized the Peruvian Indians, and within a short space of time the Spaniards, consisting of only 190 men and 500 Indian *Yanaconas*, found themselves besieged in Cuzco by thousands of Indians.[33] A short time after, the same thing happened to Francisco Pizarro in Lima.

The final battle for the ancient city of Cuzco lasted six to eight months — sixteen months according to some versions. It represented a crisis for the Conquest of the Tahuantinsuyu and finally dispelled the assumption still widely held in Europe that the Spaniards had overwhelmed the peaceful Indians by effortless surprise attacks. There is a strong analogy with Cortés's struggle for the Aztec capital Tenochtitlan. In both cases the Spaniards were confronted with the nobility rallying to newly emerged, dangerous leaders, who had taken the place of the defeated kings Montezuma and Atahualpa — in Mexico Cuautémoc, and in Cuzco Manco II — and the Spaniards were compelled to witness the sad spectacle of the Indian metropolises they had so admired going up in flames.

Manco Inca belonged to the generation of Huáscar and Atahualpa. While Quizquiz and Rumiñahui were still moving about the country, virtually nothing was heard of him, unlike his brothers Paullu and Huayna Palcon, except that he had shown himself to be a willing tool of the Spaniards. The latter permitted him to reside with Inca splendor in Cuzco, which was as yet still more or less undamaged, and he remained in close contact with Almagro and Hernando Pizarro, even when individual uprisings flared up in different parts of the country.

The actual organizers of the great revolt appear to have been the *villac-humu*, the high priest, and Tici Yupanqui, both brothers of Manco. Little as the Spanish accounts may convey of the background to the rebellion and the continuing loyalty to the Inca in the vast areas of land away from the Inca highways, which the Spaniards could not control, their descriptions of individual incidents are vivid and extremely dramatic.

"... the captured Manco ... sent emissaries to the *curacas* and military leaders in various major towns in order to discuss with them how best to throw off the Christian oppression ... and had rich sacrifices made to the ancient gods at the major shrines ...

"One night, with the utmost secrecy, he left Cuzco carried in a litter, together with his wives and servants. But Juan Pizarro had been told something was afoot. He rushed to the palace, and no sooner had he found it empty than the Spanish soldiers started to loot. No doubt he ordered them not to, but at this stage he could no longer stop them ...

"Finally he dispatched his brother Gonzalo and several companions in pursuit of Manco ...

"Almost the whole night had passed before they came upon the Inca, hidden in the rushes. He had abandoned his litter in order to conceal himself better ... They brought him out, showing the greatest courtesy, placed him back in his litter, and brought him back to Cuzco, where the sight of his devastated palace caused him great sorrow. He tried to escape a second time, but Juan Pizarro recaptured him with ease and from then on placed an even stricter guard over him ..."[34]

There are further descriptions of various uprisings in the county, which preceded the great revolt and brought Manco into increasing difficulties, so that in the end, in order to prove his loyalty to the Spaniards, he contributed to the destruction of these independent groups and permitted his office of Inca to be exploited for base intrigues, as emerges from this passage, quoted partly verbatim from the *Varones ilustres*:

A Spaniard named Pedro Mártir, on his *encomienda* in Colla territory in the southeast, was murdered by some Indians. Fleeing the inevitable reprisal, they took themselves, their women and children, and ample supplies to a mountain fortress. Their leadership was superb and they resisted every attack. The Spaniards then destroyed their artifically constructed water supply, but heavy rain saved them from dying of thirst and they once more felt confident in the support of their gods. "The captain of the Inca auxiliaries in the Spanish camp kept the men under seige informed as to all the white men's plans," and at every attack the Spaniards were repulsed by a storm of stones raining down on them. "Juan Pizarro had this *orejón* burned to death and informed the Inca in Cuzco that he was to see to it that the fortress should surrender, otherwise he would be treated as responsible for the treachery of the *orejón*.

Pre-Columbian terraces at Matucana watered by the glacier of the distant Nevado de Coriocpa.

"Manco feared for his life and sent one of his most trusted leaders . . . to the besieged with the sanctified battle-ax of the sun . . . When he realized that the besieged would not consider surrendering, he resorted to subterfuge, claiming that he had been sent by the Inca to help them. He informed them that he had with him the sanctified ax of the sun in order to swear an alliance. The occupants of the fortress were to admit him and his four companions the following night. Then they would settle how best to destroy the Christians.

"On his return from the fortress, he disclosed to Juan Pizarro that it was only out of love for his master Manco that he had agreed to a course of action wherein he would certainly lose his life. He needed four Spaniards for the venture. They were to shave off their beards, dye their hair with black pitch like the Indians, and accompany him to the fortress, dressed in Indian clothes. Juan Pizarro was to follow them with the other Spaniards and the auxiliaries.

"This was the plan . . . and at the prearranged time that night the five men climbed up to the fortress. The men under siege feared betrayal and were already regretting the agreement. They did not wish to break their word, but appeared most suspicious and looked carefully at each one of the men in turn and noted that there were no more than four men accompanying the envoy. They were taken through the first door, but only the *orejón* was permitted to pass through the second door so that he could swear on the holy ax. The four companions remained in the outer ring. As the commander of the fortress was about to close the inner door, the *orejón* admitted the four men with a loud cry, and pulling his club from under his garment, he began to fight . . . he called to the Spaniards, but they were not in time to save him from death. Owing to the darkness and the narrowness of the place, the intruders were able to conceal themselves in the fortress until Juan Pizarro and the others arrived . . . When the Colla saw that they could no longer hold their hill, they gave up."

The Spaniards' Indian auxiliaries are said to have been responsible for the worst excesses of brutal slaughter. The looting of the fortress yielded "5,000 castellanos in gold," which the Spaniards used to build the city church of Cuzco.[35]

The chronicler justified such punitive retaliation with the example of the "great caudillo of the people of Israel, Joshua," at the fall of Jericho, and with quotations from the Church Fathers.

Inca Manco's release, as stated earlier, arose out of Hernando Pizarro's greed for gold. The Spanish sources of information are full of mutual recrimination and attempts to conceal the truth, so that it is difficult to reconstruct the actual course of events.[39]

One anonymous account relates that Pizarro was bribed by a gift of gold from the *villac-humu* in person, although it was already generally known that his men had killed over thirty of Almagro's companions who had just returned from Chile. According to Zárate, the Inca is supposed to have been granted permission to go to Yúcay to attend a great religious festival, in return for a promise that he would bring back the solid gold statue of his father Huayna Cápac — the *huaoqui*. He is said to have returned once more, but then he finally made his escape.

The rebellion, which Manco's brother, the *villac-humu* had been preparing for so long, now had a secular leader, and all the vassals and all the auxiliary peoples were summoned to recapture Cuzco and Lima.[36]

Straightway, Garcilaso relates, thousands appeared outside the city of Cuzco and overran it "with a fearful clamor and din. Most of them had bows and shot burning arrows into the houses in the city, even into the king's palaces, sparing only the Sun Temple and its annexes and immediate surroundings and the house of the *mamacunas*." Their main target was the palace of Viracocha, where the Spaniards were encamped. It burned down room by room. Only the great hall, in which they celebrated Mass, remained standing. The survivors subsequently erected the Church of the Assumption on this spot.[37]

Half the city burned down, as even the solid stone buildings had roofs of esparto grass.

The fortress of Sacsayhuaman fell to the *villachumu*. Cuzco was full of Manco's men, "who erected barricades everywhere and drove the Spaniards first into the central square and then herded them together into two houses about a hundred paces apart. Stones rained as thick as hailstones from the slings and flew into the doorways, and the war cries and the blowing of the conch trumpets was so loud and persistent that it was quite deafening and struck everyone there with terror."[38]

The problem of supplies became increasingly desperate in the burning city: "They went in groups to drink at the stream and in groups they ransacked the burnt-out houses for maize. Their chief concern was for their horses. They did manage to find some food, although it had been spoiled in the fire, but in their extreme hunger they ignored this. Their Indian servants were of great help to them at this time of need, bringing them maize to eat and herbs for their wounds ... The Spaniards later said that without the active support of these Indians, they would not have survived the siege ...

"The *Yanaconas* also acted as guards and spies and kept them informed by day and night of their enemies' intentions ... After eleven or twelve days of confinement the Spaniards and their horses were so weakened by the constant fighting,

Lower falls of the Rodadero (approach to the fortress of Sacsayhuaman).

tumult, and hunger, that they could scarcely remain upright. Thirty Europeans had already fallen and practically every soldier was wounded, and it was hard to know what could be done for them."

They decided not to wait "until they were so weak that they could no longer hold their weapons" and the Indians "slaughtered them like pigs," but to attempt to break out and "to die fighting together ... Whoever found it possible under the constant Indian assault, went to confess to one of the three priests; the remainder confessed their sins to each other; they all called on God and His saints and hoped to die as Christians."[39]

Part of a water conduit at Sacsayhuaman.

They were now fighting with the *Yanaconas* in the burning alleyways. Manco's troops continually ensnared the Spaniards and their horses with *bolas*, which had three stones attached to one end (the gauchos still use these *bolas* in ostrich hunting today), and "showered them from above with stones and masonry from the walls of houses.[40] Garcilaso describes Manco standing on a hill and addressing his Indians, calling on them by province and tribe, saying that the hour of liberation for his empire was approaching. The Spaniards ascribed the fact that they did not perish on that or the following days to the miraculous personal intervention of their national saint, St. James. The worst threat still came from the mountain fortress of Sacsayhuaman, occupied by the Inca and the *villac-humu*. Juan Pizarro launched an initial, unsuccessful attempt to storm the terraces of the fortress, in the course of which he was wounded on the chin. Disregarding all protests, with his head bandaged and wearing no helmet, he made a second attempt. This time he was hit on the head with a stone and died three days later. His companions buried him secretly by night, so that the Indians should not know about it. When they did discover that the "invincible son of the sun," or "Viracocha," so feared by them, had fallen, they are supposed to have burst into their *haylli* (victory hymn).

Sacsayhuaman was recaptured allegedly by the audacious surprise attack of a single-handed Spaniard, working his way up the cyclopean walls of the fortress with ladders and ropes and pushing at the walls with his feet.[41]

Inca Manco led his attacks on horseback. A group of his Indians were armed with European weapons. It is remarkable, however, that he would launch major attacks only on nights when there was a full moon.[42] Even at this late stage, for the Incas the battle still appears to have been allied to a cosmic or cultic rhythm, while the Spaniards remained under arms by day and night.

No news whatever of the beleaguered Spaniards in Cuzco reached the outside world, and all that they themselves received were the severed and shrunken heads of their soldiers who had fallen into the hands of Manco's troops. The envoys and auxiliaries sent by Francisco Pizarro in Lima to Cuzco were intercepted by bands of armed peasants and killed. Some 300 Spaniards lost their lives in the Yuracmayo pass between Lima and Jauja. The Indians belonging to Manco's brother Tici Yupanqui occupied the exits to the pass and the mountains overlooking the ravine and sent down avalanches of stones on the foreigners as

Corner bastion of Sacsayhuaman.

they appeared. They then seized their equipment, and having removed all traces of their presence, they would then lie in wait for the next group of unfortunate victims. Soon after, their weapons and horses were used by Manco's troops in Cuzco; seven or eight Spanish slaves had to prepare the powder for them.[43]

Francisco Pizarro himself was imprisoned for a long time in Lima by Tici Yupanqui, and many Spaniards thought of fleeing to the ships. In a plaintive, desperate letter to Alvarado in Central America, Pizarro revealed that the colony which they had considered to be pacified was now as good as lost; there was no longer a single obedient *kazik*, and poor Almagro was either far away or dead. Manco did not achieve his great aim of liberating the Inca empire from foreign domination. The heights overlooking Lima were suddenly abandoned by Tici Yupanqui's Indians.

One of Pizarro's subordinates, Francisco de Chaves, mounted a punitive expedition in the vicinity of Huaylas. He set upon the peasants with bloodhounds and devastated villages and fields. He is supposed to have hung 600 children between the ages of three and sixteen, stringing them up in rows and compelling them to shout his name "Chaves" before they died. This action left such an indelible impression that in 1551, fifteen years later, Emperor Charles V revealed his great personal distress by issuing an order in Innsbruck for the maintenance of 100 children of the former *encomienda* of Chaves and for the building of schools in that area.[44]

Manco himself left Cuzco.

References to the revolt in the Spanish texts become less frequent.

It was now the harvest season and the Inca's camp must have been encountering difficulties with supplies. The Peruvian peasants could no longer be kept away from the fields.

The Inca is said first to have taken shelter in the fortress of Ollantaytambo and finally to have retreated to the inaccessible Andes at Vilcabamba, south of the Apurímac, with several thousand Indians and a few families of the nobility. There he instigated the working of hitherto uncultivated mountain valleys and hillsides, laying the agricultural foundation for further resistance.

Manco's tragic resignation and the gradual extinction of the revolt may puzzle the modern reader. The background to the failure is not immediately evident. Manco's loyal bands of peasants had achieved more by their own brand of guerilla warfare than the organized mass armies of Atahualpa, Quizquiz, and Rumiñahui.

The old Inca empire, however, had not ruled its vast territories with patriotic warriors, but with the aid of a sophisticated and broad-based organization implemented by an upper caste of aristocrats and priests. This upper stratum had steadily decreased over the last decades as a result of Huayna Cápac's war in Ecuador, the plague, and, finally, through the acts of vengeance perpetrated in the course of the Inca civil war between the brothers Atahualpa and Huáscar. The mighty *ayllus* of Túpac and Huayna Cápac's day, each comprising hundreds of people, had now been reduced to scarcely more than a few families, and in some instances to one single individual. Manco and his brothers now faced a mass of Indians and a great number of *curacas* who had acquired autocratic stature, in apparent isolation. Finally, the idea that the whites could never be exterminated, since the ships on the coast never ceased to unload fresh weapons and forces from other colonies and from Europe, and also because of the foreigners' superior strength in arms, may have strongly influenced the Inca in his decision.

Manco remained undefeated in Vilcabamba, the reservation of his choice, which also housed the imperial Inca palladium, the golden sun idol, which had been rescued from Cuzco and brought there. This last remnant of independent Inca rule survived for more than two generations, even though Vilcabamba was not far from the road to Cuzco and Lima. The Andes and the raging rivers protected the Inca like a natural fortress.

The Indians of the region supported the Inca with exemplary loyalty. When, two decades later, he fell victim to Pizarro's assassins, whom he had asked for asylum, the Indians did not allow any white man who ventured into the region to leave it alive.

The Spaniards who had remained behind in Chile, under the leadership of Pedro de Valdivia, had been waging a minor war for more than eight years, and as they had been thrown back entirely on their own resources, they had also had to cultivate the fields as well.[45]

There, as in the Anglo-Saxon settlement areas of North America, fighting with the Indians continued until well into the 19th century.

Quarrels between the Spaniards themselves continued to smolder during the Manco rebellion. There was no dearth of sensible persons who tried to prevent things from going to extremes. Among these was the gray-haired old man who had promoted Pizarro and Almagro's original expedition — Gaspar de Espinosa. In his younger days, this learned jurist had himself used base intrigue to gain what he had been unable to achieve by legitimate means; he instigated proceedings against the discoverer of the Pacific, Vasco Núñez de Balboa, and drew up the death sentence of this famous man. He then took over his fleet, and since 1533 he had acted as a silent partner in the conquest of Peru. But all his life he had hoped in vain for a government of his own. He lost his son, who was serving under Pizarro, in the Manco rebellion, and abandoning his own plans for the conquest of northern Ecuador, he set out from the port of Paita with a small force and advanced overland to bring help to Pizarro in Lima.[46]

He arrived in Lima to find that the rebellion had ended, but that civil war had broken out between the followers of Pizarro, Almagro, and Alvarado. Almagro had returned from Chile a sick and embittered man, and after Manco's departure, he had appointed prince Paullu Túpac as Inca and had Hernando Pizarro taken prisoner and tortured.[47]

Espinosa hurried to Cuzco in order to mediate. He managed to exact certain promises from Almagro, but the very next day his advisers dissuaded him from honoring them. Espinosa had been so weakened by altitude sickness by the time he arrived that within a few days he died in Cuzco. Cieza ascribes the following words to him, allegedly addressed to Almagro: "Do you know what I think of this whole affair? That the victor will be just as much a loser as the defeated."[48]

In the end Almagro set Hernando Pizarro free and thereby paved the way for his own downfall. Then came the battle of Salinas and its shameful concequences; Almagro's defeated and disarmed men suddenly found the victor's muskets and catapults trained on them, and with the slaughtered and the wounded lying on the ground in rows, the *Yanaconas* of both parties rushed at them, stripped them, and left them lying there naked.

Hernando Pizarro now took Almagro prisoner and put him on trial. When the seventy-three year old co-discoverer of Peru heard his death sentence being read out, he "tried every possible way of arousing Pizarro's pity. He pointed out to him that Pizarro and his brother owed the greatness and power they had attained at least in part to him; that he (Almagro) had borne the major part of the cost of the expedition to Peru, which they were now ruling; at the same time, he reminded him that he had voluntarily released Pizarro and had disregarded the advice of his own commanders to kill him; if Pizarro had been badly treated during his captivity, this had not been at his command, nor had he known about it; he asked him to have respect for his advanced age, which would bring him to the grave soon enough in any case." Hernando Pizarro refused to be moved; he replied abruptly, saying that "such whining phrases were not becoming to a man of understanding and courage. Almagro countered this by saying he should not be surprised that he was afraid of death, for he was only human and a sinner, and Christ himself had feared death. After these words, Pizarro's sentence against him was carried out and his head was cut off."[49]

In Lima, the aged Francisco Pizarro is said to have done all he could to dissociate himself from the murder. He tried to effect a reconciliation with Almagro's son, the young Diego, but without success.

The one thing that rigidly bound Almagro's followers together was the fact that they had absolutely nothing.

They had been stripped of all their properties and rights and they lived a communal existence like the early Christians. The half-Indian conquistador's son also had an immense following among the natives. The tiny "Chile party" became increasingly dangerous and daring, especially as they saw quite plainly that Pizarro's anxiety was increasing and that they were obviously worried about the repercussions that Almagro's execution would have in Spain. We have the written opinion of Oviedo, the royal correspondent, about Atahualpa's trial; he severely condemns Hernando Pizarro for the execution of Almagro, with whom his sympathies lie.

Hernando Pizarro now traveled to Spain in order to try and prevent the anticipated measures. He never returned to Peru.

In the same year, 1539, Gonzalo Pizarro mounted an expedition to the lowlands of the Amazon. This period was to be fatal for Francisco Pizarro in Lima.

The plotting Chile party now set to work quite openly. They no longer greeted Pizarro in the street and went "so far as to attach three bars to gallows that stood in front of Francisco's home, with one of them pointing at his house, the other at the house of his lieutenant Juan Velásquez, and the third at the home of his secretary Antonio Picado. Rumors of a conspiracy against Pizarro grew so loud that several people warned him once again." He replied, "the heads of others were protecting his own," and told those who advised him to go about with his bodyguard that "he did not want to provide any pretext that would justify the suspicion or charge that he was taking precautionary measures against the judges sent by the king." As Pizarro went to Mass regularly in the main church of Lima, the assassination was planned for a Sunday. On the Saturday one of the conspirators disclosed the plot to the priest in the main church during confession. His secretary brought the news to Pizarro, who was dining with his sister-in-law Inés Múñoz and his Indian children. "When he was told of the confession that had been made to the priest, he was at first alarmed, but later he remarked to his secretary that he believed it to be a fabrication, as Herrada had searched him out only a few days earlier and had showed himself to be very loyal. Someone, he thought, probably had an eye on his office."[50]

Pizarro did not go to Mass after all on that Sunday, the 26th of June, 1541, but had it celebrated in his home. Meanwhile, the conspirators stormed noisily through the streets shouting, "The tyrant is dead!" Scarcely anyone ventured out into the streets, believing that the conspirators had already taken over.

It was Chaves who admitted the assassins to the house of the Marqués. He was supposed to have bolted the door, but had opened it a fraction, allegedly in order to see what was going on outside. He was the first to be stabbed, and his dying words are said to have been: "What! Will you not spare your friend?" Pizarro did not have time to buckle his armor. His lieutenant Velásquez jumped out of the window, clenching the commander's mace between his teeth. Abandoned by almost everyone, Pizarro fought until he could barely wield his sword. "Finally, he fell, struck by a fatal dagger thrust in his throat. Even as he was falling he called out for the last sacraments, and when he could no longer speak, he made the sign of the cross on the floor with his hand and kissed it. So doing, he committed his soul to God."[50]

During the night of the assassination, Bishop Vicente Valverde fled from Lima with his brother-in-law and other followers. They found a sailing vessel, loaded it with their treasures, and sailed north along the coast. The young Almagro sent a ship in pursuit, but it did not catch up with them. "Thus God ordained that the time had come and the Indians were prepared to avenge the capture and death of prince Atahualpa, in which the prelate Vicente had figured so prominently," writes Oviedo. However, Oviedo was biased in his judgment of the preacher of Cajamarca. A letter, which as Bishop of Cuzco, Valverde wrote to Charles V, shows his deep concern for the improvement of the living conditions of the Indians in his care, especially the utterly impoverished and enslaved *Yanaconas* in Peru.[51]

The bishop, his brother-in-law, and all who were with them were driven off course on to the island of Puná, whose chieftains had seized on the dissension among the Christians as an opportune time for mounting their own uprising in conjunction with some neighboring tribes.

Valverde and his companions were murdered and sacrificed. Their great gold booty was retained by the chieftains. According to the early Dominicans in South America, Fray Vicente de Valverde was massacred as he was about to read Mass at the altar of the little wood and bamboo church that he himself had erected there.[52]

The expedition of the young Gonzalo Pizarro, then governor of Quito, to the jungle of the Amazon basin in search of gold and spices beyond the Cordilleras, consisted of 300 Spaniards, half of them mounted, and 4,000 Indians. They took 1,000 dogs with them, which were used for manhunts, and vast quantities of provisions, including a herd of pigs.[53] As soon as they crossed the Andes and entered the tropical forests, they encountered innumerable difficulties.

Part of the time the men advanced by using rafts and had to face currents and cataracts.

Once they reached the plain they had to wade through miles of flooded jungle. When the rivers became navigable, by dint of great effort, Gonzalo Pizarro had "a brigantine built in order to transport the provisions and the baggage and the sick more easily ... They had to construct furnaces in order to heat the iron that they needed, which they obtained from horseshoes of the fallen horses. Gonzalo ordered all his men to take part in the work and set to work himself with hammer and ax. Instead of pitch they used rubber, which they got from the trees, and instead of tow, the Indians' old cloaks and their own tattered, half-rotted shirts. They finally finished the ship and could now transport their baggage with ease. In addition they built several canoes, which followed in the wake of the brigantine."[56] Humboldt's famous discovery of the rubber tree had thus been anticipated and had even been given a practical application.

Captain Orellana was sent ahead with thirty men in the ship for reconnaissance, while Gonzalo Pizarro followed on foot with the main party. Orellana never returned. He let the ship containing all the provisions and the most vital equipment drift downstream for almost 2,000 miles and reached the mouth of the Amazon in the Atlantic Ocean virtually without incident. From there he sailed to Europe. Thus he gained a mention in history as the first person to cross the equator on that continent. In reward, Francisco de Orellana was granted permission by the Crown to colonize the Amazon region. He died on the return journey to South America.

With the disappearance of their ship, Gonzalo Pizarro and his men faced extreme privation and found themselves compelled to return to their bases. Forty Spaniards wasted away with hunger, and it was impossible to help them; with cries of distress, they leaned against the trees and fell dead to the ground." The party barely survived the crossing of the icy Andean passes. Pizarro and his men were almost totally naked, for the constant rain and the ravages of the journey had reduced their clothing to tatters, and it hung about them in rags.

The remnants of the expedition reached Quito draped in animal skins, with old rotted boots on their feet. Their daggers hung at their hips unsheathed and were eaten away with rust.[54]

Two and a half years had passed since their departure from Quito, 2,000 Indians had perished, and of the 300 Spaniards only 80 were still alive.[53]

The mission of Gonzalo Pizarro and Orellana was not an isolated one. The Spaniards' passion for discovery knew no bounds and considered no sacrifice too great. "Let us remember," writes the geographer Ernst Samhaber, "that since the earliest times, the source of the Nile was one of the major geographical mysteries for mankind. It was not solved until the 19th century. The continent of Africa, too, was not crossed until the second half of the last century. However, scarcely four decades had elapsed since the discovery of America, and the Spaniards had explored both northern South America, from Peru across the Amazon River to the Atlantic, and from the Pacific coast of Chile to the La Plata River." When Pizarro had set out to discover Peru, he had expected that the crossing of the country would present no more difficulty than others had experienced in Mexico and Nicaragua, and that he would then once more reach the Atlantic in the south.

"In North America Spanish expeditions set out from the Gulf of Mexico and explored far along the upper reaches of the Mississippi and the Missouri, from Florida to Mexico. It was a full century before a handful of bold Frenchmen succeeded in penetrating this region, and even then they kept close to the river courses. It took the English settlers in North America a century and a half before they mastered the narrow strip of coastland and pushed forward into the broad regions beyond the Alleghenies. It is easy to assume that the terrible greed for gold was the sole incentive for all these voyages of discovery and campaigns of conquest. It is only by comparing the written descriptions left by the conquistadors themselves with the accounts of other colonial peoples that we are able to assess the intellectual achievement in the opening up of America" (Samhaber).

Philipp von Hutten, a young German traveling to India, set out for Venezuela with some fishing vessels in Holy Week of 1546 and lost his life in the most savage way at the order of a Spanish conquistador, Juan de Carvajal; at the latter's command, he and his young companion from Augsburg, Ehinger, had their heads cut off by a Negro with a blunt knife. In the last letter written to his father in 1541, he said: "God knows, it is no lust for money that had induced me to make this voyage, but a strange desire that has long been with me, and which, methinks, would not have died easily without my seeing India first, and I truly do not rue it. For this reason, I do beseech you not to be displeased at my voyage and to comfort my dear mother and my sister."

The newly-discovered lands excited the longing of many men who had lost their roots in the course of the European wars. In 1590, Cervantes, who could describe better than any other Spanish writer the lot of the soldier who had out-served his usefulness, made an unsuccessful application to the king for a post in the New World. His application can still be seen today in the Indian Archive in Seville: "Miguel de Cervantes Sahavedra... requests and entreats most respectfully that His Majesty should do him the favor of entrusting him with a post in Las Indias (America) in one of the three or four which are at present vacant — the position of accountant in the New Kingdom of Granada (Colombia), or the position of governor of the province of Soconusco in Guatemala, or the position of paymaster of the Cartagena galleys, or that of *corregidor* of the city of La Paz. Any of these posts would be a great kindness on the part of His Majesty; it was his desire to continue to serve His Majesty and to conclude his life in the way of his ancestors ..."

The 100,000 or so conquistadors who sailed to the New World in the course of the 16th century took into exile with them a legacy of the Middle Ages, including the mercenary system, which persisted there for a long time.

There was a curious mingling of knights of the Cross and robber knights, fanatical piety and harsh realism, high-flown plans and deep pessimism, generosity and petty greed in this small national group that scattered throughout the new continent and forced its own imprint on the native population.

Colloquial speech in the languages of Latin America retain to this day echoes of the softer medieval accents of a Berceo, sounds that have been banished in the mother country by classical purists.

Apart from the polemic writings, Spanish colonial literature is a treasure trove. The contemporaries of Pizarro often lapse into personal detail, yet there is a whole array of audacious men with fluent pens. The most significant of these is, without any doubt, Cieza de León. The untiring interest of this soldier in the lands of the equator and the Tahuantinsuyu, and his gift of portraying the men and women that lived in them fairly and without prejudice, make his writings timeless. In the 17th century it was mainly monks who, emulating Las Casas, studied with scientific thoroughness the many religious and historical texts and the reflection of animate and inanimate nature in the Indian imagination. The most comprehensive ethnological, religio-historic, and politico-historic assessment is the *Historia del Nuevo Mundo*, the product of thirty years' work by the Jesuit father Bernabé Cobo. This was preceded by detailed and painstaking investigations of the Inca cults, such as the writings of Santillán and the *Relación anónima*.

By contrast, even though their knowledge of the Inca tongue enables them to portray many things much more vividly, the writings of the Indian chroniclers are more tendentious than the works of the monks. Garcilaso and Santa Cruz Pachacuti heavily emphasize their newly acquired Christianity, whereas the missionary activities of the clerical orders sought a much more gradual approach to the spiritual world of the different peoples in the hope of achieving a lasting effect.

Unfortunately, most of the chronicles devote a lot of space to the endless personal feuds of the Spaniards and their political attitudes.

The murder of Francisco Pizarro had a sad sequel — the death of Inca Manco.

The group of conspirators around Almagro's son were soon among the outlawed and hunted once again. One of Pizarro's assassins, the mestizo Diego Méndez, and some companions took refuge in the territory of the Inca, in Vilcabamba. Inca Manco is said to have received them hospitably and even to have invited them to a ball game.

"As the Inca seemed withdrawn and sad, the Spaniards tried to make him laugh and began teasing each other . . . the Inca's spirits really seemed to rise . . . As the *chicha* beer was being passed round, Diego suddenly rushed at the Inca and attacked him with his dagger, until he sank to the ground, to all appearances dead. The other Spaniards had done nothing to stop him. Now the Indians rushed forward to defend their lord . . . The Spaniards killed several of them and then

Facsimile of the poet Cervantes' application on the 21st of May, 1590, for a post in America, with marginal notes by various administrative officials.

155

hurriedly mounted their horses — night was approaching — to make their escape before the news of their crime spread further.

"That same night they covered a fair portion of the way to Cuzco, crossing a river by a hanging bridge, which they then cut adrift to save themselves from the pursuing Indians. However, the news spread like wildfire and the murderers were now pursued from all directions . . . A group of *orejones,* who were at that time escorting a noble lord, left him and immediately rushed off to participate in the hunt. They tracked the Spaniards down in a cave sanctuary, where they took them unawares and killed them all.

"After they had avenged their lord, they set off for Vitico, where the assault had taken place. They found the Inca still alive — it was now five days after the attack — and they appeared before him with a display of such passionate grief that they accelerated the death of the Inca."[55]

60 *Inca noblewoman
(colonial period).*

61 Blasco Núñez Vela (1544–1546), first Viceroy of Peru.

62 D. López de Zúñiga y Velasco, Conde de Nieva, fourth Viceroy.

63 Alcalde's (mayor's) staff decorated with Indian figures from the time of the viceroys.

64 a *Here three generations are brought together in one scene; the wedding of Martín García de Loyola and the daughter of Inca Sayri Túpac; right, the marriage in Spain of their daughter to a Borja; above, left, the Incas Sayri Túpac and Túpac Amaru.*

64 b *Detailed study from the same scene.*

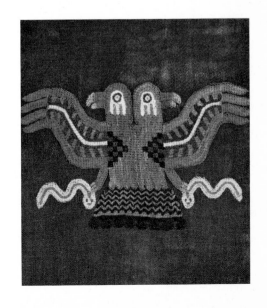

65a   Funeral procession of Charles V, on the 24th—25th of February, 1559, in Augsburg. The emperor died on 21st of September, 1558, in San Yuste, and was buried in the Escorial. It was during his reign that Peru was discovered and all but lost to the crown once more with the promulgation of the Nuevas Leyes, which defended the human rights of the Indians against the interests of the conquistadors. Mourning ceremonies continued in the empire until 1559. Counts and dukes carried the royal insignia — the golden imperial flag in front, followed by Charles' favorite horse shrouded in a dark shabrack with the Burgundian Cross; then came the golden helmet with the crown and feathered plume, the escutcheon and the mantle emblazoned with the coat of arms with the double eagle and the two-edged sword. The Inca funeral ceremonies were very similar — here, too the ruler's insignia (scepter, throne, litter, and feather sunshade) were borne through the land by the nobility.

65b   Emperor Charles V.

66   Double-headed bird of prey on an ancient Peruvian tapestry (right).

de Castizo ₃ y Española
Español.

de Español ₃ y Alvina
Negro Torna atras.

67—74   The mixture
of races in Spanish
America.

de Español'e Yndia
Mestiza

de Mestiza 2 y Español

de Español 4 y Negra
Mulata

de Español 6 y Morisca
Albino

12
De Tente en el Aire
y Mulata, Albarrasad.

Frutas dla Nue Esp:
Chirimoya, 1. Vña, 2. Sandia, 3. Aguacate
4. Chico-4. Sapote Blanco, 5. Zapote prieto
6. Mamei, 7. Camote, 8. Pera, 9. Me-
xipa, 10. Higos. 11. Piña, 13. Guayaba, 14. Platano

De Yndio 1º y Mestiza
Coyote.

75 *Inca converted
to Christianity.*

CHAPTER VI

Charles V's New Laws (Nuevas Leyes, 1542) for the protection of the Indians —
Revolt of the conquistadors — First viceroys (1542) — Execution of the last Inca
of Vilcabamba, Túpac Amaru (1572).

During these years a storm was brewing for the conquistadors in Spain. In 1542, Charles V issued the *Nuevas Leyes*, the New Laws, which ordered the severest restrictions of conquistador privileges ever to have come from the Crown. After decades of campaigning and setbacks, when he was almost seventy, the Dominican "Apostle of the Indians," Bartolomé de las Casas, made a personal request to the king and finally succeeded in persuading him and the Council for Indian Affairs to take decisive action in the legislation of the colony. Earlier, in 1518, he had already temporarily aroused the sympathy of the young King Charles and his adviser, the governor cardinal, who later became Pope Adrian of Utrecht, for the reforms planned by the Dominicans. The terrible oppression and extermination of the Indians in the Antilles by Christopher Columbus and his associates — by 1510 there were only 46,000 left of the original native population of about one million in 1492 — had filled many in the New and Old World alike with outrage and distress.

The movements of great religious and intellectual revival and the consciousness of the moral responsibility of the individual (which in Europe also unleashed social upheavals such as the German Peasant's War) were forcefully interpreted by the missionaries who appeared in America. In 1511, the Dominican father Antonio de Montesinos preached a sermon in the straw-covered church of Santo Domingo that echoed around the world: "You are all in mortal sin and live and die in it because of the cruelty and tyranny that you practice against these innocent people. Can you tell me, by what right and by what justice you keep these Indians in such cruel and appalling servitude? . . . Are they not human beings? Do they not have reasoning souls? And are you not obliged to love them as yourselves? Don't you understand this? Don't you feel this? You oppress and torment them, without feeding them or tending them when they fall sick as a result of the inordinate amount of work that you burden them with . . . They die, or rather, you kill them, in your daily scrabbling for gold."
"Montesinos called on the Spanish settlers to set the Indians allotted to them free and threatened to refuse absolution at confession to those who would not do so."[1]

The sermon caused such a scandal that nearly all the Dominicans were apparently recalled to Spain. This was still in the time of King Ferdinand, and he expressly let it be known to the Spanish settlers that they had acted in accordance with royal instructions. Lawyers and theologians had pronounced the Indians' duty to work as consistent with the natural and divine right, "and if there were any question of a guilty conscience, he and his advisers would bear the responsibility."[2]

But the Dominican cause had not entirely failed. Ferdinand V gave Montesinos a personal audience, and in 1512 he issued the Burgos Laws, which may be regarded as the precursors of the *Nuevas Leyes* of 1542. They ordered certain improvements in the Indians' lot, such as provision of food and clothing, the avoidance of work damaging to health, and facilities for Christian instruction. The compulsion to work was not removed, but curtailed. In practice, these first Indian laws were largely disregarded, for what could the Spaniards achieve without Indian labor. Las Casas accompanied Montesinos back to Spain and now showed how effective he could be.

Las Casas had been familiar with the New World since he was a young man. His father, an unsuccessful Seville merchant, had sailed with Columbus and had brought back a young Taino slave from the West Indies — one of the 800 who, one and a half years later, had to be set free and repatriated, so far as they could still be traced by then. As a student, Bartolomé de Las Casas used to roam through Seville by night in the company of this Taino slave.[3] In 1502 Las Casas went to the West Indies himself, first to La Española as a catechist and then to Cuba. Like many others, he was given land and Indians there and he became commercially successful. His partner, Pedro de Rentería, would take the agricultural produce grown with the aid of Indian labor to Puerto Rico and La Española and sell it there. Las Casas also made a habit of taking in and feeding numerous refugees from other territories that were in a state of turmoil, while all around him the Spaniards, in their indiscriminate hunt for gold, drove the Indians entrusted to them to death and ruined themselves financially.

Stirred by the sermon delivered by Dominican missionaries on a visit to La Española in 1514, Las Casas and his partner felt that even this moderate form of self-enrichment at the expense of the Indians was unjustified, and in 1515 they handed the *encomienda* back to Governor Velásquez.[4] In 1522 Las Casas entered the Dominican order, and from then until the end of his life he devoted all his energy, learning, and organizational talent to the services of Indian welfare.

His attempts to interest Spanish peasant farmers in emigrating to the New World to establish integrated Spanish-Indian settlements there met with strong resistance from the owners of latifundia, resident in Spain, and from the *encomenderos* overseas, and consequently came to nothing.[5]

It was not until 1542 that the decisive breakthrough came with the promulgation of the *Nuevas Leyes*. In fulfilment of the king's earlier promises, these now specifically laid down that the Indians were just as much free men and direct sub-

Bartolomé de Las Casas: portrait and autograph (1552).

jects of the crown as the Spaniards. They insisted on the eight-hour day and restricted female and child labor. The hard core of the laws was Article Thirty, which prohibited the distribution of new *encomiendas* or the passing on of existing ones as legacies or gifts; it also decreed that when an *encomendero* died, the Indian tribute allotted to him should revert to the Crown. Thus, within a foreseeable space of time, this whole highly disputed "institution of Spanish native policies was to disappear."[6] In future all higher posts were to be reserved for members of the Spanish nobility.

This radical pronouncement by the king, proclaiming the ideal of the equality of all men, was made in the Old World before the period of the Enlightenment and the French Revolution. In those same years, when Las Casas was interceding on behalf of the oppressed natives of a world that had yet to be pacified, rebellious peasants in Central Europe, who had interpreted Luther's writings of freedom literally, were being forcibly compelled by the privileged orders, by secular and religious lords, who spoke the same language as their subjects, to submit to an even harsher yoke than before, as they lost the last privileges remaining to them from the Middle Ages. Serfdom was not abolished until 1781 in Austria, 1807 in Prussia, 1818 in Bavaria, and 1861 in Russia. In the prosperous Germany of 1900, the workers had no eight-hour day like the Indians. They, and often their

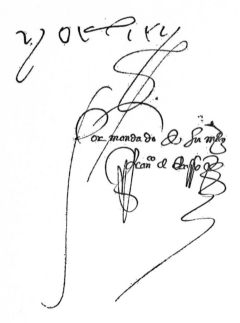

"yo el rey:" signature of Charles V on a Real Cédula of 1548, sent from Brussels to the Council for Indian Affairs.

wives and children with them, had to work fourteen hours. To this day there are sulfur mines in southern Italy where those accepting employment have to give a signed undertaking that they are entrusting themselves to the primitive and perilous equipment at their own risk.

These comparisons are not so much an illustration of how free the Indians were — even Alexander von Humboldt was astounded at the social position of the Indian worker when he traveled through the "Equinoctial regions of the New Continent" between 1799 and 1804 — as of how unfree Europe remained until very recent times.

In the Inca state, compulsory labor in the mines, on the Inca plantations, and on the construction of roads, fortresses, and temples, was dictated by the seasons. The eight-hour day was not always observed, and in the tropics and in the mountain heights, it was the asbolute maximum that could be exacted from the Indian constitution. In Central America and Ecuador, and for a while in Trujillo and Lima, Negro slaves now filled the places of the Indians, so that the vacated lowest rung on the social ladder was once more filled, grotesquely enough, with the approval of those same religious groups who had worked so hard for the equality of the Indians with the whites. However, in the highlands of Peru and Bolivia, all the burdens continued to be shouldered by the poor Indians.

The regime of the conquistadors in Peru had fallen into disgrace at the Spanish court, following Almagro's execution and the continuing vendettas between the parties. In consequence of the *Nuevas Leyes,* many of the privileges previously granted to the Pizarro family by the Crown were now revoked. The governorship of Peru was abolished and now became a non-hereditary post of viceroy, as in Mexico.

The man sent across the ocean to implement these orders and to be the first viceroy was the elderly Blasco Núñez Vela. He had been especially urged to bring about a reconciliation with Inca Manco and to convey the thanks of the king to Inca Paullu.[7]

He landed at Paita, and on his way to Lima he would not allow Indians to carry anything for his column; at every Spanish settlement he passed he gave instructions for the *Yanaconas* (those Indians obliged to act as personal servants) to be set free.[8]

Juan de Barbarán, already known to us as a well-established businessman and *encomendero,* a friend of Pizarro and until then a cool-headed mediator in all disputes, was chosen by the municipal council to ride out and greet the first viceroy. At the "*tampu* of the partridges," he met a courier bringing the menacing order to the *encomenderos.* Barbarán hurried back to Lima, stormed into the city, and called down from his horse, "Off with you to your freedom! See what orders the viceroy has brought!"[9]

The settlers must have been utterly dismayed and embittered. They regarded the abolition of the hereditary privileges primarily as a threat to the livelihood of their progeny.

Whereas previously the clash of individual interests had led to civil war, now the settlers were in outright revolt against the Crown. Loyal subjects turned into rebels. R. Porras Barrenechea gives a good impression of the mood of the Peruvians at the time: "When the king attacked the *encomiendas* and sent the unpopular, ill-humored Núñez Vela to the country to implement the *Nuevas Leyes*, the *encomenderos* urged Gonzalo Pizarro to be their caudillo. First he was pronounced 'Capitán contra el Inca' and attorney for the *encomenderos*, and he was subsequently made governor. The *audiencias* (largely autonomous provinces, approximately equivalent to present-day political states) entrust him with supreme power and the *cabildos* (communities) greet him as their savior."

These are the days of the "muy magnífico señor don Gonzalo Pizarro," who enters Lima under a canopy, the days when the streets echo to the cheers of blindly devoted followers, calling, "Curse those, who deny you, to the death!"[10]

However, it was Gonzalo's eighty-year old military commander, Francisco de Carvajal, who first introduced method into the confusion and set things on a demonic course. He had made his way through the whole of Europe and had been present at the Sack of Rome and at the capture of Francis I in Pavia, had then gone to Mexico, and finally landed in Peru. It was rumored that he was a bastard son of Cesare Borgia or a renegade monk. At first Carvajal wished to have nothing to do with an open conflict with the Crown. However, once he had enlisted in Gonzalo's cause, with his Negro guard, he soon became the "Demon of the Andes."[11]

"He rode about on a gigantic russet mule, dressed in a violet-colored Moorish burnoose . . . a black taffeta hat on his head, with a silk band in which many black and white hens' feathers were arranged in a criss-cross pattern all the way round."

His men strode about in bright red cloaks and red cape, similarly stuck with feathers.[12] *Caballeros* hanging from the trees were always a sign that they had passed by. Following the Inca custom, Carvajal threw the monk Pedro de Ulloa into the Sancay prison, where there were poisonous snakes, for distributing royal circulars. This was his way of driving the waverers into Gonzalo Pizarro's camp.

The Church's reply was excommunication. The priests in the main church of Cuzco interrupted their celebration of Holy Mass as Carvajal entered with fifty armed men.

Gonzalo, who felt the excommunication more keenly, gained absolution for himself and his followers by doing penance in front of the doors of the church and undertaking to send a mission with a large donation of money to the pope in Rome within the space of three years.

The cynicism of the aged Carvajal is best illustrated by his dry comment on these conciliatory efforts, which were quite meaningless to him, saying a period of four years would have been better, for by that time there would no longer be a pope in Rome, as the mighty Turk would long since have taken over the city and whole of Italy, thus making the voyage and the pardon altogether unnecessary![13]

R. Porras Barrenchea describes how echoes of the Peruvian uprising reached Spain, and the hesitant moves that followed: "Zurbano, formerly a follower of Almagro and an opponent of Pizarro, set out to fetch help for the viceroy, sailing first to Panama, and from there to Spain, to intervene with Prince Philip. He and another man, Cueto, spoke up for Núñez Vela, while Francisco Maldonado put Gonzalo Pizarro's case . . . The Prince does not commit himself and so Zurbano, Cueto, and Maldonado travel to Germany to see Charles V. The emperor receives them in Cologne and is particularly pleasant to Zurbano; in view of the delicacy of the situation, however, he refuses to make a definite statement. He later selects the highly educated cleric and administrative expert Pedro de la Gasca to solve this problem. Zurbano and Maldonado sail back to Peru with La Gasca."

Meanwhile, the fate the unfortunate viceroy Núñez Vela had, however, already been sealed. Driven out of Lima, he again tried to gain a foothold in Ecuador and advanced by way of Tumibamba to Quito.

Gonzalo Pizarro and Carvajal pursued him with their army and challenged him at the equator.

Exhausted, and by now incapable of sound judgment, Núñez Vela plunged into an encounter in the Iñaquito plain and was defeated. Taking flight, he fell from his horse and was decapitated by one of Carvajal's Negro slaves. His gray beard and hair were handed round as trophies for admiration by the ladies of Lima.

The viceroy's followers, who on his instructions were wearing white Indian outer garments, had to find shelter among the Indians in the hills and in the monasteries of Quito. Carvajal's men even dragged them out from under the church altars.[14]

For four years, from 1544 to 1548, Gonzalo Pizarro wielded power such as few mortals enjoy. The Peru over which he ruled stretched from Quito well into Chile and Argentina, and an armada of twenty-three small ships, then the most powerful fleet ever seen on the west coast of America, gave him mastery over the entire Pacific from Panama to the Magellan Straits. The Atlantic port of Nombre de Dios was also his, and consequently the whole isthmus. His counselors advised him to marry an Inca princess and proclaim himself king of Peru, but a remaining shred of loyalty held him back.[15]

Even as he was reaching the peak of his power, which was based on terror and financed by the newly-discovered silver mines at Potosí, the foundations of his authority were already beginning to crumble. The king's deputy, Pedro de La Gasca, had meanwhile arrived in America and gained support by proclaiming a general amnesty in conjunction with an appreciable relaxation of the *Nuevas Leyes*. In a letter from the king,[16] Gonzalo had been offered an opportunity for himself and his followers to return to loyal support of the king. He rejected this, even though Carvajal had been in favor of accepting. This compelled La Gasca to throw in his troops and financial resources,[17] which he had kept secret until then, and take up arms against the Peruvians.

Sacsayhuaman.

Gonzalo and Carvajal won the first engagement, but after that, in spite of an increasing use of terror against all "traitors," their power rapidly began to decline.

The troops of La Gasca and Gonzalo were ranged opposite one another for the last time on the plain outside Sacsahuaman. Whole divisions of Gonzalo's men ran over to the royal camp, until finally he found himself alone with his friend Acosta, who advised him to die in battle, like the ancient Romans. Gonzalo replied, "No, it is better to die like a Christian,"[18] and rode across to the royal camp "on a magnificent chestnut-colored horse, wearing a satin garment over his leather armor, with a golden helmet on his head" and handed over his dagger.[19] The dialogue between the royal official and the aging conqueror brother of the explorer provides an insight into the mental outlook of the insurgents. La Gasca reproached Gonzalo with his ingratitude towards the king, who had permitted him and his brothers to become rich and had "raised (them) out of the dust." Besides, Gonzalo had not taken any part whatsoever in the discovery of these territories. Whereupon, the discoverer of the northern sources of the Amazon retorted with a hint of contempt: "All this ground was indeed discovered by my brother; but it is we who conquered them, at our own expense and by risking our lives, and it took the four Pizarro brothers to do so, and all the relatives and friends who were with us. His Majesty certainly gave my brother the title of Margrave, but he didn't give him the march that went with it. And the king did not raise us up out of the dust. For since the Goths came to Spain, we *hidalgos* and our house have been known. It is those that do not belong to it, that need the king, with his offices and honors, to raise them up out of the dust in which they crawled. And what if we Pizarros were poor — that was the very reason why we went out into the world and won this empire and gave it to His Majesty.

171

We could well have kept it, like many others who conquered new lands have done."[19]

He knew that his life was over. La Gasca, who had previously tried repeatedly to provide him with a way out, now had to sentence him to death.

Pizarro accepted the sentence with composure, and before his death, like a true son of Estremadura, proclaimed the greatest veneration for the Virgin Mary. His head was impaled on a lance, like that of a traitor; his gigantic fortune was confiscated by the Crown.

Carvajal was discovered by his own men, hiding in the rushes, and they handed him over. When he was informed that he would be hanged and quartered, he is supposed to have replied laconically, "It's enough if you kill me once."[19]

Historians have been fascinated by the figure of Gonzalo Pizarro, and his death on the executioner's block in the prime of life surrounds him with glory. Some see in him a pioneer of the independence of South America, while others dream of the king he might have been.

Pedro Pizarro described him in the following words: "Gonzalo Pizarro was courageous, knew little, had a fine face and splendid beard; he was thickset, not tall, and rode extremely well." Zárate writes, "He had an inordinate passion for women, regardless of whether they were Indian or Castilian."

In the midst of all this upheaval, the old customs of the Indian village communities and tribes were still practiced in many areas. As a result of the widespread need and hunger in the country, the importance of ritual festivals and sacrifices increased. In 1547, Marcos Otazo, a priest, attended one of these festivals in the ancient tradition that was held in the Lake Titicaca area, and at the express wish of Cieza, the chronicler, he recorded the proceedings:[20]

". . . It was at the time of full moon, in May, 1547, when I was missionary in a place called Lampaz. The *curacas* and village elders of the surrounding area came to me and begged me on their knees to permit them to perform their rites which were customary at this time of year. I told them that I would have to be present, so that nothing would take place that conflicted with our Catholic faith. They agreed and all hurried to their homes. I believe it was exactly midday when the drums began to sound from various directions — there they strike them with only one stick. Then the plaza began to fill up. Ponchos were spread out like carpets on the ground and the two *curacas* and their village elders, wearing their finest clothes, their hair arranged in the customary two long plaits, took their places on them. Both chieftains of the two halftribes[21] were each approached by a strikingly handsome twelve year old youth, advancing from the right. From the knees and elbows down, their clothing was hung with red fringes, in the manner of the savages, while gold and silver plaques decorated the rest of their clothes. In the right hand they carried a halberd and in the left a woollen *coca* bag. After them, two equally beautiful ten-year old girls approached from the left-hand side. They were dressed almost exactly the same, except for the long skirt with a train, which the Indian women do not usually wear, and a puma skin, hanging all the way down their backs. Each of them carried a fine woolen

76   *Church of Ichupampa in the mountains to the north of Arequipa.*

77 *Church of Pomata on Lake Titicaca. The stone reliefs in the dome, especially the radiating angels' heads framed in squares, still show strong influences of the Tiahuanaco culture.*

78 *Beheading of Inca "Don Juan Atahualpa." (Inaccurate portrayal. This was the manner in which Túpac Amaru, the last Inca of Vilcabamba, was executed in 1572. Atahualpa was strangled to death in 1533.)*

79 18th-century portrait of the wealthy Don Marcos Chiguan Thopa. The head fringe and the gold and feather ornament above it, the sunturpaucar, are the only reminders of his pure Inca descent.

bag in the right hand, filled with gold and silver sacrificial gift offerings. Each train was carried by an Indian noblewoman, with many maids of honor walking behind her. Then came six Indians dressed as peasants, with digging sticks over their shoulders and bright feather decorations, followed again by six youths, carrying sacks of potatoes and beating drums . . . The youths and the girls bowed by inclining their heads, and when this was reciprocated they stepped back twenty paces without turning their heads from the chieftains.

"The peasants now stuck their digging sticks in the ground in a row and hung on them their sacks of specially chosen large potatoes . . . To the accompaniment of the drums, the various groups now performed their dances . . . rising on tiptoe and swinging their sacks in the air from time to time without moving from the one spot . . . while the tribal elders and all the others sat on the ground in strict order and watched in complete silence . . ." While they were all seated, a one-year old unblemished llama, the same color all over, was led in front of the main chieftain . . . suddenly they all crowded round it in a close circle, so that I could see nothing, and forced the animal to the ground with its limbs outstretched, and while it was still alive they tore the entrails out and handed them to their sooth-sayers, the *huacacamayos*.

"I saw several Indians hurriedly scatter as much blood as they could scoop up with their hands over the potatoes in the sacks."

"Then one of the leading Indians, who had only recently become a Christian, rushed forward . . . cursed them on account of their devilish cult — without any sign of fear as dogs and other things that I did not understand . . . so that when I rebuked them in turn, the Indians became quite anxious and ashamed and broke off the sacrificial ceremony, in the course of which they would have predicted the harvest and the events of the coming year in their customary way . . ." The agitation of the Christianized Indian nobleman, and the splendid attire and the honor paid to the children described in this passage, makes us suspect that human sacrifices may have been about to take place, although it is repeatedly denied in the texts that this ever occurred.[22]

Almost all the Spaniards living in Peru had half-caste children. This was not just because of the scarcity of Spanish women and the resignation and compliance of Indian women. A factor that weighed heavily in this was that the *curacas*, unlike the conquistadors, could pass their property down to sons and daughters alike. The alliances most coveted by Spaniards and *mestizos* were with princesses from the Inca *ayllus*, which had been stripped of their male population.

Particularly tragic was the fate that befell the sole legitimate daughter of Sayri Túpac, granddaughter of Manco and Huáscar. She had been baptized with the name of Beatriz de Mendoza, and at the wish of the Spanish authorities, she was later to have become *coya* of the Inca in Vilcabamba. However, at the age of seven, she was dragged out of the convent of Santa Clara in Cuzco by two mestizo *encomenderos*, the brothers Arias and Cristobal Maldonado — according to legal documents, they were probably the trustees of her fortune. Cristobal rav-

Llama sacrifice.

ished the child and blackmailed her mother, the widowed *coya*, into giving her consent to the irregular marriage.

However, the ambitious *mestizo* was put on trial for high treason. He lost all his rights, was made to pay a heavy fine, and was banished and sentenced to serve as an unpaid horseman in Oran. The same thing happened to his brother and to other *mestizos* who were reputed to have taken part in intrigues. A few years later, the Inca princess Beatriz was married to a nephew of Ignatius of Loyola, Captain Martín García de Loyola, notorious for his part in the capture of the last Inca of Vilcabamba.[23]

Francisco Pizarro had four children by daughters of Huayna Cápac. The mother of the first two children — whom he married to another Spaniard three years before his death in order to be able to turn his attentions to the second daughter of the great Inca — was descended on her mother's side from the Chimú *curaca* of Huaylas in the Santa Valley. She bore Pizarro her first child, a girl, called Francisca Pizarro y Yupanqui, in 1534 in Jauja. In 1540, Pizarro made over the *encomienda* of Huaylas, with its 3,000 Indians, to this daughter, together with the severely depopulated area of Conchucos, thereby ratifying a decision of Huayna Cápac. The Inca had assigned Ñusta Contarguacho, the grandmother of Francisca Pizarro, three "huarangas" with 1,000 Indians each. The Indians of Huaylas worshiped the six-year old child as their queen. Francisca Pizarro and her brother Gonzalo, who was regarded as his father's future successor, were both recognized by the Spanish royal house as legitimate children, and after the initial afflictions and persecution suffered as a result of their father's murder, they were permitted to live in Trujillo and enjoy the fruits of their estates for some years. The brother died early, and many conquistadors courted the child heiress, including her own uncle Gonzalo.

All the Pizarros devoted a large section of their wills to assuring the future of their half-caste children. None of them make any provision for their mothers, who were all Inca princesses, for the leading conquistadors would have been content with nothing less. The crown discouraged legal marriages for political reasons.

Francisco Pizarro lived a family life with his Indian children, his half-brother Martín de Alcántara, and his wife Doña Inés. She had been the first married woman to accompany her husband to Peru. She tried to assuage her grief at the loss of her three small children, who had died on the voyage, by her untiring devotion to her brother-in-law's children and for the welfare of the settlers. Her supreme womanly qualities emerged at the time when Jauja was the first small colony. She was the first to plant wheat in Peru and she introduced the olive, the cultivation of flax, and many Castilian fruits into the country. She was known as the Peruvian Ceres.

After the assassination of Pizarro, she and Barbarán, together with other women and monks, brought the bloody corpses of Pizarro and her own husband to safety. She safeguarded the lives of the children, after her house had been plundered and destroyed, and would not abandon them when she married for the second time and bore a son. After the death of her second husband, she and twelve women and girls withdrew to a nunnery which she herself had founded and endowed with her own possessions.[24]

In 1549, two of Gonzalo Pizarro's children, Francisco and Inés, and two daughters of Juan Pizarro, were taken to Spain, together with the young Garcilaso de la Vega, also a *mestizo*. This son of Gonzalo is supposed "to have been inclined to get up to every conceivable kind of escapade. When he was taken away, he is supposed to have said that he would take his revenge on the men who had done this evil to his father!" He was then twelve or thirteen years old. "It was probably high time that this wild Inca offspring of Gonzalo's was taken in hand."

House of Garcilaso de la Vega el Inca in Cuzco.

The enormously rich inheritance of the Pizarro family was contested in private and public legal proceedings for a long time. Hernando Pizarro, the only legitimate one of the four brothers, put up the most stubborn fight against the Crown for every single item of the family possessions under dispute. At the age of fifty, after obtaining the necessary dispensation, he finally married his young niece Francisca Pizarro y Yupanqui, in order to hold the inheritance together. The daughter of the old explorer is said to have been a good wife to him. She never ceased to keep the memory of her father alive in her heart. Whenever she signed anything, she would carefully execute the same two calligraphic flourishes with which Francisco Pizarro used to sign documents.[25]

She defended the honor of her family with great energy against the outside world. In 1578, when the Pizarro coat of arms was being redesigned and the designer was careless in his work, she made her notary protest.[26] The coat of arms itself betrays not a hint of the humility that might have been expected of the illegitimate children of a family outlawed by the Crown, but bears the pillars of Hercules, with Charles V's motto of "Plus ultra." It shows the city of Cuzco, with the crown above, and hanging from it, the *borla*. All the way round are white llamas, alternating with a line of Indians, tied together by ropes around their necks, and the motto, "Indefesso labore meo, fidem, prae oculis habens, tot comparavi divitias" (With untiring effort, and always remembering the faith, have I won this great wealth). (For the coat arms, see p. 127.)

Gonzalo's daughter Inés married Francisco Pizarro, the last son of the old Francisco.

With the fall of Gonzalo Pizarro, the worst threat of succession had been averted. But after Pedro de la Gasca's departure, renewed uprisings and feuds among the conquistadors broke out again. The king's amnesties and the partial repeal of the *Nuevas Leyes* had created a state of legal instability that was exploited by the adventurers in order to increase their power.

The difficulties facing a representative of the Crown, who wanted to recapture lost ground and was not prepared to be surrounded with a web of corruption or be appeased by good living, are outlined in a letter written to the king in 1556 by Viceroy Marqués de Cañete in Lima.[27] ". . . I found this country in an even

The Spanish rebel Francisco Hernández Girón (1553).

Francisco Hernández defends himself in a *pucara* (Inca fortress) against the royal troops.

more hopeless condition than I had ever expected . . . Doctor Saravia and the cleric Santillán (both subsequently famous chroniclers) officiate as *oidores* (chief inspectors) . . . they are forever at loggerheads, so that each of them has accused the other in secret petitions to His Majesty, as must be well-known at court . . . in addition they are quite corrupt and not at all used to having someone in authority above them . . . They gave twenty-two persons authority to dip into the royal purse, using the money to purchase weapons, horses, and goods, so that now there are more than 200,000 pesos missing, 60,000 alone being from the assets of the deceased . . . Soldiers and *vecinos* (citizens) receive large loans from these funds; some of them barter in anticipation of hoped-for royal awards of land . . .[28] In Cuzco, this center of perpetual unrest, Garcilaso de la Vega is corregidor . . . a highly suspect man, as far as political intrigue is concerned, who has even put down in writing his assertion . . . that he would curse his sons if they obeyed Don Carlos (Charles V).[29] In addition to the fortune he already had, this man has been further enriched by a *repartimiento* of 12,000 pesos, with one of 6,000 for his deputy. He squanders these incomes in the company of 150 to 200 dinner guests, each of whom has been involved in the most recent uprising of Francisco Hernández or in some earlier ones . . . two of this Francisco Hernández's military leaders round up all the old companions, live on their country estates, and, whenever they enter Cuzco, they always have between sixty and eighty armed men with them . . . In the newly-founded *pueblo* (town), which they call La Paz, I found a certain Juan Remón installed as corrigedor and supreme judge — a soldier who acts the strong man there . . . from the start he has been supporting over 200 fellow combatants, spends all his earnings, and even runs into debt . . . now he is asking me for another *repartimiento*, which he needs on account of his 200 friends, and insists on it, without the least show of courtesy . . .[30]

"I am already resigned to the prospect of war, and I might almost welcome it. If it costs me my life, which could easily happen, I ask His Majesty to bear in mind that the gentle remedies and amnesties applied before are no longer adequate. For it has already been made public here roughly how much a viceroy costs and similar forms of insolence . . . and if we do not take drastic action, His Majesty will lose this beautiful rich land and the souls of its people . . .[30a]

"The *encomenderos*' treatment of the natives is worse than ever. It would take one viceroy for every *vecino* to make sure that he did not rob, exploit, and torment the natives . . . Although I am a hard man, it breaks my heart to have to witness what goes on here. Things are very bad since the limitation on tributes has been publicly suspended here and the imposition of individual labor duty reintroduced, and the Indians are dying out. If God does not intervene here, then things will go the same way as on the island of Santo Domingo . . .[31]

"His Majesty should send men of some standing to be officials out here, for their heads would not be so easily turned, unlike these people, who were sailors or stable boys in Spain and suddenly find themselves with an annual income of ten to twelve thousand pesos."

"I really should have written all this in code . . . but because I have not been allowed this privilege, I can only give this letter to a trusted person who will hand it over personally to His Majesty. I earnestly request His Majesty to keep the secret . . . for if the Seville merchants should get to hear of this, their agents in Peru will soon make it known throughout the whole of the country. It is these very merchants who are out to perpetuate the wars and feuds in this country, for it is under these conditions that their business interests profit most, and in the end all the wealth accrues to them . . ."

"In the short time that I have been in this country, I have arranged for the foundation of settlements in five different areas, set well apart from one another: in the area of Tumibamba . . . the city of Cuenca in the region of Guarco . . . the city of Cañete — I have named it after my home town — 20 miles from Trujillo, the village of Santa . . . When the plans are ready, I shall send copies to His Majesty and shall report the other details. This will be of great help to the many married people. It will settle them and they will no longer wish to be soldiers, but farmers . . . this alone will guarantee the security of the land! Little has been done in this direction until now . . . everything seems to be built on sand . . . I am using the tributes that have now been released to try and promote the construction of roads, bridges, and buildings . . .[32] There are also many *mestizo* women in this empire, the daughters of deceased conquistadors and other settlers . . . who suffer great hardship, both physically and mentally; Spanish women without means are also frequently arriving; I have founded a home for all these women, where they can also receive instruction, and I have provided it with landed estates and servants . . . I have established a similar institution for the many deserving poor that exist in Lima to provide charitable relief for them . . ."[33]

Cañete himself described the means which he employed against the rebellious settlers as harsh. The chronicler Poma de Ayala praises him as a particularly mild and Christian viceroy who gave his money to the poor, built bridges of stone, and befriended humble Indians and noble Incas alike, and held the conquistadors in check; Bernabé Cobo refers to him as "Padre de la patria."[34]

It was probably in answer to a specific wish of the emperor Charles V that he succeeded in gaining the confidence of Sayri Túpac, the son and successor of the murdered Inca Manco, and persuaded him to leave his refuge of Vilcabamba and visit him in Lima, the City of the Kings. Poma de Ayala has an impressive description of the meeting of the two rulers — the Inca in his litter with a large retinue and the viceroy on horseback — and the great banquets and honors in the new city, and in a drawing he shows the two in intimate conversation.

Sayri Túpac then permitted himself to be baptized in Cuzco, where, by papal dispensation and amidst great ceremonial, his marriage to his sister Doña Beatriz Coya was celebrated in the presence of the assembled Spaniards and the Inca nobility. He allowed himself to be persuaded not to return to Vilcabamba, but to take up residence in Jauja under Spanish protection. He died soon after, probably poisoned by his own countrymen, fanatical defenders of the independence of Vilcabamba.

Battle of Chuquinga: the Emperor is defeated with the aid of Indian troops.

Francisco Hernández is captured at Jauja, taken away by Indians, and later beheaded at Lima.

181

The town of Cañete, founded by Viceroy Cañete (1536).

Garcilaso, whom the Marqués de Cañete had so harshly attacked in his letter, was the father of the later chronicler and owed his fortune not only to the above-mentioned conspiracies, but also to his union with the Inca princess Chimbo Ocllo, the mother of the chronicler. Every week this niece of Huayna Cápac and granddaughter of the great Túpac would assemble her Inca relations; the conversations around the table in his parents' home provided the son with information which he later used in his famous *Comentarios Reales de los Incas*. However, he left for Spain at an early age and it was only after many years spent in Flanders and North Africa in the service of Philip II that, still far from home, he could turn to his life's work. Consequently his chronicle rests largely on reports by other eyewitnesses.

His parents' home broke up and his mother was driven out to marry some impoverished Spaniard. His father remained in Peru and married a rich Spanish woman. Garcilaso, the chronicler, died in Andalusia on the same day as Miguel de Cervantes, whose fate bore some resemblance to his own. In a side chapel in the Mezquita of Córdoba, with its thousand columns, a lamp has burned for centuries and a stone plaque proclaims that "here rests an illustrious man who was experienced in the art of writing, and a hero in battle, and in whose veins the noble blood of the dukes of Feria was mingled with the royal blood of the *emperadores* of the New World."[35]

With the end of the Marqués de Cañete's period of office, favoritism and corruption flourished again for several years in the viceroyalty of Peru. When the most famous of the Spanish crown officials, Viceroy Toledo, took up office in 1569, Philip II's bureaucratic principles of order were established, and with them a totally different concept of administration and Indian policy.

Francisco de Toledo was closely related to Alvárez de Toledo, better known as the Duke of Alba, who has gone down in history and literature for his rule of terror in the Netherlands. Alba was in command in the Netherlands in the same years that Francisco de Toledo, the fifty-five-year-old administrator, who had proved his worth in all parts of Europe, ruled the New World as the instrument of Philip II. In his efforts to stamp out anarchy, he soon proved himself to be the enemy of any form of independent development in Peru, especially of the integrated Indian-Spanish culture that was just beginning to emerge. Despotic behavior by Spaniards and the persisting privileges of the indigenous *curacas* and Inca descendents were a thorn in his flesh. Marriages between Spaniards and Indian noblewomen soon came to be regarded as against the interests of the state, and even missionary work, which was officially recognized as of the highest concern to the Spanish Crown, became a source of offense as soon as there was any evidence of a cooperative spirit between the priests and the Indians.

In 1572, impressed by the mighty bastions of the Inca fortress of Sacsayhuaman, Francisco de Toledo writes to King Philip II: "I saw your father (the Emperor) erecting the same kind of fortress on Spanish soil. His Majesty will recall the Alcázar of Toledo, which curbs that city community like a magnificent bridle . . .

The Spanish town of Nazca.

182

Uprisings and rebellions that used to be the order of the day here in Peru call for sharp measures to hold the community in check . . . The bulwarks of the law are not sufficient unless they are reinforced by such material means . . ." In his political testament he refers with great pride to the citadel of Cuzco: ". . . its construction caused great resentment in this city, to the Indians as well as the Spaniards, when they realized that it represented a curb and an instrument of diminishing the freedom that they had hitherto enjoyed." (Letter and political testament of Francisco de Toledo.)

During his term of office, the viceroy sought by means of an administrative system that intervened in the smallest details, to tap all the resources and strength of the country and make them yield the highest possible fiscal increase in revenue.

The unabating financial requirements of the king made it essential for Toledo to concentrate above all on remitting satisfactory amounts of gold and silver.

Between 1557 and 1572, the king's share of one fifth of the yield of the Potosí mines had fallen from 468,534 pesos to 216,517, namely by more than half. When Toledo left Peru in 1581, it had risen to 1,276,872 pesos. This was largely due to Toledo's introduction to Peru of a new process employing mercury in the working of the mines, which produced a substantial increase in the silver output. The process had previously been tried out in Mexico.

Nevertheless, although Peru was the country of precious metals, Toledo maintained that the two cornerstones of Peru's prosperity were the maize plantations and the llama herds.[36]

One of his decrees forbade the Spaniards to use the Indians as beasts of burden, a practice which had still not been eradicated and later prompted Humboldt to the sad observation, "In these climates, the whites are so lazy that every mining manager has one or two Indians in his service who are called *caballitos* (little horses). Each morning they allow themselves to be saddled and bent forward and using a stick to support themselves, they carry their master about. Travelers are recommended to use *caballitos* who are surefooted and have a gentle, even walk. I find it really distressing to hear people given attributes normally ascribed to horses and mules."

The Indians are supposed to have spoken well of Toledo, saying that the country had not been governed so well since the days of Túpac Yupanqui. Admittedly the Incas, and consequently their subjects, had their own very special concepts of what good government entailed. One important principle, based on experience, was that the Indians had to be urged to work. "Left idle, they went to ruin and became rebellious."[36] Cieza maintains that Huayna Cápac thought it good to mobilize the inhabitants of his lands for community projects in order to make them remain good subjects, even if it meant "moving a mountain from one place to another." For example, he is supposed to have had masonry for building brought from Cuzco to Quito. Even if this is an exaggeration, nevertheless the gigantic hewn stone blocks, some of them weighing over 1,000 tons, which were transported across deep valleys and were then piled up one above the other and fitted

The Indian women, practicing their art of weaving at home, soon provided the monks with a profitable subsidiary income.

to one another to form the fortresses and temples of Sacsayhuaman and Ollantaytambo, are evidence of levies of compulsory labor, just like the pyramids of the Egyptians.

"Viceroy Toledo widely adopted the Inca policy of resettlement (*mitmac*), and thus became the founder of the infamous *mita* system. Until then the Indians had lived in settlements at great distances from each other, sometimes quite alone in virtually inaccessible dwellings, preferably always in the proximity of a mountain, rock, spring, or some such holy place, from which they believed they had originated." In order to facilitate the conversion of the Indians to Christianity, and to simplify administration, these scattered settlements were now amalgamated into the larger locations that were customary in Spain.

In the centuries that followed, the irrigation installations and the agricultural terraces deteriorated. Restrictions were imposed on the private employment of Indian manpower, and instead one seventh of the entire male population was now condemned by law to forced labor and to the most appalling form of slavery and physical hardship. It sowed the seeds of embitterment, which bore fruit two hundred years later with the bloody Indian uprising, led by the insurgent José Gabriel Condorcanqui, Túpac Amaru II.[36]

Toledo took his duties very seriously and considered it necessary to go on a journey of inspection through all parts of the rugged empire. He was accompanied by a great body of technical advisers and was away for five years. The total distance covered by Toledo amounted to about 5,500 miles. During this "Vista General," he ruled the empire from the various places at which he stopped, as had been the practice of the Inca rulers. Toledo is said to have attended to about 2,000 official matters during this time.

Polo de Ondegardo, the notorious grave robber — the seated mummies of almost all the great Incas were discovered and burned by him — was on Toledo's staff. He was also an expert in Indian cults and religions, and the chroniclers Acosta, Garcilaso, and Cobo made extensive use of his notes and copied lengthy passages from them.

It was he who sponsored the famous "Informaciones de Toledo sobre el Imperio Incaico." With the help of interpreters bound under oath, a series of interrogations was conducted in front of witnesses, ranging over the most varied aspects of life in the conquered land. The reasons for the inquiries into burial customs and grave gifts are all too transparent. The catch questions about sexual "vices" and ritual human sacrifices were intended to provide the lawyers with the necessary material not only to justify the forceful imposition of a Christian government, but actively to promote it. The investigations of the compulsory labor traditionally performed for the Incas and *curacas* were closely related to the shaping of the Indian service obligations to the Spaniards, and to the legal formulation of the *encomiendas*. The remaining rights of the *curacas*, or "reyezuelos" (petty kings), as they were called by the Spaniards, were intended to guard against the continuing overwhelming prestige of the Inca descendants.

*IX   Detail from a cloak of the colonial period, with objects and stylistic elements
of ancient, Spanish, and Peruvian origin.*

Yet the information yielded by these investigations tend to make us overlook their motives. Even a sober administrator such as Toledo displayed such great interest in the curiosities and the history of the conquered land that he suggested, in a letter to Philip II, the founding of a museum devoted to the nature and art of ancient Peru. He recommended the sun disk, seized during the destruction of the Inca reservation of Vilcabamba, to the monarch's special care, saying that it would be worth sending to the pope in Rome as an emblem of the culture that had been won over to Christianity.[37]

The Spanish authors who were left to sift through these findings were highly individual characters. One of them was Pedro Sarmiento de Gamboa, the "cosmograph," seafarer, discoverer, mathematician, astrologer, and conquistador, who compiled the first coherent chronicle dealing with the history of the Incas. Although a very vigorous, worldly, rough conquistador, his mind was haunted by the most amazing fantasies and adventurous plans. Setting out from Peru, with his unerring instinct, he would undoubtedly have discovered Australia, whose existence had been suspected since antiquity, had it not been for his superiors and his crew, who had no confidence in the southwesterly course. As a result, only the Solomon Islands were discovered. During his unsuccessful pursuit of Francis Drake — who had attacked Spanish ships on the 13th of February, 1579, in the port of Callao near Lima, in the course of his audacious expedition around the world — he compiled maps of the Magellan Straits by making boat trips and climbing mountains, and left settlers there. They all perished of hunger, because Sarmiento fell into the hands of the English in the Atlantic and was therefore unable to send them supplies. During his internment in London, he made a very favorable impression on Walter Raleigh and Queen Elizabeth, and on his release he was entrusted with secret dispatches from England to Philip II. However, on the way from France to Spain he was captured by the Huguenots and languished for three years in a dark and damp prison. His hair went white and his teeth fell out. Philip finally succeeded in securing his release.

Signature of "Captain Sarmiento de Gamboa".

In the twenty years he spent in Peru, Sarmiento came into conflict with the Inquisition on several occasions. The main cause of his difficulties was astrological speculations, cabalistic practices, and magic manuscripts. The case of the Dominican monk Francisco de la Cruz, who had completely given himself up to occultism, became mentally deranged, and was finally put on trial by the Inquisition, as well as the sudden death of Sarmiento's first patron, the viceroy Nieva, made such arts, which until then had been very much in vogue, suspect. The Conde de Nieva, "a man of the world and a fatalist," was interested in astrology. It is told that on his arrival in Peru, he had his horoscope prepared by an astrologer, who predicted his imminent death to the day and hour. Nieva had accepted this with composure, and on the day and at the appointed hour, he had even reminded the astrologer of his prediction; the reply had been that the dangerous constellation had not yet passed. Leaving the Franciscan garden, where the conversation had taken place, the viceroy had then returned to his palace, left it again in the middle of the night, and was found dead in the street on the morning of the 19th of February, 1564. It is generally believed that he was beaten to death by hired assassins with sand-filled leather bags, at the instigation of a jealous husband.[36]

The mixture of more or less exact sciences and practices indulged in by this chronicler is remarkable. One witness maintained, "Sarmiento had shown him a finger ring and had stated how, by following secret preparations with this ring on his finger, while reciting an invocation aloud, he could look in a mirror and discover whatever he wanted to know."[36]

This was why Sarmiento's chronicle showed such an interest in all the Inca myths that touched on occult phenomena. It was his notes that preserved for us the story of the famous vision of Pachacútec, who saw his future empire in a crystal.

During an interrogation, when Sarmiento was being questioned by the Archbishop of Lima, a heated exchange took place. The Archbishop, who had been acting as Inquisitor for half a decade before the introduction of the Santo Oficio, quite openly said to the accused, that in dealing with his case he did not feel himself bound by any law. After six months' imprisonment, "when the opinions of various priests had also been consulted, sentence was finally passed on Sarmiento, who was to attend Mass in the main church of Lima as a penitent, candle in hand, wearing no outer garments." Further, the penalty of "banishment from all His Majesty's Indies and return to the Spanish empire," a sentence frequently imposed in Inquisition matters, was pronounced for immediate enactment ... Sarmiento at first appealed to the pope, but then recanted in the Audiencia on the 24th of May, and heard the required Mass ... and was allowed to remain."

But he continued to make no secret of his dislike of the clergy. Their distress at the scanty instruction of the Indians in the Christian faith left him unmoved, and on one occasion prompted him to the biting comment that Spain was none the better for the centuries of religious learning that had gone on there.[36]

Sarmiento's history of the Incas, like the pronouncements made throughout his life, is a belated product of the Renaissance — the crusading spirit had receded. The legal and political outlook dictated by his office are contained mainly in the preamble to his chronicle. His chief interest, however, is in the immense bulk of material dealing with the Inca legends and traditions, which he recommends to the readers as the "most remarkable and interesting reading about a barbarian nation."[39]

How little the prejudiced views of Francisco de Toledo were influenced by the understanding of the Inca world gained from the researches of Sarmiento and his colleagues can be seen from the maxims drawn up by his administrative officials:

"1. The lawful ruler of these lands is the King of Spain. The Incas and *curacas* are tyrants who have come to power by the oppression of the natives.

2. The King of Spain has the right to fill the *curaca* posts at his discretion, without waiting for resignations.

3. The King of Spain has the right to present and distribute land to Spaniards, as seems most beneficial to the administration of the land, without regard to objections that may arise out of the false assumption that the Incas are the lawful kings and the *kaziks* hereditary authorities.

4. In his position as the ruler of the land, and in the absence of legitimate successors to the Incas, who have become illegal, the King of Spain is the owner of all mines and minerals, of all possessions of the sun and the idols, of all treasures placed in graves, and of all estates and herds belonging to the Inca mummies, these being vacant and unowned and abandoned possessions.

5. As ruler of the land and lawful king, the King of Spain is responsible for the welfare and protection of the Indian population, and in fulfilling his obligations towards them as their guardian, which is made necessary by their weak-mindedness and lack of insight, he is entitled to make laws for their own good and to enforce the observation of these laws, against their will and even, if needs be, at the expense of their liberty: for example, to deter them from laziness and to keep them at an occupation beneficial to themselves or the state, since otherwise they will not, as has been proved, do anything at all; to rule them by intimidation; to forbid them to start legal proceedings without the permission of the law, or of their *curacas;* or to sell property, and whatever follows from this."[36]

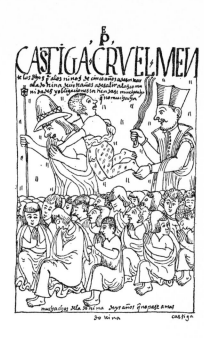

Christian instruction for the Indians in the time of Viceroy Francisco de Toledo.

The points listed above contain echoes of the *requerimiento,* which in Pizarro's time was read out to the natives by Fray Valverde at the very first landings in San Mateo, Manta, and the Gulf of Túmbez, and finally to the Inca Atahualpa himself in the market place of Cajamarca.

At that time, they still said that the Inca could enjoy the protection of the king, provided he submitted to the Spanish throne.

The Marqués de Cañete still abided by these rules in his dealings with Sayri Túpac. However, in Garcilaso's version, the Inca's reaction, as he sat at the archbishop's sumptuous table, while the details of the honors and incomes being granted to him were read aloud, was to take one of the silk fringes of the tablecloth between his fingers and say, "Previously, this whole tablecloth and all that is on it belonged to me, and now I and my house are being fobbed off with this little thread."[37]

Viceroy Toledo wanted nothing more to do with Inca authority, even though it persisted only in the impoverished reservation of Vilcabamba. Francisco de Toledo wrote to the King of Spain saying that the presence of this offensive fortress would inevitably lead to untoward occurrences and that the natives would be looking perpetually in that direction.

Titu Cusi Yupanqui and Túpac Amaru, the sons of Manco, were regarded as the lawful heirs to the throne of Cuzco, not only in the shelter of Vilcabamba, but by the Indian population and many of the half-castes of mixed Spanish and Indian blood living in large areas of Peru.

Toledo's guiding principles and maxims of government, and his conduct towards the last Inca, were not endorsed by all the Spaniards. They provoked intense protest from a large section of the clergy in Peru, particularly from the Jesuits, who had defended the principles of Bishop Las Casas in word and deed not only in the well-known Guaraní missions in Paraguay, but throughout the whole of South and North America.

It was against the spirit of Las Casas and the advocates of Charles V's "New Laws" — regarded as exaggerated and dangerous by Philip II's officials — that the gigantic paper war, with all its inquiries, evidence, and dedications, was unleashed by Toledo's faction. The *Nuevas Leyes* were held responsible for everything that had gone wrong since the arrival of the first unfortunate viceroy, Núñez Vela. One of the appointed experts writes angrily: "The influence of Father Las Casas and the scruples that he aroused in the consciences of the emperor and the theologians were such that His Majesty was almost prepared to let these empires slip back into the hands of the Inca tyrants. This father convinced the whole of Spain, from the king and his council down to the most insignificant little monk, that the Inca, the *kaziks,* and the *curacas* were entitled to rule the land and wield royal power, and he even designated the Incas as the legitimate kings of these lands and the *curacas* as rightful lords." In his dedication, Sarmiento goes so far as to say that this difference of opinion was inspired by the devil and that Las Casas was prompted by personal grievances." We see how the royal forces and the priesthood, who were friendly to the Indians, had both initially been united in their attack on the Spanish overlords, but now split up into opposing camps.

In the words of one of the above-mentioned testimonies, "The attempt to prove the tyrannical nature of Inca rule distressed the clergy as much as if it were their own kingdom that was coming under the hammer."

The clergy used every means at their disposal in their opposition to Toledo. Like Montesinos in Española and Las Casas in Nicaragua before them, they refused to give absolution to participants in campaigns of the viceroy's of which they did not approve.

The Jesuit José de Acosta, a man who came into close contact with the viceroy, enlivened the debate surrounding the maxims of Toledo's men with a no less massive retaliatory document.[40] Here are just a few of his statments: ". . . the use of arms against Indians is only permissible in cases of genuine need . . . the arguments put forward by a few advisers — one if almost inclined to call them flatterers — at court to support the king's orders . . . are completely illogical and legally indefensible in their reference to the authority of the Incas and Aztec rulers and in their pretention that Inca rule was a tyrannical usurpation and the earlier system of small state rule only an interim arrangement in anticipation of a lawful king . . . To wrest sovereignty from the oppressors — if such they be — of the Indians in this way is surely no better than retrieving stolen property from a thief and then keeping it oneself . . . Do the crimes of others entitle us to act likewise? . . . This is quite absurd and is all too reminiscent of some of Aesop's fables!" . . . "Moreover," Acosta maintains, "the sovereignty in these lands, whether usurped or no, has lasted for more than 600 years." This happens to be untrue in the case of the Aztecs; the submission of her tribute peoples had only been effected a short time before, and even the great Inca empire did not have such an exceptionally long tradition. Yet this hardly detracts from the argument of this cleric, an argument inspired by similar feelings to those voiced by 19th-century scholars, in particular the Anglo-Saxon ones, that anticipates many fundamental principles of modern international law. Acosta concludes, "The example of most other empires will confirm that when a power has ruled for a very long time, this in itself is enough to make it obsolete, but in changing it, it is not necessary to shatter all the existing human institutions. Admittedly, there is hardly any kingdom that has not come into existence by violence. It is no coincidence that in antiquity the same word was used for 'king' and 'tyrant.' But to install an absent prince in a community of a polycratic structure without the consent of its members and against their express wishes — if that is not oppression, then no tyrant has ever existed."

So we see that those who shared the views of the saintly zealot Las Casas, had in no way been shaken in their convictions by the testimonies and inquiries into the history of Peru. The doctrine of the Bishop of Chiapa remained a powerful force.

The same standards by which Toledo had condemned the Incas were now applied to him.

It was not his merits as an administrative official, or his scholarship or legal ability, that earned Toledo his place in history, but the detestation that he incurred by having the last Inca, Túpac Amaru, ferreted out from his hiding place and making him die on the executioner's block. This was the one single successful military campaign of Toledo's term of office.

In 1572, a troop of twenty men penetrated the Andes of Vilcabamba. Their leader was the same Martín García Oñaz de Loyola who had married the daughter of Sayri Túpac. Sarmiento de Gamboa was also present. The warlike Titu Cusi had meanwhile died, so they captured Manco's youngest son, the timorous Túpac Amaru, and took him back to Cuzco, together with his relations and sundry followers. "Loyola led the Inca through the streets with a golden chain around his neck, in faithful imitation of ancient Peruvian military custom . . . When the procession reached the house of Viceroy Toledo . . . who was watching the spectacle out of the window, in the company of several church dignitaries . . . Captain Loyola ordered the captives to remove their *llautus*, and the Inca his *borla*. However, they refused to do so and only touched their *llautus*, inclining their heads in the direction of the viceroy's window. Túpac Amaru answered the command by saying, 'This viceroy is nothing more than a *yanacona*, a subject of the king!' Whereupon, Loyola let go of the gold chain in a fury and struck him twice on the neck, probably in the belief that he was thereby performing a service for His Majesty and doing the viceroy a favor. Instead, his behavior struck all those who saw it as unworthy of a noble *caballero*."[41]

Despite violent resistance, Túpac Amaru was put on trial. Francisco de Toledo had decided on the death sentence from the outset, as he wanted no one in Peru to recognize any king other than Philip II.

Martín García de Loyola follows the ancient Peruvian custom (see below) and leads the captured Inca Túpac Amaru to Cuzco with a chain around his neck. A second Spaniard carries the *huaoqui* and the golden image of the sun.

"The religious orders in Peru interposed on his behalf, but in vain; the Bishop of Popayán came from Colombia to implore the viceroy on his knees, but in vain; the entreaties of the unfortunate Inca begging to be sent to Spain as a *yanacona* of the king were also in vain. Nothing succeeded in averting the decision to execute the Inca ... The Inca allowed himself to be baptized. In the great square in Cuzco, a tall scaffold was erected and swathed in black. An endless mass of Indians had rallied together there."[42] "... it was scarcely possible to make one's way through the streets. Cuzco had never been so near to disaster as now. Even the Spaniards, who had also moved out on to the balconies in large numbers, cursed the viceroy and his counsellors aloud, and Toledo himself appeared wearing mourning ... As the Inca mounted the scaffold ... the screaming of the Indians in their thousands echoed round the square ... and remarkable to relate ... when the execution squad ordered the crowd to be silent, poor Túpac Amaru raised his hands and gave a quick clap. At this everyone fell silent and became calm; it was now as if there were not a single living soul in the whole square, and there was no lamentation and no sound to be heard as the head of the Inca fell. Such was the obedience, the fear, and the reverence the Indians had for their lord."[43]

With the death of the last reigning Inca of Vilcabamba, the great Peruvian kingdom had been extinguished. Throughout almost the entire subsequent colonial period, members of the collateral lines and a series of *curacas* kept certain of the hereditary privileges guaranteed by the crown, which apart from considerable incomes — the taxes of large areas passed through their hands — were chiefly nominal. They were given coats of arms and titles such as "Maestre de Campo," "Cacique Principal," and "Alférez Real" (royal standard bearer). In this capacity they were allowed to head the procession with the flag at the feast of Saint James.[44] At first, they continued to wear the full Inca attire, but gradually this was modified by European fashion, until it was hard to distinguish them from a *hidalgo* of what had meanwhile become Bourbon Spain.

In the late 18th century, when educated and enlightened Spaniards, mestizos, and Indians delighted in the Spanish theater and French literature and turned with reawakened interest to the cultivation of the Quecha language and drama,[45] and the masses, despite repeated reforms, were sinking into ever more oppressive economic enslavement, the name of Inca suddenly gained new strength and a menacing ring. José Gabriel Condorcanqui, a mestizo highly esteemed by the church and officialdom, was a *curaca* of the region between Cuzco and Lake Titicaca, an area hallowed by ancient Inca tradition, and a direct descendent of the last Inca of Vilcabamba. After lengthy hesitation, in 1780 as Túpac Amaru II, he placed himself at the head of a rebellion against the corrupt tax administration, which shook the whole of Bolivia and half of Argentina. He relied on Indians, mestizos, and creoles (Spaniards born in Peru), but was defeated by the resistance of the *curacas*, who feared for their incomes. Túpac Amaru did not enter Cuzco as a victor, but like his ancestor, to be executed.[46]

One generation later the white settlers brought the rule of the Spanish crown to an end in Central and South America. But as South America developed its independence, conflict between various conceptions of constitutional government arose. The idea of Inca supporters for a constitutional monarchy along British lines, with a parliment of Indian *kaziks* as representatives of the nobility, once again gained favor. The Argentinian politician Manuel Belgrano made such a suggestion to the Congress of Tucamán in 1818 and, according to a contemporary letter, Manco Capác Inca "a descendant of the old kings of Peru," brought "his claim into play."

However, as with the ambitions of princes' sons and daughters arriving from Europe to claim thrones in the New World, this project too foundered, for the republican Americas allowed no enforced restorations, and the Indian nobility lost the rights it still possessed under the Spanish crown, or died out.

Even today, social structures from pre-Spanish times have persisted in many places in the Andes and as the British archaeologist G. Bushnell has observed ". . . in Peru there are still many pure Indian communities reflecting the traditions of the ancient *ayllus* that once formed the basis of the social pyramid of the Inca empire."[47]

In 1954, I chose "Huayna Cápac, Huáscar, and Atahualpa — Investigations into the History of the Last Decade of the Inca Empire," as the subject for my doctorate in Munich. That work was the point of departure for this book. The next years, my husband, who is an architect, and I worked together in libraries and institutes at home and abroad. We extended the range of our subject to include the early period of the Spanish colonial period, in which the economic, social, and religious conflicts between the conquerors and the defeated really emerged.

From 1948 to 1954 we were greatly assisted by my supervisor, Professor Ubbelohde-Doering, who placed the whole of his private library freely at our disposal and permitted us to live and work in Toerring Castle at Seefeld, surrounded by the Peruvian textiles and ceramics of the Völkerkundemuseum of Munich, which were housed there. We also recall with pleasure the hours spent in conversation with Dr. Disselhoff, who was Professor Ubbelohde-Doering's assistant in Seefeld at that time.

We wish to express our sincere thanks to the institutions and individuals who have contributed to the making of this book by their advice and information and by supplying photographs:

The Foreign Ministry, Bonn; the Ministerio de Educación, Lima; the German Embassies in Madrid and Lima; the Peruvian Embassy, Madrid; the Spanish Embassy, Bonn; the consulates of Peru and Bolivia in Munich; the Archivo General de Indias, Seville; the Biblioteca Nacional del Perú, Lima; the Biblioteca Nacional, Madrid; the Biblioteca del Palacio, Madrid; the Bavarian State Library, Munich, the Museo de América, Madrid; the Museo Naval, Madrid; the Museum für Völkerkunde, Munich; the Museum für Völkerkunde, Berlin; the Lindenmuseum, Stuttgart; the British Museum, London; Juan M. Baca, publishers, Lima; Imprenta Góngora, S. L., Madrid; Paul Haupt, publishers, Bern; Gebrüder Mann, publishers, Berlin; Thames & Hudson, publishers, London;

In particular we should like to mention by name Mrs. P. Fernandez Vega, Vda. de Ferrandis, Miss M. L. Vazquez de Parga and Mrs. Rostworowski de Diez Canseco of Madrid; and also Mr. F. Anton, Munich; Prof. Ballesteros Gaibrois, Madrid; Dr. Briesemeister, Munich; Captain Cabrera, Madrid; Dr. Eisleb, Berlin; Dr. Fauser, Munich; Dr. Finke, Munich; Fritz Jäger, Stuttgart; Dr. Kutscher, Berlin; Dr. Lommel, Munich; Dr. Modesto Suarez, Bonn; C. Morales Arnao, Lima; José de la Peña, Seville; Baron von Reitzenstein, Munich; Hans Reutimann, Männedorf, Switzerland; Colonel Schwarz, Madrid; R. A. Skelton, London; Prof. Dr. Trimborn, Bonn; Prof. Luis Valcarcel, Lima; Prof. Dr. Zerries, Munich.

Our especial thanks go to Mr. Karl Baur, head of the Callway publishing firm in Munich, and to his wife Dr. Baur-Heinhold, and particularly to his assistants, Dr. Hermann Rinn, Mr. J. Thierry, and Günther Mehling. *Lieselotte Engl*

Chronological list of Peruvian styles (according to Kauffmann-Doig) referred to in this book.

Paracas-Necropolis 200—900 A.D.
(Paraxas Peninsula on the south coast of Peru.) The multicolored, embroidered cloths used to wrap the bodies found in the Paracas Necropolis are among the finest textiles not merely of ancient Peru, but in the entire world.

Recuay (Huaylas) 200—900 A. D.
Recuay is a small locality on the upper reaches of the River Santa in the northern highlands of Peru. The main places for this style are situated in the surrounding area. Negative painting with the aid of wax is characteristic of this region. The pattern was overlaid with wax, and after the vessel had been dipped in dye, the wax layer was removed, thus revealing the design.

Mochica 2d—9th century A.D.
(Northern coast of Peru, for the most part in the valleys of Chicama, Moche, and Virú.)
The potters of the Mochica culture, in addition to portraying their many gods and demons, also depicted their own world in realistic scenes of everyday life. Portraits of warriors in particular occur frequently.

Late Chimú 13th—15th century.
By the fifteenth century the Chimú empire extended along the 550 miles of coast from the border of present-day Ecuador down approximately as far as Lima, and was annexed by the Inca empire in about 1460, shortly before the Spanish conquest.

Inca (Imperial) 14th—16th century.
The syncretism in the areas of art, religion, mythology, and philosophy was achieved in ancient Peru under the rule of the Incas. This is characterized by a humanization of the themes portrayed, by strong stylization and ultimately by a departure from figurative forms.
The cultural periods listed here overlap to a considerable extent. Their exact dating is only gradually and partially being established by means of a combination of archaeological and technological means, by the radio-carbon process.

1492	Discovery and colonization of South America and Peru. On the 12th of October, Columbus discovers the island of Guanahani in the Bahamas and names it San Salvador.
1502	As a young priest, Las Casas arrives in the New World for the first time under Governor Ovando. He never reaches Peru.
1513	Vasco Núñez de Balboa discovers the Caribbean Sea, east of present-day Panama.
1517	Execution of Vasco Núñez de Balboa after a sham trial.
1519—1521	Hernando Cortes conquers Mexico.
1524	14th of November, Francisco Pizarro's first voyage of discovery with two ships along the west coast of Colombia. Two cartographers map the coastline.
1526—1527	Pizarro's second expedition; a trading *balsa* is captured and three Indians are retained as interpreters; first major spoils of gold, silver, vessels, and textiles from the Inca empire; discovery of the coast of Ecuador (Esmeraldas and Coaque); major losses through hunger, sickness, and hostile Indians; thirteen Spaniards maintain their position on the Isla de Gallo; visit to Túmbez and other north Peruvian coastal towns; return to Panama; emissaries report the Spanish ship's call at Túmbez to Huayna Cápac. Two Spaniards, who remained on land, are supposed to be taken to him, but never arrive in Tumibamba.
1527	Huayna Cápac dies of the plague.
1528—1529	Francisco Pizarro in Spain. Imprisonment for debt in Seville. Audience with Charles V in Toledo. 26th of June, 1929, *Capitulación de Toledo* (treaty with the Crown, wherein conditions and payments are set out). Appointment as viceroy and commander-in-chief of the expedition for the conquest of Peru.
1530	Francisco Pizarro returns to Panama. His brothers Hernando, Gonzalo, and Juan and his cousin Pedro, sail with him.
ca. 1530—1532	War between the brothers Huáscar and Atahualpa.
1531—1532	Third expedition sets out from Panama with 130 men; unsuccessful attempt to conquer Ecuador; seven months' march overland from the equator to the Gulf of Guayaquil; fruitless attempts to establish strongholds on the island of Puná and at Túmbez.
1532	Atahualpa sole ruler of the Tahuantinsuyu. 24th of September, Francisco Pizarro sets out from San Miguel de Piura for the interior.
1532	15th of November, arrival in Cajamarca. 16th of November, Inca Atahualpa taken captive.
1533	The Inca treasure assembled in Cajamarca; Spaniards visit Pachacámac and Cuzco in small groups accompanied by escorts selected by Atahualpa. June, 1533, Hernando Pizarro returns to Spain and delivers the royal fifth part of Atahualpa's ransom to Charles V.; execution of Atahualpa. 15th of November, Pizarro and Inca Manco enter Cuzco.

Two more Spanish conquistadors appear in Ecuador. Benalcázar gains access to the highlands, founds Riobamba and Quito; Pedro de Alvarado from Guatamala lands with the largest invading army yet, a fleet, and 4,000 Indians from Puerto Viejo in Central America. Armies of Atahualpa's generals Quizquiz and Rumiñahui wiped out in Ecuador by Benalcázar, Alvarado, Almagro, and Hernando de Soto, with the aid of Inca auxiliary troops. Alvarado paid off by Francisco Pizarro and leaves Peru.   1534

18th of January, foundation of la Ciudad de los Reyes (Lima).   1535
Almagro's expedition to Chile. Return of Hernando Pizarro to Cuzco. According to the *Real Provisión* (decree of special importance) he brings back with him, Cuzco falls under the jurisdiction of Francisco Pizarro. Massive Indian uprising led by Manco. Hernando, Juan, and Gonzalo Pizarro, with 200 Spaniards and 80 horses, besieged for one year in Cuzco.

Inca Manco abandons the siege of Cuzco and retreats to Vilcabamba in the highlands.   1536

Francisco Pizarro made "Marqués." Almagro seizes the city of Cuzco, takes Hernando Pizarro prisoner, and appoints Paullu Túpac as "Sapay." Temporary reconciliation of parties and Hernando Pizarro set free.   1537

Pizarrists win at Salinas, and Almagro executed in Cuzco. Hernando Pizarro falls into disfavor at court and serves a twenty-one year prison sentence in Spain.   1538

The Bogotá plateau is discovered simultaneously by three conquistadors — Benalcázar (setting out from Quito), Quesada (from the north), and Nikolaus Federmann (from the Dutch colony in Ecuador).

Further isolated encounters with Manco's forces.   1538—1540
Gonzalo made governor of Quito.   1538
Gonzalo makes expedition into the Amazon region in search of the legendary Eldorado (Orellana discovers the mouth of the Amazon).   1539—1542

Francisca Pizarro murdered in Lima on the 26th of June by followers of Almagro.   1541
C. Vaca de Castro arrives in Peru. Succeeds Pizarro as governor.

Short-lived rule by the Chilean party under the mestizo Diego de Almagro. The royal president Vaca de Castro gradually gains control. Execution of the young Almagro. Blasco Núñez Vela, the viceroy, brings Charles V's *Nuevas Leyes* from Spain for the protection of the Indians.   1541—1542

Uprising of the *encomenderos* against the Crown. Gonzalo Pizarro leads the rebels. Assassination of Manco Inca.   1544

Charles V sends Pedro de la Gasca to Peru as plenipotentiary extraordinary.   1545

Defeat and murder of the viceroy Blasco Núñez Vela in Ecuador. Gonzalo Pizarro is uncrowned king of western south America, from Panama to the Magellan Straits.   1546

Pedro de la Gasca arrives in Túmbez in June; unsuccessful attempt to avert civil war by a general amnesty.   1547

Defeat of Gonzalo Pizarro at Sacsayhuaman. Executed, 9th of April.   1548
Pedro de la Gasca returns to Spain.   1550

1553	Part I of Pedro Cieza de Leon's chronicle, commissioned by Pedro de la Gasca and published in Seville.
1550—1556	Antonio de Mendoza's year of office as viceroy followed by interregnum; second uprising by *encomenderos*, under Francisco Hernández Girón; continuing instability caused by feuds among the Spaniards and attacks by Negro deserters. The Indians, oppressed more than ever before, leave their fields and settlements.
1556—1560	Third viceroy, Andrés Hurtado de Mendoza, Marqués de Cañete: "True security will be achieved in this country when men no longer call themselves soldiers, but farmers." Peace treaty with Inca Sayri Túpac of Vilcabamba.
1558	Death of Charles V, on 21st of September in San Yuste.
1560—1564	Conde de Nieva, fourth viceroy.
1569	Fifth viceroy, Francisco de Toledo, takes office.
1572	Abolition of Inca autonomy in Vilcabamba; execution of Túpac Amaru in Cuzco.
1780—1781	Rebellion, defeat, and execution in Cuzco of José Gabriel Condorcanqui (Túpac Amaru II).
1810—1825	Wars of independence and secession from Spain by the South American colonies.

INCA RULERS

For want of exact dates, those listed below are only approximate.

1. Manco Cápac (ca. 1200)
2. Sinchi Roca
3. Lloque Yupanqui
4. Mayta Cápac
5. Cápac Yupanqui
6. Inca Roca
7. Yahuar Huácac
8. Viracocha
9. Pachacútec Yupanqui (1438—1471)
10. Túpac Yupanqui (1471—1493)
11. Huayna Cápac (1493—1527)
12. Huáscar, in Cuzco (1527—1532)
13. Atahualpa, from 1527 regent in Quito; assumed the royal insignia in approximately 1528 in Tumibamba. Condemned to death by a Spanish court martial, headed by Francisco Pizarro, and died by the garrote in Cajamarca in 1533.

Notes on the religious and mythical motifs that appear in the illustrations and color plates

For the ancient Peruvians art was the magic-religious language by means of which they could communicate not only with other men, but above all with the gods.

To interpret ancient Peruvian art, it is necessary to have a knowledge of the Andes and of the neighboring cultures. Here, we are still at the very beginning. Let us start by taking two of the mystical religious symbols of ancient Peru that have been interpreted — the mythical figure with the two scepters, and the votary holding the sacrificial instrument in one hand and the severed human head in the other. These two archetypes of religious primeval experience have been artistically portrayed in the ceramics, sculpture, and textiles of the varying periods and regions of ancient Peru. Instead of the two scepters, the figure sometimes carried weapons or sprouting branches, always as a sign of omnipotence — "might in both hands."

The sacrificer either holds the severed head in his left hand, lets it hang down (sometimes there are whole chains of them), or has it fastened to his own body. The weapon may be a club or a knife. The figure with the scepters is often surrounded with rays in the form of scrolls and snakes — symbols of light, lightning, and other meteorological phenomena. The most famous example of this is the Raimondi monolith. According to some archaeologists, this is Viracocha, the creator of the world, while others maintain it is the sun.

Both these beings emerge early on throughout Peru; they are also portrayed at the height of the Inca empire and live on in a Christian guise in post-Columbian painting and architectural sculpture.

The meaning of the figure with the severed head is also puzzling. Its feline teeth relate it to the myth of the creator, or "huari." The head it carries in its hands is not always an enemy trophy head and symbol of war, but is frequently a straightforward blood offering to make the earth fruitful again. In the figurative sense it represents the fruit and nourishment that man earnestly longs for and hopes to win from the gods by sacrifice. Textiles from the Paracas period portray fertility as such in a quite uncanny and horrific manner. Here the arms are no longer the only carriers of trophy or animal heads. The phallus becomes a snake with a triangular head, its tail ending in a feline creature, while the other snakes emerge from its head, radiating outwards like the rays of the sun, with animal or human heads or even bodies at the ends, which in turn again have trophy heads hanging from the hips or the arms.

The single- or double-headed snake is also a common symbol. The one-headed snake personifies the primeval mother of water, river, and lightning. She descends from the divine regions, and as a result of her efforts, men and animals come into the world, distinguished by six fingers, a harelip, or some other such abnormality. Such people frequently become soothsayers or medicine men.

The two-headed snake is the primeval mother of the plant world, symbol of the tree and the rainbow. Disease and decay are the plagues with which she afflicts people, animals, and plants. (cf. Valcárcel I, 66, 74 ff. and 80 ff.).

I Mummy mask, height 10¹/₄ in., found in a chamber in the base of the so-called "Moon Pyramid" (Huaca de la Luna) near Moche on the north Peruvian coast. Approx. 500 A.D. The pierced ears probably held ornamental plugs, which are now lost. The Mochica masks aimed at a highly realistic portrait-like effect. "They are placed on the face of the dead person, and preserve his features beyond death" (Eckert, p. 20). The gold masks of the Inca mummies, described by the early Spanish chroniclers, are unfortunately no longer in existence.
Lindenmuseum, Stuttgart. Photo: Ferdinand Anton, from his book, *Alt-Peru und seine Kunst*, Leipzig, 1962.

II God or demon in animal and human form, from a textile from the Paracas Necropolis, with *tumi* (knife), ruler's staff, *llautu*-like mask, and numerous snake-like extremities, symbolizing fertility and power. (The large crown on the head and the two smaller ones on the extremities are in Nazca style.)
This very stylized portrayal corresponds in detail to the religious and mythological beliefs of ancient Peru and even to the visionary experiences attributed to individual persons, such as Inca Pachacútec's encounter with the sun god at the Susurpuquio source, described by Bernabé Cobo (see p. 13).
Length of the strip 8¹/₄ in. Norbert Mayrock Collection. Museum für Völkerkunde, Munich. Photo: Braunmüller.

III Above: four figures in rich apparel, wearing headdresses in the shape of a crescent moon, are pictured on the earplugs. Each holds a bird and is accompanied by a monkey and a poorly-dressed man. Possibly a sacrificial scene. Diameter about 5¹/₂ in. Length of the plug, which looks like a hole in the center, 4³/₄ in. Textile Museum, Washington, D.C. Photo: F. Anton, Munich.

III Below: Gold figurines, one male and two female, ranging in height between 2²/₅

and 3³/₅ in. Inca style. They were mostly dressed as dolls, with only the head visible. Textile Museum, Washington. Photo: F. Anton, Munich.

IV Mummy of a noblewoman, partly unwrapped and again prepared, from the Paracas Necropolis. In 1925, Julio Tello and his assistants found 429 well-preserved crouching mummies in a confined area of the Paracas peninsula on the south Peruvian coast. They varied in size and in the richness and amount of grave gifts with which they were buried, according to the social rank of the person concerned. This unique find was preserved by the dry climate and the saltpeter content of the soil in this region.
The large mummy bundles consisted of many layers of delicate cloth covering the actual corpse — these cotton wrappings are often up to 65 ft. long and 13 ft. wide — and were accompanied by numerous burial gifts such as dried meat, maize, and beans, as well as jewelry and again, delicately embroidered cloths, folded very small. In the uplands it was also customary to preserve the mummies artificially, especially members of the royal Inca dynasty, but even so, they did not keep well because of the dampness of the climate. The mummies of the Inca kings — one of them was vividly described by the first three Spaniards to visit Cuzco (see p. 122) — were all burnt at the time of Viceroy Toledo.
Museo de América, Madrid. Photo: Oronoz, Madrid.

V Above: Fragment of cloth from the Paracas Necropolis.
Museo de América, Madrid. Photo: Oronoz, Madrid.
Below: Painted wooden goblet (*kero*).
Museo de América, Madrid. Photo: Oronoz, Madrid.

VI Details from three Paracas Necropolis cloths. Mayrock and Hart Collection.

Museum für Völkerkunde, Munich. Photo: Braunmüller, Munich.

VII Detail of a cloth in the style of the Tiahuanaco coast, ca. 900—1200 A.D. Transitional stage leading towards the complete abstraction of the later Inca style. In this textile, the essential characteristic of the jaguar (eye and fang teeth) are still just recognizable and are portrayed in sophisticated and partly reciprocal geometric shapes. The design is extremely attractive.
Museum für Völkerkunde, Munich. Photo: Braunmüller, Munich.

VIII Dancer in a condor mask. In vol. 2, XX, of his "Comentarios," Garcilaso gives a vivid description of how, even in the late Inca period, the regional lords (*curacas*) appeared and danced, wearing animal masks at the Inti-Raymi festival. "Some of them came dressed exactly like Hercules is usually portrayed, namely in a lion's skin and head, in which the Indian would insert his own head, because they prided themselves on being descended from lions (pumas) ... and others appeared with the huge black and white wings of the bird they call "kuntur" (condor) ... The Yuncas delighted in the most repulsive masks and figures imaginable ... and behaved like madmen and simpletons ..." Woven fabric from the Paracas Necropolis.
C. D. O. Collection, Lima. Photo: F. Anton, Munich.

IX Detail from a vicuña fabric covered in small figures, early colonial period. Indians with bows and arrows, Spaniards with daggers, a mermaid with a guitar, the famous *kantu* plant, and many American and European animals (llamas, monkeys, birds, cattle, horses) and strange vases are worked into the design.
Museum für Völkerkunde, Munich. Photo: Braunmüller, Munich.

1 *Manco Cápac*, and 2 *Mama Ocllo*, colonial oil paintings from the Copacabana Monastery in Lima.

The attributes of the Inca office shown here correspond fairly accurately with Inca tradition, even the puma heads on the shoulders, knees, and instep of the feet, although these are regarded as Spanish features by J. H. Rowe in his very instructive essay on similar portraits of the Cuzco school (*Colonial Portraits of Inca Nobles*). Describing Inca attire, Bernabé Cobo (14, II) expressly mentions "mascaroncillos de oro y plata, y también de lana" on the shoulders, the knees, and the insteps; lion or puma heads frequently appear together with the figures of men or gods in ancient Peruvian textiles and ceramics, and are also described in the legends of divine apparitions (see p. 13).
Photo: A. Guillén, Lima.

3 The existing literature does not make it plain for whom Machu Picchu, 2625 ft. up in the Urubamba valley, was built. Could it have been an independent temple city, or one that was subject to Cuzco and later taken over by the Incas (Sarmiento mentions a whole list of centers such as these in the neighborhood of Cuzco), or was it a late Inca frontier fortress against the Chanca who had been driven back into the eastern Andes? Photo: Paolo Koch, Zurich.

4 The construction of agricultural terraces of closely fitted stones was known since antiquity in Peru, especially in the coastal region. According to the chronicler Pedro Sarmiento (10th chronicle), it was Inca Pachacútec who first promoted them on a large scale in the uplands, where the soil often had to be brought from far outlying areas.
Photo: Hans Reutimann from his book, *Reich der Sonne*, published by Katzmann KG, Tübingen, and Paul Haupt, Bern.

5 Bastions of Sacsayhuaman.
Photo: Paolo Koch, Zurich.

6 Tampu Machay. The building consists of two lower terrace walls, and two upper ones supported by the actual mountain. The stream is ingeniously trapped in a ledge above them and runs down from there. The upper wall contains four regular trapezoid niches.

We are reminded here of the myths about the origin of the highland peoples and tribes, and in particular of the first appearance of Mancho Cápac in Pacaritampu "out of the central one of three windows" (see p. 11). Springs and caves were the *pacarinas* (places of origin) and thereby favored *huacas* (places of veneration). The Inca Pachacútec, after much fasting, had had his famous vision of the sun god by the spring of Susurpuquio.
Photo: Hans Reutimann.

7 Wooden jaguar's head, Inca style.
Larrea Collection, Museo de América, Madrid.
Photo: Oronoz, Madrid.

8 Wooden ritual container (*paccha*), Inca style. The liquid (water from holy springs, or *chicha* beer) flows out of the beak protruding from the round container, which symbolizes both a spring and a voracious bird, and rests on the back of a (painted) jaguar. The liquid is caught in the square drip cup below and from there it flows under the second creature (in other *pacchas* this is devoured by the larger creature, symbolizing sacrifice) and then follows the winding water course until it comes to the end.
Larrea Collection, Museo de América, Madrid.
Photo: Oronoz, Madrid.

9 R. Carrion Cachot has this to say (p. 13) about the great stone of Sayhuite, or Concacha: "... Geographical phenomena are depicted on the [natural] uneven surfaces of the block — mountains, valleys, ravines, perpendicular precipices; lakes at high altitudes, rivers, and watercourses ... canals and irrigation installations flowing in various directions, reservoirs, ponds, cascades, etc. ... Pumas and monkeys watch over these holy places ... At the sources of the streams and rivers, and in the reservoirs there are deities, sometimes in the form of a human couple (some of them personify sun and moon), and on platforms and terraces animals mate as a cult symbol of the fertility of the fields. ... Side by side with the anthropomorphic deities, maize plants ... llamas ... and other creatures are portrayed on sacrificial altars ..." Various forms of aquatic animals (e. g. crabs) suggest that the sea coast is also represented on this stone.

Four large feline creatures appear along the edge of the stone where the channel opens into holes facing the four points of the compass. The best preserved part, depicted on the upper surface, are various temples, houses, terraces, steps, and the irrigation canals. These were not simply intended to enhance the map-like quality of the stone, but provided channels for the sacrificial liquid (water, or *chicha*) to run down, similar to the pipe-shaped sacrificial container described above.
Photo: A. Guillén, Lima.

10 Over life-size portrait head of grey granite, popularly referred to as "Inca Viracocha".
Museo de América, Madrid.
Photo: Oronoz, Madrid.

11 The Spaniards found gold treasure weighing approximately 2,200 pounds in the pyramid of Etén. The early chronicler Lizárraga writes: "What happened to this gold, I don't know; it vanished like smoke."
Photo: Museum für Völkerkunde, Berlin-Dahlem.

12 Chanchán.
Photo: Museum für Völkerkunde, Berlin-Dahlem.

13 Paramonga, about 125 miles north of Lima, probably built shortly before the Inca conquest.
Photo: Otto Zerries, Munich.

14 Mangomarca.
Photo: Otto Zerries, Munich.

15 Vessel. Mochica culture.
Museo Nacional de Arqueología, Lima.
Photo: Braunmüller, Munich.

16—17 Scene with many figures (worship of a war god, battle scene or victory celebration with captives, herald with horn, and counting board); dark brown flowing drawing on a light grey stirrup vase, from the north Peruvian coast, ca. 500 A.D. The moon crescent decoration on the helmets is characteristic of the Mochica culture.
Museum für Völkerkunde, Munich.
Photo: Braunmüller, Munich.

18—19 On the clay reliefs at Chanchán the rainbow is combined with the form of a two-headed snake (symbol of fertility).
Photo: Otto Zerries, Munich.

20 Portrait of Huayna Cápac. Colonial oil painting. Copacabana Monastery, Lima.
Photo: A. Guillén, Lima.

21 The Sun Temple of Vilcas was already half in ruins and "overgrown with grass" by the time the chronicler Cieza saw it in about 1550. But Cieza knew some Spaniards who had still seen the temple intact and who told him of the gold and jewel decorations on the holy seats and of the other treasures. Vilcas lay in the heart of the Inca empire between Cuzco and Jauja. In front of the temple there was an enormous polygonal area, some 500 ft. across and 650 ft. long, where the three major Inca roads merged — the highway of Inca Yupanqui, that of Túpac, and the "royal highway" of Huayna Cápac. Apart from the trapezoidal portal, the construction was quite different from the Inca buildings in the Cuzco region. The perpendicular style and the great flight of steps going all the way up are reminiscent of the temple pyramids of Central America, though not of the same quality, and of the ziggurats in Mesopotamia. Ruins of similar terraced pyramids, such as at Vilcas, but dating from a much earlier period, have been found in the highlands of central and northern Peru and Bolivia. They are also mentioned in the texts as fortresses hostile to the Incas during Huayna Cápac's war against Quito.
Photo: A. Guillén, Lima.

22 "Intihuantana" in Machu Picchu. The irregular but precisely sculptured pillar and its socle create a very awe-inspiring atmosphere. Its name alone, "sun seat", shows that it was one of the famous sun huacas. It is thought that it was used as an observation point for watching the position of the sun and shade. Apart from this, there seems to be a certain similarity with the stone pillars, known as "usnu" in the center of the great square in Cuzco and elsewhere, where the Inca himself used to offer sacrifices at major festivals.
Photo: F. Anton, Munich.

23 Pictorial map of Sacsayhuaman. This watercolor of 1778, measuring approximately 32 1/2 in. by 19 1/4 in., by the Spanish "Sargento maior de Ynfanteria don Ramón de Arechaga y Calvo," is not just amusing on account of its figures; it also has an instructive accompanying text explaining the various monuments, water reservoirs, and water supplies above and below ground. He expresses profound regret "that the town has been reduced to such a ruinous state and . . . the finest sculptured stones have been wrenched away for the building of portals, churches, towers, and houses."
According to tradition, the Incas Pachacútec, Túpac, and Huayna Cápac are all said to have contributed to the planning and building of Sacsayhuaman; however, the original layout dates back to earlier times. There are numerous highly symbolic stone buildings and holy springs, and the legends surrounding Sacsayhuaman refer to it as a holy mountain. Viceroy Toledo admired this "defiant fortress," where the Spaniards almost perished during the insurrection of Inca Manco in 1536. Nowadays, the Inti-Raymi festival is again celebrated there every year on the 24th of June (winter solstice) by great crowds of people in Inca dress.
Archivo de Indias, Seville.

24 Dances performed with animal masks. These pictures from the ethno-historical work by Baltasar Jaime Martínez Compañón, Bishop of Trujillo (1778—1788), show how the rites that originally derived from the concept of a fraternal being in the animal kingdom still persisted long after the Spanish conquest. According to Garcilaso (6, XXI and XXII), in the time of Huayna Cápac various groups (probably representatives of the ayllus or provinces) in puma skins or decked out with black and white condor wings danced at the major festivals in the presence of the Inca.

Ms. 344, Biblioteca de Palacio, Madrid.
Photo: Oronoz, Madrid.

25 Thirty-nine turquoise figurines from Piquillajta near Cuzco.
Larrea Collection, Museo de América, Madrid. Photo: Oronoz, Madrid.

26 Sacrificial knife, showing the god-king Naymlap (?), found near Lambayeque.
Museo Nacional de Arqueología, Lima.
Photo: A. Guillén, Lima.

27—28 Stone sculptures from Ecuador. Museum für Völkerkunde, Berlin-Dahlem.
Photo: Graf, Berlin.

29 The shape of the "counting board" from Tumibamba (approx. 13 1/2 x 11 1/2 in.) is highly reminiscent of the temples or fortresses in Ecuador described in the Spanish texts, some of which have actually been excavated.
Museum für Völkerkunde, Berlin-Dahlem.
Photo: Graf, Berlin.

30 The small wooden box with the lid (4 1/4 x 4 1/4 x 9 1/2 in.) is hard to place historically, despite the unity of the chip carving. The "putti," which according to the legend, Inca Huayna Cápac is supposed to have opened shortly before his death, may have been similar to this piece.
Museum für Völkerkunde, Munich.
Photo: Braunmüller, Munich.

31—33 Skeletons or spirits of the dead portrayed on Mochica vases. Not only in this early culture of the north Peruvian coast, but also later in Cuzco and in the whole Inca empire, in Colombia and Central America, life and religion were molded by the belief that the dead lived on, danced, made music, and held banquets. In Cuzco the royal mummies were washed at regular intervals, fed with burnt offerings, and given chicha to drink. The dead were expected to produce the life-giving force from under the earth, to make the seeds germinate and the plants grow.
Museum für Völkerkunde, Berlin-Dahlem.
Photo: Graf, Berlin.

34—36 Figures of gods, men, and animals on burial cloths from the Paracas Necropolis (ca. 200—800 A.D.). For a more detailed explanation, see the notes on color plates II, V, VI, VIII.
Museum für Völkerkunde, Munich.
Photo: Braunmüller, Munich.

37—39 Peruvian gold jewelry, and part of a mummy from Paracas with nose and breast ornament.
Museo de América, Madrid.
Photo: Oronoz, Madrid.

40–41 Portraits of Atahualpa and Huáscar. Museum für Völkerkunde, Berlin-Dahlem. Photo: Graf, Berlin.

42 Map of America, drawn by hand (1535). The northern part of North America and the southern part of South America have not yet been discovered. Ms. Sloane 117, British Museum, London.

43 Detail from Waldseemüller's map of the world (1507). This is the first large printed map on which the new discoveries of the Spaniards and Portuguese appear (Spanish possessions are marked by flags bearing the coat of arms of Castile), as well as being the first printed large-scale attempt to supplement the Ptolemaic picture of the world with the information gained by Marco Polo on the one hand, and from the Portuguese charts on the other. Photo: Bavarian State Library, Munich.

44 Photo: Museo Naval, Madrid.

45 Photo: Museo Naval, Madrid.

46 It was Juan Pérez, the fervent missionary prior of La Rábida and former father confessor of Queen Isabella of Castile, who gained Christopher Columbus the patronage of the Spanish kings and the introduction to the shipowners in the nearby port of Palos de la Frontera. He had previously made unsuccessful attempts in Portugal, France, and England to enlist support for his plans for voyages of discovery. Oil painting in the Museo Naval, Madrid. Photo: Museo Naval.

47 "Atahualpa, 14th Inca, the defeated son of Mama Chachapoya, Queen of Quito, proclaimed king of Cuzco. He was defeated and taken prisoner by conquistador Francisco Pizarro and beheaded in Cajamarca. He was first baptized and given the name Don Juan in 1533." This text translated here, which can be seen under the portrait of Atahualpa, dating from the colonial period, contains several inaccuracies. He was not beheaded, but garroted, and there is no mention of his being the son of Huayna Cápac. The clothes and the attributes could be authentic. Copacabana Monastery, Lima. Photo: A. Guillén, Lima.

48a Tunic of Inca origin, found in Pachacámac, Peru, 35½ x 31½ in. Neck of the garment is dark vermilion, the harebell pattern red, green, yellow, black, and white; the change from the uniform, repeated flower pattern to the richly differentiated geometric pattern, approaching an abstract form of picture-writing on the central horizontal border, is quite striking. Museo de América, Madrid. Photo: Oronoz, Madrid.

48b Simple tunic, with black and white squares, as worn according to eyewitness accounts, by detachments of Atahualpa's warriors in Cajamarca. Museum für Völkerkunde, Munich. Photo: Braunmüller, Munich.

49 Granite sculpture of a prisoner. Height: 10¾ in., width: 2½ in. From Calca in the Urubamba valley, near Cuzco. Larrea Collection, Museo de América, Madrid. Photo: Oronoz, Madrid.

50 Paracas tapestry with the by now familiar form of trophy head, held here as a symbol of public property, and the scepter, that has turned into a sprouting branch.

51 Libation container in the form of a fortress. Museo de América, Madrid. Photo: Oronoz, Madrid.

52 Sacrificial container, with separate spouts for filling and pouring out (paccha), from Recuay in the Santa valley (ca. 300–900 A.D.). This model-like pottery vessel is a further proof that two-story houses existed in ancient Peru. Ruins of some of these can still be seen in the mountain areas. Museum für Völkerkunde, Berlin-Dahlem. Photo: Graf, Berlin.

53 Seville and the Guadalquivir. Oil painting attributed to Sánchez Coello (approx. 6 ft. 6 in. x 4 ft. 3 in.). This river port and the "Casa de Contratación" within the city was the only place permitted to receive the overseas gold and to handle wares on their way to and from America. Originally the reason for this was to facilitate the supervision of payments to the Crown. As a result the monarch became dependent on the monopolies controlled by the Seville merchants, and later found himself unable to break free of them. The importance of the remaining Andalusian ports consequently diminished. Museo de América, Madrid. Photo: Oronoz, Madrid.

54 Signatures of illiterate fishermen from Puerto de Santa Maria (Cádiz). Francisco Pizarro's signature. Museo Naval, Madrid, and "El Peru Virreinal."

55 The "Marqués" Francisco Pizarro. Small portrait in the Museo de América, Madrid.

56 Church doorway in Cochabamba. From the book South America by Hans Mann, published by Thames & Hudson, London.

57 "The most illustrious Señor Don Fray Vicente de Valverde of the Order of the Predicadores, first Bishop of Cuzco, a native of Oropesa near Avila. His father, Francisco de Valverde, was a citizen of Trujillo in Estremadura, and his mother, Donna María Alvares de Valtejeda, a sister of the Count of Oropesa. He studied at the University of Salamanca and was 'Lector en Artes y Teologia' in the Colegio de S. Gregorio in Valladolid, came to Peru with Francisco Pizarro, and was present at the death of Atahualpa, whom he instructed in the faith and baptized in Cajamarca on the 31st of May, 1533. On the instructions of Pizarro and the other conquistadors, he sailed to Spain in 1543; at the suggestion of Charles V he was ordained bishop of all Peru by a papal bull of Paul III in 1536, and as such entered the city of Cuzco in June, 1538, where on the 4th of September of the same year he dedicated the cathedral 'to the resurrection of our Beloved Lady.' On the 14th of June, 1536, he was proclaimed protector of the Indians by royal decree. At the end of October, 1541, he suffered a gruesome death at the hands of a Caribbean [?] Indian in the river valley of the Guayaquil. He held office in his see for three years and four months." (This legend appears on the portrait of Valverde in the Museum für Völkerkunde, Berlin-Dahlem.) Photo: Graf, Berlin.

58 Catechism belonging to Pedro de Gante. Museo de América, Madrid. Photo: Oronoz, Madrid.

59 Portal of the baroque church of Santa Cruz in Julí, Peru. Photo: Hans Mann, from the book, South America, published by Thames & Hudson, London.

60 Inca noblewoman from the colonial period, the earliest of a series of five life-size portraits, at present in Cuzco, of descendents of the Inca ayllus. Whereas the later pictures show increasing Spanish influence (see illustration nos. 75 and 79), this princess still wears the original costume, as described by the first Spanish eye witnesses. Museo de Arqueología, Cuzco. Photo: A. Guillén, Lima.

61—62: Two viceroys, after portraits in Lima, copied by the Augsburg artist Johann Moriz Rugendas, who traveled through Mexico and the western part of South America from 1831–1847. Nuñez Vela was murdered in the Peruvian civil war; López de Zúñiga y Velasco died in mysterious circumstances. Pencil drawings in the Graphische Sammlung, Munich, inv. nos. 17 333 and 17 337.

63 Alcalde's (mayor's) staff overlaid with silver. Museo de América, Madrid. Photo: Oronoz, Madrid.

64a and b Marriage of Martín García de Loyola to the daughter of Inca Sayri Túpac. Pencil sketch and watercolor study by J. M. Rugendas after an anonymous oil painting in Cuzco.
Graphische Sammlung, Munich, inv. nos. 17 586 and 17 585. In the early conquest and colonization period, the descendants of such marriages were far more highly regarded than later on and occasionally occupied military posts as *vecinos, encomenderos,* and priests (cf. Rosenblat 2, III, p. 151 ff.). After the insurrections of the first and second generations of conquistadors, their rights were severely curtailed.

65a Funeral procession for Charles V in Augsburg, 1559. Six folios from a series of pictures consisting of twenty-one folios in the Austrian National Library, Vienna (cod. 7566²). Folio size, 13¹/₂ in. x 9¹/₂ in.
"On the 21st of September, 1558, Emperor Charles V died at his villa in the Hieronymite monastery of San Yusta in Estremadura. The funeral ceremonies held for him as king of Spain did not end with his burial in the Escorial. His son and successor appeared again as 'chef du deuil' in the *pompe funèbre* which he arranged in Brussels on the 29th and 30th of December, 1558, in honor of Charles V as the deceased sovereign of the Netherlands. But Charles' younger brother Ferdinand I, and his successor on the imperial throne, also arranged a great memorial celebration, which was held in Augsburg on the 24th and 25th of February, 1559..." (Bruno Thomas in *Waffen und Kostümkunde,* 1959, Book I).

65b Charles V according to the colored drawing of an unknown German master of the 16th century.
Graphische Sammlung, Munich, inv. no. 1908: 336.

66 Two-headed bird of prey on a tapestry from the Paracas Necropolis, south Peruvian coast (ca. 500 A.D.) It is surprising how often this mythical creature appears as a heraldic emblem in many different cultures of the world.
Museum für Völkerkunde, Munich.
Photo: Braunmüller, Munich.

67—74 Picture series of families of different "colors" were extremely popular in the New World. The often curious names given to the blood mixtures and the drastically portrayed situations and social levels show the attentive observer much of the tragedy of the colonial caste system. Spanish, Indian, and African blood perceptibly raised or lowered social standing. The examples included here are numbers 3, 7, 1, 2, 4, 6, 12, and 15 from the Madrid series of sixteen small *Cuadros de Mestizaje* (approx. 19 x 14 in.). The complete series is:
1. Spaniard and Indian woman: mestiza
2. Mestiza and Spaniard: castizo
3. Castizo and Spanish woman: Spaniard (thus the so-called *cuaterón* counts as a full Spaniard again!)
4. Spaniard and negress: mulatto
5. Spaniard and mulatta: morisca
6. Spaniard and morisca: alvino
7. Spaniard and alvina: negro torna atrás (a little negro "comes back again," and possibly in the fourth generation at that!)
8. Indian and negress: lovo (wolf!)
9. Lovo and negress: chino
10. Chino and Indian woman: canbujo
11. Indian woman and canbujo: Tente en el aire ("in the balance")
12. Tente en el Aire and mulata: albarrazado
13. Albarrazado and Indian woman: barsino
14. Barsino and Indian woman: canpa mulato
15. Indian and mestiza: coyote (little wolf)
16. Indios Apaches.
Museo de América, Madrid.
Photo: Oronoz, Madrid.

75 Picture of Don Alonso Chiguan Inca from the *ayllu* of the third Inca Lloqui Yupanqui. In his essay, *Colonial Portraits of Inca Nobles,* J. H. Rowe places the picture and the man in the same period as the portrait of Don Marcos Chiguan Thopa (see illustration no. 79).
Yet the picture of Don Alonso contains more Inca elements (feather collar, ear plugs, sun disk pectoral, cut of the clothing,

geometric design on the fabric) and in our view must belong to an earlier period, whereas the style of portrayal and the legend on the portrait of Don Marcos are clearly characteristic of the 18th century.
Museo de Arqueología, Cuzco.
Photo: A. Guillén, Lima.

76 Church of Ichupampa.
Photo: H. Reutimann, from his above-mentioned book.

77 Interior of the church of Pomata (17th century).
Photo: Hans Mann, from his above-mentioned book.

78 Popular portrayal of the execution of Atahualpa as a bloody beheading. Beneath the rainbow, the ancient Peruvian symbol of fertility, and the stars, the execution of the Inca takes place in the presence of the priest Vicente Valverde; above is the tribunal, headed by Francisco Pizarro. Atahualpa's brother Huáscar and his father Huayna Cápac appear in litters in their full Inca finery (below, right and above, left); left, the famous Mama Ocllo, and above right, Atahualpa's mother with her women attendants; the rest of the picture is filled with Spanish soldiers with lances and firearms, Indian warriors, and Inca nobles.
Museo de Arqueología, Cuzco.
Photo: A. Guillén, Lima.

79 An 18th-century portrait shows us a later Inca descendant dressed in the European fashion, with lace-edged sleeves of brocade and a gold chain. Below, on the right, the legend reads: "Don Marcos Chiguan Thopa, Coronilla Inca, Catholic *caballero* of God's grace, royal standard bearer, and one of the twenty-four chosen representatives of the Inca assembly of the eight communities of the great city of Cuzco, descended from the blood of Inca Cápac Lloqui Yupanqui, the third king of these empires... Cacique Principal... of Guaillabamba... and Paucartambo..." Five viceroys awarded and confirmed these and other titles and revenues respectively. He was allowed to maintain a bodyguard of Cañari and was subject to no local court of law, but could appeal direct to a specially appointed judge at an *audiencia* in Lima.
Museo de Arqueología, Cuzco.
Photo: A. Guillén, Lima.
(There is a similar painting in the Landesmuseum of Lower Saxony, Hamburg.)

NOTES ON THE FIGURES AND MAPS IN THE TEXT (the numbers refer to the page numbers)

15 Ground plan of a palace in Chanchán according to Squier, p. 192. Recent aerial photographs have confirmed the accuracy of the drawing.

16 Below: only high-ranking individuals learned the art of using the *quipus*.

27 Impression from a Peruvian wooden goblet *(kero)*. Museum für Völkerkunde, Munich.

28 Quotation from Poma de Ayala, p. 145.

32 The church and monastery of Santo Domingo today stand on the ruins of this sun temple.

34 Growth of the Inca empire (map) and altitude areas.

36 The old and the new Cuzco, according to Squier's survey, p. 583.

38 Network of Inca streets (map).

51 Mochica ceramic. Museum für Völkerkunde, Berlin-Dahlem.

58 Ceramic, approx. height, 2 in. Museo de América, Madrid.

83 Tiara in the Relación Anónima (in *Tres Relaciones...*, p. 159). In a footnote to this work, Marcos Jiménez de la Espada writes that this is a faithful copy of a pen drawing that he had seen. The shape of the headdress, he maintains, coincides with similar insignia of the Inca kings in the »Decadas« of the Herrera.

85 Map of the Yucay valley according to Squier, p. 602.

86 Battle scene on a Mochica vase (according to Kutscher).

86 Trephined skulls. (It is thought that damage sustained as a result of a stroke may have been cured by this operation, which was very delicately performed in ancient Peru.) Squier, p. 568.

94 Viceroyalty of Peru, conquistador campaigns, and foundation of cities (map).

109 "The initial legal titles of European colonial foundations overseas were: first discovery and occupation, followed by papal bestowal and state covenant of the two occupation powers of Spain and Portugal... Symbolic actions accompanied the formal act of taking possession. After landing on the island of Guanahani, Christopher Columbus unfolded the royal standard and two flags with the Cross, and in front of witnesses delivered the required declaration, and made the clerk take down a record of it." (Konetzke, p. 31)

115 Copper engraving from the Biblioteca Nacional, Madrid.

125 Small Inca vase. Museum für Völkerkunde, Berlin-Dahlem.

126 Drawing on a Mochica ceramic (Kutscher, p. I. 25). Prisoners' weapons and clothing hang from the club slung over the shoulder of the victor.

137 Plan of the city of Riobamba according to Poma de Ayala. Riobamba was one of the first cities to be founded in Ecuador, even before Quito. "There is here field produce and fruit in plenty, but little gold and silver" (quotation from Poma de Ayala, p. 1005).

142 Quotation from Poma de Ayala, p. 554.

167 Letter written by Bartolomé de Las Casas in 1552: "... I request the royal counsel not to allow Negroes to be sent to the Indies, and especially not to Peru, as they are so lazy..." Copper engraving portrait in the Biblioteca Nacional, Madrid.

168 The emperor's signature under a decree, dated 9. 10. 1548. It empowers a Seville merchant to ship 100 Negro slaves to America.

182 The viceroy Marqués de Cañete named this colony founded by him after his native town in Spain. Poma de Ayala, p. 1037.

182 The city of Nazca on the south Peruvian coast. Poma de Ayala, p. 1043.

DRAWINGS IN THE TEXT BY:

E. M. Engl: p. 51.

H. Engl: p. 11, 12 below; 26, 33 right; 39, 50, 84, 91, 93, 122 after a drawing in the chronicle of Fray Martín de Murúa, ca. 1600 (first published in full in 1962, after being found by M. Ballesteros-Gaibrois in Ciudad Rodrigo in the possession of the Duke of Wellington); p. 14 after the helmet and leather armor in the Museum für Völkerkunde, Berlin.

Th. Engl, p. 13, 27, 34, 58, 94, 125, 127, 145.

Gerdt Kutscher (from Mochica ceramics in his book, *Chimu — eine altindianische Hochkultur*, published by Gebr. Mann, Berlin, 1950): p. 15 above, 25, 55, 126.

Poma de Ayala (some are details from drawings, and the page of text is taken from the Paris facsimile edition of his handwritten account of 1600): p. 16, 28, 29, 49, 113, 135, 137 below; 142, 177, 180, 181, 182, 183, 187.

Wood engravings from *Peru — Incidents of Travel and Exploration in the Land of the Incas* by E. George Squier, New York, 1877: p. 10, 12 above; 15 below; 32, 33 left; 36, 85, 86 below; 89, 114, 137 above; 146, 147, 148, 171, 179.

Sources of other Figures in the Text:

Woodcuts from the *Instrucción Nautica* (16th century): p. 56, 57.

Drawings from the *Relación Anónima* (p. 159) in *Tres Relaciones...*: p. 83.

Map by Sebastian Münster (wood engraving): p. 109. Portrait engraving from the Biblioteca Nacional, Madrid: p. 115.

Wood engraving from the first edition of the chronicle of Cieza de Leon (1553): p. 131. Facsimiles of autographs in the Archiv de Indias, Seville: p. 155, 167 left, 168.

Portrait engraving from the Biblioteca Nacional, Madrid: p. 167 right.

Facsimile signature from the chronicle of Sarmiento, Pietschmann ed. (p. XXXIV): p. 185.

NOTES TO THE TEXT

Unless otherwise indicated (by vol. for volume, or p. for page), the arabic figures following the author's name stand for the volume or book number, and the Roman numerals for the relevant chapter concerned.

Exceptions: with Valcárcel the Roman numerals indicate the volume, and the arabic figures, the page; the Roman numerals following D. I. A. (Documentos Inéditos del Archivo de Indias) indicate the series, the subsequent arabic figure, the volume number, and the final arabic figure, the page number.

CHAPTER I

1 Cieza 2, III; Valcárcel II, p. 369.

2 Sarmiento VII; Gregorio García, in Valcárcel II, p. 375.

3 Sarmiento VII.

4 Cobo 12, XIX; see also Prittwitz, note 295 (p. 310 ff.); Prittwitz has gone into the mythological and philological significance of the character and name of Viracocha in great detail.

5 Bushnell, p. 93; Trimborn, p. 102.

5a One of the best known versions of landings from overseas is that of the origin of the royal dynasty of Lambayeque on the north Peruvian coast: King Naymlap came from the ocean with his harem and a strong clan, arriving in *balsas*. He had a temple built inland for the image of the deity that he had brought with him, and a palace »after his fashion«, in which he held court with his cook, his cup bearer, his valet, his cosmetician and bath master, his conch blower, and other officials.

His death was kept secret and interpreted as an ascent to heaven; his successor had himself buried in a subterranean vault. When the dynasty died out, the "kingdom" is said to have fallen to the Chimú. (Balboa in Valcárcel II, p. 463 ff.) The numerous legends about immigration from the region south-east of Lake Titicaca suggest that Bolivia was a gateway for invasion by the peoples from the eastern plains of South America and possibly even from the Atlantic. Later, in historical times, the Chiriguanos made repeated advances in this direction. They continued until recent times to drive an ethnic group by the name of Guarani into migrating, and in the curious religious legends of these people the Atlantic coast and the world across the sea feature prominently (see Mètraux, *La Religion des Tupinamba*, as well as unpublished investigations by Jürgen Riester, Bonn).

6 R. Porras Barrenechea, *Los Cronistas del Perú* (1528—1650), p. 398 f.

7 A. Oliva, in Valcárcel II, p. 406; According to most of the texts, Manco Cápac was not the sole founder of the Inca dynasty, but three or four brothers and sisters emerged from the cave together with him.

8 Ramos Gavilán, in Valcárcel II, p. 416; Lommel illus. 18 and 19 (*tungu* shamanite apparel).

9 Sarmiento XIII.

10 Cobo 12, X.

11 Cobo 12, X; Sarmiento maintains that the Chanca attack took place one generation later in the reign of the eighth Inca, Viracocha.

12 Sarmiento XXVIII.

13 Sarmiento XXVI.

14 S. C. Pachacuti, p. 270 ff.; Betanzos VIII; Garcilaso 2, vol. 5, XVIII. It should be remembered that in the Inca story of creation men were fashioned not of clay but of hard stone.

15 Sarmiento XXVII.

16 Cobo 12, XII; Lommel (p. 47, 48) has some interesting observations in this connection about the invocation of shamans by dreams and about the rituals performed at springs or wells, especially in Australia. There the shaman novice dives into a water hole to catch a talking snake. He returns to the surface with crystals endowed with magical powers and thereby proves his authority to his tribe.

17 Sarmiento XXX; Cobo 12, XII.

18 Sarmiento XXXVIII.

19 Betanzos XVIII.

20 Cobo 12, XI; Sarmiento XXXII.

21 Sarmiento XXXVIII, XLVI.

22 Rowe, "The Kingdom of Chimor."

23 Bushnell, p. 119 ff.; Bennett, p. 84 ff.; Ballesteros, in *Historia Social* I, 463.

24 Sarmiento XXXVIII. Pachacútec granted the defeated Chanca extensive privileges in order that they might help him to conquer new provinces. After the military objectives had been achieved, he wished to do away with their leaders. Warned by the wife of Inca Cápac Yupanqui, who was a Chanca, the Chanca fled to the eastern Andes and were never again conquered by the Incas. The relationship between them is similar to the later dealings between Inca Manco and the Spaniards.

25 Disselhoff, p. 338.

26 Whether it was the Chimú empire that fell first, and then Ecuador, or whether it happened in the reverse order has yet to be examined in detail.

27 Sarmiento LXVI.

28 S. C. Pachacuti, p. 284 ff.

29 Sarmiento XLIV; Polo de Ondegardo, in Valcárcel II, p. 227 .

30 Cieza 2, XXXI. the complex subject of sister-marriage and succession had been examined afresh in the thesis by L. Engl (1954).

31 Sarmiento XLIII; Cieza 2, LXXXI; Cobo 12, XVI. "Mama Ocllo was an important and clever woman. While she lived, her son Huayna Cápac ruled according to her advice."

32 Sarmiento LI.

33 S. C. Pachacuti, p. 283 f. The *Anónima* gives more exact information about the hierarchy of the priesthood and about the "humu" and "laica", mentioned by S. C. Pachacuti. (*Tres Relaciones*) 156. "Ministros mayores" (higher servants of the cult), 153 "Adivinos" (soothsayers), 170 ff. "humu" (priests).

34 Cieza 2, LXI; Cobo 12, XVI.

35 Balboa XII.

36 The chronicles tell us of a highly organized assassination attempt led by his uncle Hualpaya, who had ruled as regent while Huayna Cápac was a minor. Cobo 12, XVI; S. C. Pachacuti, p. 294; Balboa X); Sarmiento and Cieza relate intrigues by bastard sons of Túpac who make claims to the throne.

37 Sarmiento XVI and XLII; Santillán 24: ". . . no venía la subcessión forzosamente al mayor sino a aquel que el padre quería . . ." It is known that tribal chiefs in Peru frequently appointed the most "capable" of their sons as successor (Cobo 12, XXV). In his introduction to the chronicle of Sarmiento, Pietschmann summarizes the conditions that had to be fulfilled in the selection of a new Inca: "He who became Inca was acknowledged as king by the leaders of the tribes and the heads of the twelve *ayllus* of the royal house, and was granted the *borla* by the oracle of the sun god." The *calpa* played a decisive

role in this, as is described in detail in chapters two and three; in later times the queen mother's influence in this is supposed to have been strong. The course of events following Huayna Cápac's death shows that Huáscar's accession to the throne was not acknowledged until his position had been secured by marriage to his sister. This marriage was almost prevented by the intervention of the old Coya Mama Rahua Ocllo. See also Chapter III, note 37.

38 Sarmiento LXII.

CHAPTER II

1 and 2 S. C. Pachacuti, p. 296 ff.

3 See Chapter I, note 38.

4 and 5 Cobo 12, XVI; Balboa, XI; Sarmiento LIX. "... He founded a provincial capital in the valley of Cochabamba, which he settled with *mitmacs* (deportees) from all areas, as the existing population there was small."

6 See Chapter I, notes 1 and 2.

7 Cobo (12, XVI) writes: "He sacrificed those who had rebelled..." These were probably members of tribes, who had not obeyed the call to capitulate. Because this kind of intimidation by terror and superiority in numbers frequently prevented the outbreak of major wars, much is made of the Incas' peaceful conquest of South America.

8 Velasco I.

9 Krickeberg, p. 223.

10 Krickeberg, p. 226.

11 Valcárcel I, p. 367.

11a In a letter from Ecuador, written by Humboldt in 1802 after he had climbed Chimborazo, he comments on some ancient Ecuadorian records in the "Puruguay" (probably puruhá) language, belonging to an Indian friend: "It has provided us with information of inestimable value, mainly about the strange time of the eruption of the so-called Nevado del Altar, which must have been the highest mountain in the world, higher than Chimborazo, and which was known to the Indians as Cápac Urco (head of the mountains). At the time of the catastrophe, the priests declared: "the earth is changing its shape; other gods will come and drive away our own! Let us not resist the command of fate"! Elsewhere he writes, (*Kleinere Schriften*, vol. I, p. 133 ff.): "This terrifying natural phenomenon occurred shortly before the capture of Quito by Inca Túpac Yupanqui."

12 S. C. Pachacuti, p. 300.

13 Cobo 12, XVI; S. C. Pachacuti, p. 301.

14 Cieza 2, XXIX; Cobo 13, XXV; Valcárcel II, p. 226. The mummies were honored just like a living monarch. Betanzos describes how every *curaca* who came to Cuzco paid homage, first to the sun, then to the Inca mummies, and finally to the reigning Inca. Each mummy had its own singer, who would celebrate the deeds of the deceased at major festivals in order to keep alive his memory. These legends formed the basis of Inca history, which the Spaniards recorded in their chronicles.

15 Cieza 2, LXIII. "... Huayna Cápac mandó hacer sacrificios, y la ofrenda de la Capacocha se hizo bien grande..." Sometimes apparently a ten-year-old girl was sacrificed; in some areas, where the social order consisted of two half-tribes, such as Hanancuzco and Hurincuzco, there were two pairs of children. If a *curaca* gave up his own child for sacrifice, he could expect special favors from the Inca; thus the Capacocha also had political significance (Valcárcel II, p. 335). See Chapter I, note 11.

16 Molina, in Valcárcel II, p. 252 ff., 298 f. and 301.

17 Cieza 2, XXIX; Garcilaso 2d vol., 6, XXI; Sarmiento XVII, LXII; the most detailed treatment of the *calpa* appears in *Relacion Anónima* (*Tres Relaciones*, p. 170 f.).

18 and 19 Molina, in Valcárcel II, p. 253.

20 Pachacútec appointed only close relatives as high-ranking officers, and Túpac almost always did the same (Sarmiento XXXVIII, XLIV, L, LII, and other chroniclers).

21 S. C. Pachacuti, p. 301; Sarmiento LX; Balboa XI; Cobo 12, XVI.

22 Balboa XI.

23 Sarmiento (XLIV) reports that on his long journey through Chinchasuyu, Túpac wore the appropriate regional costume in each of the provinces he visited. Huayna Cápac may have done the same. While he was in Cajamarca, Atahualpa is known to have worn a cloak that was made in the region of Puerto Viejo, on the coast of Ecuador.

24 Cieza 2, LXIII.

25 Garcilaso 2d vol., 6, XX, XXI.

26 S. C. Pachacuti, p. 282 f.; Balboa XI; Sarmiento LX; Cobo 12, XVI.

27 and 28 Balboa XI; Cobo 12, XVI.

29 Cieza 1, XLIV; Montesinos, in Valcárcel III, p. 320; Cobo 12, XIV.

30 See also notes 10 and 11.

31 Balboa XI; Cobo 12, XVI.

32 Montesinos, in Valcárcel III, p. 321; Cieza 1, XLIV.

33 Cieza 2, LXVI; Cobo 12, XVII; S. C. Pachacuti, p. 303, also p. 283, 302, and 304.

34 S. C. Pachacuti, p. 304; Cieza 2, LXI.

35 Sarmiento LX.

36 and 37 Balboa XI; Cobo 12, XVII.

38 Balboa XI.

39 Balboa XII; Cobo 13, XV; S. C. Pachacuti, p. 305 ff.; Sarmiento LX; Murúa.

40 Balboa XII; Cobo 12, XVII.

41 Cobo 12, XVII; Balboa XIII; S. C. Pachacuti, p. 306; Cieza 2, LXVII; Sarmiento LX; *Relación de 1572*, signed by Sancho de Paz Ponce de León, in Valcárcel I, p. 370; *Relación anónima de la ciudad de Quito 1573*, in Valcárcel I, p. 371.

42 Sarmiento LX; Balboa XIII; cf. Eckert, p. 19: (they believed that) "with the acquisition of the head and skin of the slain enemy, his being had also been delivered into their power. If the dead man had first been made obedient by magical invocation, then he could be expected to render help of all kinds; the enemy thirsting for vengeance was transformed into an obedient slave, whose continued existence (through preservation of the body) was of great value."

43 Balboa XII, XIII; Sarmiento (LXII) describes a meeting between the Inca and a hostile army, and Balboa an encounter with primitive savages. It is possible that S. C. Pachacuti's descriptions of Huayna Cápac's night visions of a ghostly army (see note 51) could be an interpretation of these encounters. Whether these were the ghosts of those who had died of the plague, or whether they were real people, or whether the events are totally unrelated remains an open question.

44 Sarmiento LXI; Disselhoff, p. 316.

45 The eye witness, Mena, says four to five months.

46 Cieza 1, LIV, XLVII, XLVIII.

47 Cieza 1, LIII; Balboa XIV.

48 Montesinos XXVIII.

49 Cieza 1, LIII.

50 Eckert, p. 18.

51 Cieza 1, LIII; Cobo 12, XVII.

52 S. C. Pachacuti, p. 307.

53 Valcárcel I, p. 85, 86.

54 Sarmiento LXII; Balboa XIV.

55 Garcilaso 2d vol., 9, XIV.

56 Garcilaso, 2d vol., 9, XIV; Montesinos XVIII; S. C. Pachacuti, p. 302.

57 Oviedo, 4th vol., 43, III; Sarmiento

LXVIII; Balboa XXII; *Relaciones primitivas*, p. 22—27: "... after the return of the ship to Isla del Gallo, where Pizarro had stayed for seven to eight months, he set sail again and discovered Túmbez and Payta; here Pedro de Candía jumped ashore and entered Túmbez, and told how he had seen great things ... The Indians ... were not afraid ... of them, they took them to be tradespeople ... two Spaniards remained behind of their own free will ... He (Pizarro) took two llamas away with him and returned to Spain with a report. From there he returned as governor..."

58 Cobo 12, XVII. Cobo refers here to "wooden houses". However, there was only one small ship involved at this point.

59 Oviedo, 4th vol., 43, III; Cobo 12, XVII.

60 Cobo 12, XVII. The Incas and the Peruvian peoples would shake their cloaks if they wished to ward off evil.

61 Cieza 2, LXVIII. On the subject of how far Pizarro advanced on his second expedition, see the chronicle of Trujillo, note 39, and Herrera, 3rd December, 2, VII and 4th December, 2, VII.

62 Garcilaso, 2d vol., 9, XIV.

63 Cobo 12, XVII; Balboa XIV; Sarmiento LXII; Garcilaso, 2d vol., 9, XIV.

64 S. C. Pachacuti, p. 307.

65 Cobo 12, XVII.

66 Cobo 13, XXV.

67 Cieza 2, LXVIII.

68 Sarmiento LXII; Balboa XIV; Cieza 2, LXVIII; Garcilaso, 2d vol., 9, XV.

69 Sarmiento LXII; details about the *calpa* by Garcilaso, 2d vol., XXI f.

70 Sarmiento XLVII: "Dando el ánima al diablo" ("and gave his soul to the devil"), adds the chronicler.

71 Cobo 12, XVII: "... He drank more than three Indians together, but always remained lucid. When his friends asked him how it was that he never became drunk, he said that he drank for the poor, whose welfare he had very much at heart."

72 Sarmiento LVII.

73 Sarmiento LXII.

74 Garcilaso, 2d vol., 9, XIV; Montesinos XXVIII; S. C. Pachacuti, p. 302.

CHAPTER III

1 Balboa XIV; Sarmiento LXIII; Murúa.

2 Murúa; Garcilaso 2d vol., 6, V.

3 Sarmiento LXIII.

4 Cieza 2, LXX; Zárate XV; Garcilaso 2d vol., XXXIII; Cobo 12, XVIII.

5 Sarmiento LXIII; Balboa XIV; Murúa; S. C. Pachacuti, p. 309.

6 S. C. Pachacuti, p. 309.

7 Balboa XIV.

8 Anónima in *Tres Relaciones*, p. 157 and 172.

9 S. C. Pachacuti, pp. 283—284.

10 Balboa; Murúa. It is worth noting in this context that a girl selected as a secondary wife was not asked for her consent; a girl could only be taken as a *coya*, however, if she gave her consent (Cobo 14, VII). See also Chapter I, note 37.

11 Balboa XV.

12 Cobo 12, XVIII; Garcilaso, 2d vol., 9, XXXII; Zárate 1, XV.

13 S. C. Pachacuti, p. 310; Balboa XVI; Cobo 12, XVIII; Zárate 1, XV; Cieza 2, LXX; Sarmiento LXIII.

14 Cieza 2, LXX; Cobo 12, XVIII; Balboa XVII; Sarmiento LXIII; Zárate 1, XV; S. C. Pachacuti (p. 311) writes: "... Atahualpa distributes weapons and clothing from the magazines of his father, and then they begin to conscript soldiers. And, conscious of his power, Atahualpa assumes the title of Inca, and from now on has himself carried in a litter ..."

15 Cieza 2, LXXI, XLIV; Cobo 12, XVIII.

16 Sarmiento LXIII.

17 Zárate 1, XV; Sarmiento LXIII.

18 Cieza 2, LXX.

19 Cieza 2, LXXI; Zárate 1, XV; Cobo 12, XVIII; Balboa XVIII, XXXV.

20 Cieza 2, LXXII.

21 S. C. Pachacuti, p. 312; Cieza 2, LXII.

22 *Información de Toledo*, p. 221; Cieza 2, LXXIII.

23 Cieza 2, LXXIII; Cobo XVIII.

24 Sarmiento LXIII; Balboa XVIII, XIX, XX; S. C. Pachacuti, p. 312 ff.; Cobo 12, XVIII; Cieza 2, LXXIII.

25 Cieza 2, LVI.

26 S. C. Pachacuti, p. 313; Sarmiento LXIII.

27 Cieza 2, LXXII.

28 Cieza 2, LXXIII.

29 Cieza 1, XLIV; Balboa XVIII; S. C. Pachacuti, p. 313.

30 Sarmiento LXIV; Cobo 12, XVIII.

31 Sarmiento LXIV.

32 Sarmiento LXIV; Cieza 2, LXXIII; Balboa XX; S. C. Pachacuti, p. 315.

33 S. C. Pachacuti, p. 315.

34 Sarmiento LXIV.

35 Balboa XXI.

36 S. C. Pachacuti, p. 318 f.

37 Sarmiento LXIV; S. C. Pachacuti, p. 319. The Rio Cotabamba is a tributary of the Apurímac.

38 Balboa XXI.

39 S. C. Pachacuti, p. 320 f.; Sarmiento LXIV.

40 S. C. Pachacuti, p. 321.

41 S. C. Pachacuti, p. 321 f.; Sarmiento LXV; Balboa XXI; Garcilaso, 2d vol., 9, XXXV. According to Balboa and Cobo, Quizquiz took Huáscar prisoner; according to S. C. Pachacuti, it was Quizquiz together with Rumiñahui; according to Sarmiento it was Chalcochima, with the help of Quizquiz; Garcilaso and Zárate mention no names.

42 Sarmiento LXV.

43 S. C. Pachacuti, p. 322; Sarmiento LXV.

44 Sarmiento LXV.

45 Sarmiento LXV; Balboa XXI; S. C. Pachacuti, p. 322; Murúa.

46 Sarmiento LXV; Murúa.

47 Cobo 12, XIX.

48 Sarmiento LXVI and XVI; Balboa XXI; Cobo 12, XV and XX; Garcilaso, 2d vol., 9, XXXVIII.

49 Cobo 12, XV; Sarmiento XVI; Balboa XXI; *Informaciones de Toledo*, p. 256.

50 Sarmiento LXVI.

51 Cobo 12, XIX.

CHAPTER IV

1 and 2 Xerez.

3 The numbers vary in the different texts. D. Trujillo, an eye witness, refers to 250 Spaniards and 3 monks.

4 Trujillo, p. 47.

5 Trujillo, pp. 47—48; Zárate 2, I; *Nouvelles certaines*, p. 70.

6 Trujillo, p. 48.

7 Balboa XXI.

8 Sarmiento LXVII.

9 A careful comparison of the dates given in the various chronicles can be found in the *Las Relaciones primitivas* and in R. Porras Barrenechea's commentary to the chronicle of Diego de Trujillo.

10 Xerez.

11 and 12 *Nouvelles certaines* ...

13 Zárate 2, III; Xerez.

14 Pedro Pizarro; Trujillo, p. 52; S. Huber, p. 123; Herrera, 4. dec., 9, I, 177 ff.

15 Xerez.

16 Xerez; Zárate 2, III; Trujillo, p. 51: Trujillo maintains that Alonso de Molina, one of the three Spaniards left behind at that time, had built a church on Puná, and asserts that he himself had seen a community of thirty young Indian men and women there.

17 Xerez.

18 Zárate 2, III; *Nouvelles certaines* ...; Xerez.

19 and 20 Xerez.

21 Konetzke VI, p. 167, 168.

22 Zárate 2, III; Xerez.

23 Zárate 2, III.

24 Xerez.

24a In his somewhat short description, Mena gives no further indication of who these "many people" were, with whom Atahualpa's captain would or could have attacked the Spaniards. (Mena, in *Las Relaciones primitivas . . .*, pp. 79–80).

25 Departure from San Miguel on the 23rd of September 1532; arrival in Cajamarca on the 15th of September, 1532 (Xerez).

26 Xerez; Mena. The chronicles of Trujillo and Oviedo report the excesses perpetrated by De Soto's sixty men: ". . . in Cajas . . . there was one of Atahualpa's captains with 2,000 warriors. This town also contained three houses full of women . . . who called themselves *mamacunas*; and we went in, and the women were led out on to the square; there were more than 500 and the captain gave many of them to the Spaniards; the Inca captain was very angry at this" (Trujillo, p. 56). It is hard to assess how much Mena and Xerez have suppressed in their versions, or to what extent Trujillo has exaggerated.

27 Xerez.

28 Mena.

29 Zárate 2, IV; Mena.

30 Xerez; Mena; *Nouvelles certaines . . .*

31 Mena; Xerez.

32 Xerez; Mena. According to Trujillo (p. 56), Hernando Pizarro released De Soto from his hours of waiting and provoked the Inca into coming out to them by making loud threats.

33 Xerez (literal quotation); Mena.

34 Mena; Trujillo; P. Pizarro.

35 *Nouvelles certaines . . .* (quotation); Xerez; Mena, and Zárate all record the same thing.

36 Zárate 2, V.

37 Hernando Pizarro; Xerez; *Nouvelles certaines . . .*, Mena; Zárate 2, V.

38 Zárate 2, V; Mena; Konetzke VI, p. 167 f.

39 Zárate 2, V: Xerez; Mena; *Nouvelles certaines . . .*; H. Pizarro.

40 Xerez; H. Pizarro; Mena; *Nouvelles certaines . . .*

41 *Nouvelles certaines . . .*; Mena; Zárate 2, V.

42 H. Pizarro; Trujillo, p. 58; Xerez.

43 Xerez; Mena; H. Pizarro; Zárate 2, V.

44 Xerez; H. Pizarro; *Nouvelles certaines . . .*

45 Balboa XXII.

46 Zárate 2, VI.

47 *Nouvelles certaines . . .*; Xerez.

48 Cobo 12, XIII and 13, IX; Sarmiento LXVIII.

49 Letter from H. Pizarro (Oviedo 46, XV); Xerez; Estete; Mena.

50 Mena; Pedro Pizarro.

51 Xerez; Letter of Hernando Pizarro.

52 Sarmiento LXXII (quotation). Xerez says that Huáscar was killed by his guards, shortly after Atahualpa had been taken prisoner, and that Atahualpa mourned his death. Zárate 2, VI, is of the opinion that this mourning was just a charade and that Atahualpa had himself ordered him to be put to death. Sarmiento LXVIII, Balboa XXII, S. C. Pachacuti, p. 325 f., and Cobo 12, XIX, who wrote their chronicles several decades later, in the 17th century, also claim that Huáscar was murdered on Atahualpa's instructions.

53 Zárate 2, VII.

54 Oviedo XLVII.

55 Oviedo XLVII. The Inquisition, which had already been established in the 13th century by Pope Innocent III against heretical movements in France and Central Europe, was not introduced into Spain until 1478. Permanent offices for hearings of the Inquisition were not set up in America for about another one hundred years (1570 in Lima, 1571 in Mexico); admittedly, privileged "familiares" (informers) were installed to supervise the conduct of the Spaniards (cf. Konetzke, p. 278). The religious tribunals did not deal with Indians.

56 Eckert, p. 16 and 18.

CHAPTER V

1 Oviedo.

2 Xerez. In reality, this picture of the debtor, ready to repay his debt but unable to make his creditor accept payment, is tragic rather than comic. The law concerning debt in the colonies was extremely harsh. On Española, for example, the death penalty had been introduced for the protection of the creditor, as we saw from the description of the fate of the young Vasco Nuñez de Balboa.

3 Xerez. In his foreward to M. Gallo's *Gold von Peru*, R. Porras Barrenechea includes more detailed figures of the gold booty seized in Cajamarca and Cuzco; he also mentions the extent of the individual conquistadors' shares of the gold, basing his figures on unpublished documents.

4 Cobo 12, XX.

5 Pedro Pizarro.

6 Garcilaso, 3d vol., 2, V.

7 Garcilaso, 3d vol., 2, VI. Garcilaso mentions Francisco de Chaves as a prominent figure among the Spaniards released by the Indians. He was well thought of by the Inca because he was supposed to have interceded on Atahualpa's behalf. In the *Los Cronistas del Perú*, p. 435, R. Porras Barrenechea describes the whole episode as "leyenda reparativa" by the defeated party.

8 Oviedo, 4th vol., 46, XXII; Zárate 2, VIII; Garcilaso, 3d. vol., 2, III. The assertion that it was the Indians themselves who devastated Cajamarca, as well as other Inca cities, is quite unauthenticated.

10 Velasco.

11 Sarmiento LXVI.

12 Zárate 2, VIII.

13 Zárate 2, VIII; Garcilaso, 3d vol., 2, III.

13a Oberem, in *Tribus*, 1959, pp. 191–193.

14 Zárate 2, IX; Velasco.

15 Carrera Andrade.

16 Garcilaso, 3d vol., 2, IV; Zárate 2, IX; Velasco.

17 Oviedo, 4th vol., 46, XX; Velasco.

18 Zárate 2, XII.

19 Cobo 12, XXX. Dávalos y Figuerora, in Valcárcel II, p. 211.

20 Zárate, 2, X.

21 Zárate 2, XII; Xerez.

21a Velasco.

22 Cieza 1, LXXI; Angel Rosenblat.

23 Cobo "Fundacion de Lima" 1, VIII, XIX; Konetzke III, p. 47 f.: ". . . with the appearance of Governor Ovando in 1501, the construction of planned cities began in Spanish America . . . Ovando had the city of Santo Domingo built with straight roads, crossing each other at right angles. In this he followed the example of the foundation of planned cities on the Iberian peninsula during the late Middle Ages . . . This kind of ground plan, known as the chess board system, is to be found in colonized parts of southern France and in eastern Germany. They did not follow on from the Roman city plan . . ."

Letter from Charles V to F. Pizarro: "El Rey: Capitán F. Pizarro nuestro gobernador de la provincia del Perú. S. Rodriguez en nombre de los conquistadores y pobladores de esa provincia, me suplicó vos mandase dar licencia para que en los lugares que pobláredes pudiésedes repartir entre los vecinos y pobladores . . . solares en que se edificasen casas y huertas, caballerías y peonías de tierra, o como la mi merced fuese. Y yo acatando lo susodicho húbelo por bien, y por la presente vos doy entera facultad para que así a las personas que se han hallado en la conquista y población de esa dicha provincia, como a las que de acqui adelante fueren a se avecindar en ella, les podéis repartir solares en que se edifiquen casas y huertas...; y residiendo los vecinos en quien así los repartiéredes los cinco años que son obligados, les hacemos merced de ello... Fecha en Toledo a veintiún días del mes de mayo de 1539 años. Yo, el Rey..." (In this letter Charles V empowers Francisco Pizarro to use his discretion and distribute ground in the city and country areas to deserving conquistadors and settlers, as well as to newcomers.)

24 According to S. Huber, p. 255.

25 R. Porras, Barrenechea, notes to *El Testamento de Pizarro*, p. 72.

26 Zárate 4, IX; R. Porras Barrenechea, notes to *El Testamento de Pizarro*.

27 Pedro Pizarro, p. 198; Konetzke, p. 49: "The settlement of citizens (*vecinos*) was brought about by the royal distribution of land, the 'mercedes de tierra'. Each settler was allotted a plot of land, where he had to build his house. In addition to the building plot in the city, he was also granted smaller plots of land outside the city for use as a garden, for cultivation, and for the keeping of cattle. These farming plots on the outskirts of the city were known as *chacras* on the American continent... The properties distributed by the king were not always the same size. The unit of measure employed was the *peonía*, the amount of land granted during the wars of the Spanish Conquest to the foot soldier who wished to settle in the conquered land... The *caballería*, originally the amount of land due to a knight on conquest and colonization of a place, consisted of a building plot in the city which was twice the size of the other, and the land for agricultural development was five times as big as the *peonía*." Konetzke III, p. 52: " The *encomiendas* were not accompanied by any legal rights to the property. The *encomenderos* could however receive 'mercedes de tierra' in the area of their *encomienda* or they could buy land there. In effect, they greatly abused their responsibilities towards the Indians of their *encomiendas*, in order to appropriate the land belonging to these natives."

28 Konetzke VI, p. 173 ff.

29 Konetzke VI, p. 177 and 182.

30 Konetzke III, p. 52, 53. "The *encomenderos* could ... receive 'mercedes de tierra' in the area of their *encomienda*..." This led to the development of the latifundia structure. "There were various reasons for this concentration of property in single families. The 'mercedes de tierra', which were distributed on a large scale in recognition of services performed, were frequently sold by their impoverished owners, who were reluctant to settle on them, although this was expressly forbidden by law. The lands distributed for settlement thus became saleable commodities and objects of speculation, and were bought on a large scale by wealthy people. Some people accepted these settlement lands simply in order to sell them for profit. Simple people requested a few *caballerías* and grazing rights for settlement purposes and would occasionally sell them before they had even been issued by the appropriate authorities. Others began to develop the apportioned settlement land temporarily, in order to be able to dispose of it at an even greater profit. Influential men aquired title deeds for their servants, who then surrendered their rights. By using cat's paws, the large owners gradually acquired even more of the royal undeveloped land. The 'composiciones', which legalized the possession of illegally acquired properties in return for a remittance to the Crown, contributed to the expansion and strengthening of the large estates of land."

31 Murúa.

32 Oviedo, 47th book, VII; Zárate 3, III; Velasco.

33 Anonymous account from the D. I. A. I, 42, 379.

34 *Varones ilustres*..., chapter on "Pizarro y Orellana".

35 D. I. A. I, 42, 378 f.

36 D. I. A. I, 42, 376 ff.; Zárate 3, III. The account in the *Documentos inéditos* from the Archivo de Indias describes how Hernando Pizarro countered criticism of the release of Manco by setting off with sixty horsemen in pursuit of the Inca. On the way he occupied the town of Calca, near Yucay. "There he took possession of large amounts of gold and silver and many Indian women. All night long he had great difficulties with his soldiers, who had fallen upon the women and were not to be dragged away from them." The following day they had to pay dearly for this. Manco's warriors closed in on them in large numbers on the return to Cuzco and pursued them as far as the city. This was the point at which the grip on Cuzco hardened.

37 Garcilaso, 3d vol., 2, XXIV and XXV.

38 D. I. A. I, 42, 380 ff.

39 Garcilaso, 3d vol., 2, XXIV; D. I. A. I, 42, 381.

40 D. I. A. I, 42, 381.

41 D. I. A. I, 42, 384 ff.

42 Zárate 3, III.

43 Zárate 3, V; Cobo 12, XX.

44 Porras Barrenechea, notes to *El Testamento de Pizarro*, p. 68.

45 Zárate 3, XIII.

46 R. Porras Barrenechea, notes to *El Testamento de Pizarro*, p. 70 ff. "En diciembre de 1533 muere el clérigo Hernando de Luque y en su Testamento declara que le pertenece la tercera parte de lo que se ganare en la conquista del Perú, nombrando su albacea a Espinosa. (Hernando de Luque, the priest, died in December, 1533. In his testament he declared that he was entitled to one third of the proceeds gained during the conquest of Peru. The executor of his testament was Espinosa.)

47 Zárate 3, IV.

48 R. Porras Barrenechea, notes to *El Testamento de Pizarro*.

49 Zárate 3, XI, XII.

50 Zárate 4, VI ff. and elsewhere.

51 Letter from the Bishop of Cuzco, Fray Vicente Valverde, of the 20th of March, 1539, and report by Luis de Morales made in 1541. Lissón Chaves, *La Iglesia de España en el Perú*, vol. 1, Seville, 1943, nos 2 and 3, p. 70 and 111 f. (in Konetzke, note 348).

52 Carrera Andrade.

53 A. Heim, p. 176.

54 Zárate 4, I to V; Fray Gaspar de Carvajal ("Relación" — abstract of this in *Los Cronistas del Perú (1528—1650)* by R. Porras Barrenechea); this cleric (1500—1574) has left us the only eyewitness account of Orellana's journey.

55 Cobo 12, XX.

CHAPTER VI

1 Konetzke, p. 174.

2 Konetzke, p. 175.

3 and 4 M. Giménez, p. 10, 14.

5 Konetzke, p. 181 f. Las Casas was not granted entry to Peru, the country in which he was especially interested. The monk Niza was his main source of information about the conditions there.

6 Konetzke, p. 190.

7 Huber, p. 320.

8 Garcilaso, 3d vol., 4, I.

9 *El Testamento de Pizarro*, p. 76.

10 *El Testamento de Pizarro*, p. 74.

11 Zárate 5, XIV; Gutiérrez de Santa Clara in R. Porras B. "Cronistas", p. 191, 198 ff., S. Huber, p. 322.

12 Garcilaso, 3d vol., 5, XLI, Gutiérrez de Santa Clara.

13 Carrera Andrade 70 f.; Gutiérrez de Santa Clara.

14 Carrera Andrade; Garcilaso.

15 *El Testamento de Pizarro*.

16 Zárate 6, VII. Letter of Charles V to Gonzalo Pizarro: "Gonzalo Pizarro, por vuestras letras y otras relaciones he entendido las alteraciones y cosas acaecidas en esas provincias del Perú despues que e ellas llegó Blasco Nuñez Vela, nuestro visorey dellas ... a causa de haber querido poner en ejecución las nuevas leyes y ordenenzas por nos hechas ... Y *bien tengo por cierto que en ello vos ni los que os han seguido no habeis tenido intención a nos deservir,* sino a excusar la asperaza y rigor que el dicho visorey quería usar, sin admitir suplicación alguna; y así estando informado bien de todo, y habiendo oido a... lo que de vuestra parte y de los vecinos desas provincias nos quiso decir, habemos acordado de enviar a ellas por nuestro presidente al licenciado de la Gasca ... al cual habemos dado comision y poderes para que ponga sosiego y quietud en esta tierra ... por ende yo os encargo y mando que todo lo que de nuestra parte el dicho licenciado os mandare, lo hagáis ... según y por la orden y de la manera que él de nuestra parte os lo mandare, *y de vos confiamos;* que yo tengo y terné memoria de vuestros servicios y de lo que el marqués don Francisco Pizarro, vuestro hermano, nos sirvió, para que sus hijos y hermanos reciban merced. De Venelo, a 26 días del mes hebrero de 1546 años. Yo el Rey. Por mandado de su majestad, Francisco de Eraso." (In this letter, which De la Gasca delivered to Pizarro, Charles V extended a general pardon to the insurgents on condition that they would obey the orders of his attorney.) The "Cartes Reales" (royal letters) had force of law.

17 Zárate 6, VI: "... y demás de todo esto llevó (La Gasca) las cédulas y recaudos necesarios en caso de que conviniese hacer gente de guerra, aunque estos fueron secretos, porque no publicaba ni trataba sino de los perdones y de los otros medios pacíficos que entendía tener ..." (If Pizarro and the insurgents did not obey De la Gasca's instructions, then the latter was empowered to levy troops and implement the king's will by force.) "Real Cédula" was the usual form of a legal order to the American empire.

18 Zárate 7, VII.

19 Garcilaso, 3d vol., 5, XXXVI.

20 Cieza 1, CXVII; see also Valcárcel II, p. 309 f. The festival of the maize harvest: the maize was brought in from the fields to the accompaniment of ritual chanting, and everyone prepared a *huaca* of maize — a *mamazora* (maize mother) — in their homes. It was guarded for three nights while certain ceremonies were observed. It was "adorned with the (finest) cloths" and was worshiped as the "protectress of the fields" (madre de las chacras). In the month of May, the soothsayers ask her "whether she has strength for the coming year;" in the case of a negative reply, she is burnt on her own fields amid great ceremonial; if she replies that she does still have strength, then she remains for another year. This superstition persists to this day.

21 Half-tribes ("parcialidad" in Spanish) are a common social element in many cultures, including Peru, which were usually identified with married communities which did not permit marriages between members of their own half-tribe. In Cuzco, there was the famous division into Hanancuzco and Hurincuzco (the upper and lower Cuzco). See also Chapter II, note 14.

22 Valcárcel II, p. 231 f. Chapter entitled "Ofrendas y sacrificios."

23 Pietschmann (introduction to the Chronicle of Sarmiento, p. XV, note 2) and Rosenblat, 2d vol., pp. 84, 89 and 91.

24 *El Testamento de Pizarro*; D. I. A. I, 42, 197 ff.

25 *El Testamento de Pizarro*.

26 Huber, note 113.

27 D. I. A. I, 4, 84 ff. Despite his undeniable successes, the Marqués de Cañete, the third Viceroy of Peru, was dismissed in 1561.

28 Zárate 5, IV: During the Gonzalo uprising. "... they began to take money from the royal treasury and from the funds of the deceased and other reserves, supposedly as a loan to pay the soldiers..."

29 Zárate 5, VIII. This Garcilaso, the father of the chronicler, was one of the closest family friends of Gonzalo Pizarro, but is supposed to have remained in the insurgents' party only out of fear of Carvajal, until it was almost too late.

30 D. I. A. I, 4, 87. The white settlers were forbidden by law to live on the land among the Indians. "The town is the home of all Spaniards in America" (Konetzke, p. 138).

30a D. I. A. I, 4, 93.

31 D. I. A. I, 4, 93 (reference to the murder of Nuñez Vela).

32 D. I. A. I, 4, 96 f.; Cieza's (1, LXXI) ideal of an ordinary life in his beloved Peru, within sight of the blossoming countryside around Lima, is very similar to that of the Marqués de Cañete: "... if only the tumult and all these evil affairs would come to an end, then this would be one of the finest countries in the world."

33 D. I. A. I, 4, 105.

34 Cobo "Fundacion de Lima" 1, IX.

35 See R. Porras Barrenechea, "Garcilaso en Montilla."

36 Pietschmann (introduction to the Chronicle of Sarmiento).

37 Garcilaso.

38 Letters from Francisco de Toledo to Philip II, dated 1st, 3d, and 9th of October, 1572 (in the introduction to *Tres Relaciones...*); the sun disk is mentioned repeatedly in the history of the Conquest as a rich booty. It is supposed to have been gambled away by a soldier already in the time of Francisco Pizarro. There were probably a number of these idols.

39 Sarmiento (dedication).

40 José Acosta "De promulgatione evangelii apud barbaros sive de procuranda Indorum salute."

41 Murúa LXXXIV.

42 Cobo 12, XXI.

43 Murúa LXXXIV.

44 Rowe, *Colonial Portraits of Inca Nobles.*

45 Alexander von Humboldt, who traveled through Ecuador and Peru shortly after 1800, describes in a letter the impression of richness, charm, and strength that the Indian languages make on him, and remarks that the Quechua language is so rich in subtle and varied phrases that when the young lords wish to pay the ladies compliments, they generally use the Inca language.

46 Daniel Valcárcel; Rosenblat II, p. 144: The creole Felipe Miguel Bermúdez of Cuzco was a member of the provisional government of Túpac Amaru II.

47 Arciniegas, p. 418 and 421.

SELECTED BIBLIOGRAPHY

Out of the great quantity of sources and literature, only those have been chosen which give the best general survey and which are in direct relationship with the development of this text.

Alcántara, Inés de, "Letter to the Emperor from Doña Inés, widow of Captain Francisco Martín de Alcántara, brother of Don Francisco Pizarro. Los Reyes (Lima), 8th May, 1543", in D. I. A. Arciniegas, Germán, *El continente de siete colores*, Buenos Aires, 1965.

Almagro, Diego, "Letter from Adelantado Don Diego de Almagro to Inca Manco", in Oviedo, 4th vol., 47th book, 6th chapter, p. 284 ff., Madrid, 1855.

Anton, Ferdinand, *Alt-Peru und seine Kunst*, Leipzig, 1962.

Ballesteros Gaibrois, M., "Los pueblos pre-colombinos, in *Historia social y económica de España y América*, ed. by J. Vicéns Vives, 4 vols. in 5, Barcelona, 1957—1959.

Barrenechea, see Porras Barrenechea.

Bennett, Wendell C., *Ancient Arts of the Andes*, New York, 1954.

Betánzos, Juan de, *Suma y narración . . .*, ed. by Márcos Jiménez de la Espada, Madrid, 1880.

Bird, Junius, *Paracas Fabrics and Nazca Needlework*, Washington, D. C., 1954.

Bushnell, G. H. S., *Peru*, London, 1956.

Cabello de Balboa, Miguel, *Histoire du Pérou*, Paris, 1840.

Calancha, Antonio de la, *Coronica moralizada del orden de San Augustin en el Perú, con sucesos ejemplares en esta monarquia . . .*, Barcelona, 1638.

Cañete, "Letter from the Marqués de Cañete, Viceroy of Peru, to the Emperor. Los Reyes (Lima), 15th September, 1556", in D. I. A.

Carrera Andrade, Jorge, *La tierra siempre verde*, Paris, 1955.

Carrión Cachot, Rebeca, "El culto del agua en el Antiguo Perú", in *Separata de la Revista del Museo Nacional de Antropología y Arqueología*, vol. II, no. 1, March, 1955.

Cieza de León, Pedro de, *Parte primera de la crónica del Perú, que tracta la demarcación de sus provincias; la descripción dellas . . . las fundaciones de las nuevas ciudades; los ritos y costumbres de los indios y otras cosas extrañas dignas de ser sabidas (1553)*, Buenos Aires, 1945.

Cieza de León, Pedro de, *segunda parte de la crónica del Perú, que trata del señorio de los Incas yupanquis y de sus grandes hechos y gobernación*, ed. by Márcos Jiménez de la Espada, Madrid, 1880.

Cobo, Bernabé, *Historia del Nuevo Mundo (1653)*, 4 vols., Seville, 1890—93.

Colección de documentos inéditos del Archivo de Indias, Series I, Madrid, 1864, Series II, Madrid, 1892 (Abbreviation: D. I. A.)

D. I. A., see *Colección de documentos inéditos . . .*

Disselhoff, Hans D., and Linné, S., *The Art of Ancient America*, New York, 1960.

Disselhoff, H. D., *Huari und Tiahuanaco* in Zeitschrift für Ethnologie, Bd. 93, 1968, p. 207—216.

Eckert, Georg, *Totenkult und Lebensglaube im Caucatal*, Brunswick, 1948.

Engl, Lieselotte, *Huayna Cápac, Atahualpa und Huáscar — Untersuchungen zur Geschichte der letzten Jahrzehnte des Incareiches* (Inaugural dissertation), Munich, 1954.

Estete, Miguel de, "Relación del viaje del capitán Hernando Pizarro a Pachacámac", in Oviedo, 4th vol., 46th book, chapters 11 and 12, Madrid, 1855.

Fernández de Oviedo y Valdés, Gonzalo, *Historia general y natural de las Indias, Islas y Tierra Firme del Mar Océano*, Madrid, 1851—1855.

Findeisen, Hans, *Schamanentum*, Stuttgart, 1957.

Garcilaso de la Vega, "Comentarios reales de los Incas", in *Obras completas*, 2 vols. (Biblioteca de autores españoles, vols. 132—135), Madrid, 1960.

Heim, Arnold, *Wunderland Peru*, 2d ed., Bern, 1957.

Heine-Geldern, R., "Das Problem vorkolumbischer Beziehungen zwischen Alter und Neuer Welt und seine Bedeutung für die allgemeine Kulturgeschichte", in *Anzeiger der phil. hist. Klasse der Österreichischen Akademie der Wissenschaften*, vol. 91, Vienna, 1954.

Herrera, Antonio de, *Historia general . . .* (1601), vols., Madrid, 1934—57.

González Holguin, Diego, *Vocabulario de la lengua general de todo el Perú ilamada lengua Quichua o del Inca*, Lima, 1952.

Huber, Siegfried, *Pizarro und seine Brüder*, Olten, 1962.

Humboldt, Alexander von, *Reise in die Äquinoctialgegenden des Neuen Kontinents*, Stuttgart-Tübingen, 1815—32.

Kauffmann Doig, Federico, *El Perú arqueológico*, Lima, 1963.

Kitchell, Bertha, *Seven Treasure Cities of Latin America*, New York, 1964.

Konetzke Richard, *Süd- und Mittelamerika; die Indianerkulturen Altamerikas und die spanisch-portugiesische Kolonialherrschaft* (Fischer Weltgeschichte vol. 22). Frankfurt am Main, 1965.

Krickeberg, Walter, "Amerika", in *Die grosze Völkerkunde*, by Hugo Bernatzik, vol. 3, Leipzig, 1939.

Kutscher, Gerdt, *Chimu; eine altindianische Hochkultur*, Berlin, 1950.

Lommel, Andreas, *Shamanism: the Beginnings of Art*, New York, 1968.

Manco, Inca, "Letter from Manco Inca to Diego de Almagro, in Oviedo, 4th vol., 47th book, 8th chapter, Madrid, 1855.

Markham, *The Incas of Peru*. London, 1911.

Mason, J. A., *The ancient civilizations of Peru*. Edinburgh, 1957.

McCown, Theodore, *Pre-Incaic Huamachuco: Survey and Excavations in the Region of Huamachuco and Cajabamba* (University of California Publications in American Archaeology and Ethnology, vol. 39, no. 4), Berkeley and Los Angeles, 1945.

Means, Philip Ainsworth, *Ancient Civilizations of the Andes*, New York and London, 1931.

Means, Philip Ainsworth, *Fall of the Inca Empire and Spanish Rule in Peru: 1530—1780*, New York and London, 1932.

Menzel, D., *Style and time in the Middle Horizon*, in Nawpa Pacha 2, Berkeley, 1964, p. 1—106.

Mena, Cristóbal de, see Porras Barrenechea, *Las relaciones primitivas . . .*

Molina, Cristobal de, "Destrucción del Perú", in *Las crónicas de los Molinas*, Lima, 1943.

Montesinos, Fernando de, *Memorias antiguas historiales y políticas del Perú* (Coleccion de libros españoles raros ó curiosos, vol. 16), Madrid, 1882.

Murúa, Martín de, *Historia general del Perú*, introduccion y notas de Manuel Ballesteros-Gaibrois, Madrid, 1962.

"Newe Zeytung aus Hispanien und Italien, Mense Februario, 1534", *Ibero-amerikanisches Archiv*, Series IX, July, 1935, no. 2, p. 101—108.

Nouvelles certaines des isles du Peru, see Porras Barrenechea, ed., *Las relaciones primitivas* . . .

Oberem, Udo, "Notizen über einige Nachkommen des Inka Atahualpa im 16. und 17. Jh.", *Tribus*, vol. IX, pp. 191—193, Stuttgart, 1959.

Oliva Anello, Juan, *Historia del reino y provincias del Perú (1572—1642)*, Lima, 1895.

Oviedo, see Fernández de Oviedo y Valdés.

Pietschmann, Richard, ed., *Geschichte des Inkareiches von Pedro Sarmiento de Gamboa*, Berlin, 1906.

Pizarro, Hernando, "*Letter to the Emperor*", in Oviedo, 4th vol., 46th book, 15th chapter, Madrid, 1855.

Pizarro, Pedro, "Relación del descubrimiento y conquista de los reinos del Perú", in *Crónicas del Perú*, vol. 5 (Biblioteca de autores españoles vol. 168), Madrid, 1965.

Presscott, W. H., *Geschichte der Eroberung von Peru*, Leipzig, 1848.

Poma de Ayala, Felipe, Guamán, *Nueva corónica y buen gobierno* (codex péruvien illustré), Paris, 1936.

Porras Barrenechea, Raúl, *Los cronistas del Perú (1528—1650)*, Lima, 1962.

Porras Barrenechea, Raúl, ed., *Las relaciones primitivas de la conquista del Perú*, Paris, 1937.

Porras Barrenechea, Raúl: *Fuentes históricas peruanas*, Lima, 1954.

Porras Barrenechea, Raúl, ed., *El testamento de Pizarro* Cuadernos de historia del Perú, I, I), Paris, 1936.

Prittwitz, Heinz Ingo, *Viracocha. Ein Beitrag zur Kenntnis von Mythos und Religion im alten Peru* (Inaugural Dissertation), Munich, 1957.

Relaciones geograficas de Indias, Published by the Ministerio de Fomento. Tomo I. Madrid, 1881.

Rosenblat, Angel, *La población indígena y el mestizaje en América* (Biblioteca Americanista, vol. I and II), Buenos Aires, 1954.

Rowe, John Howland, "Inca Culture at the Time of the Spanish Conquest", in *Handbook of South American Indians*, Washington, D. C., 1946.

Rowe, John Howland, *The Kingdom of Chimor* (Acta Americana, vol. 6), Washington, D. C., 1948.

Rowe, John Howland, *Colonial Portraits of Inca Nobles* (The Civilizations of Ancient America. Selected Papers of the XXIXth International Congress of Americanists), Chicago, 1951.

Santa Cruz Pachacuti, "Relacion de antigüedades deste reyno del Pirú", in *Tres relaciones* . . ., Madrid, 1879.

Santillán, Fernando de, "Relación del origen, descendencia, política y gobierno de los Incas", in *Tres relaciones* . . ., Madrid, 1879.

Sarmiento de Gamboa, Pedro, *Geschichte des Inkareiches*, see Pietschmann, Richard.

Squier, E. George, *Peru*. New York, 1877.

Toledo, Francisco, "Letter from Viceroy Don Francisco de Toledo to the Consejo de Indias, of 1st of March, 1572", in Pietschmann, *Geschichte des Inkareiches* . . .

Torres Lanzas, Pedro, *Relación descriptiva de los mapas, planos, etc. del Virreinato del Perú*, Barcelona, 1906.

Tres relaciones de antigüedades peruanas, ed. by Márcos Jiménez de la Espada, Madrid, 1879.

Trimborn, Hermann, *Das alte Amerika*, Stuttgart, 1959.

Trujillo, Diego de, *Relación del descubrimiento del reyno del Perú*, edición, prólogo y notas de Raúl Porras Barrenechea, Seville, 1948.

Ubbelohde-Doering, Heinrich, *Auf den Königsstraßen der Inka*, Berlin, 1941.

Ubbelohde-Doering, Heinrich, *The Art of Ancient Peru*, New York, 1952.

Ubbelohde-Doering, Heinrich, *Kulturen Alt-Perus*, Tübingen, 1966.

Valcárcel, Daniel, *La rebelión de Túpac Amaru*, Mexico City, 1947.

Valcárcel, Luis E., *Historia del Perú Antiguo*. Lima, 1964.

Vargas Ugarte, Rubén, *El Perú Virreinal*, Lima, 1962.

Varones ilustres del Nuevo Mundo — Pizarro y Orellana, Madrid, 1639.

Vasquez de Espinosa, Antonio, *Compendio y descripción de las India Occidentales* (Smithsonian Miscellaneous Collections, vol. 108), Washington, D. C. 1948.

Verneau, R., and Rivet, Paul, *Ethnographie ancienne de l'Equateur. Mission du Service de l'Armée pour la mesure d'un arc meridien équatorial en Amérique du Sud*, Paris, 1912 —1922.

Vicens Vives, J., ed., *Historia social y económica de España y América*, 4 vols. in 5, Barcelona, 1957—1959.

Xerez, Francisco de, "*Relación de la conquista del Perú*", in *Biblioteca de Autores españoles*, vol. 26, Madrid, 1947.

Zárate, Augustin de, "Historia del descubrimiento y conquista del Perú", in *Biblioteca de Autores españoles*, vol. 26, Madrid, 1947.

Zerries, Otto, "Die Tanzmasken der Tuhuna-Juri-Taboca-Indianer der Sammlung Spix und Martius im Staatlichen Museum für Völkerkunde, Munich", 1820, *Paideuma*, VII, 7, Bamberg, 1961.

214